Sharing the Land of Canaan

Human Rights and the Israeli–Palestinian Struggle

Mazin B. Qumsiyeh

Pluto　　　Press

LONDON • STERLING, VIRGINIA

First published 2004 by Pluto Press
345 Archway Road, London N6 5AA

USA: University of Michigan Press, 839 Greene Street,
Ann Arbor, MI4 8106

www.plutobooks.com

British Library Cataloguing in Publication Data
A catalogue record for this book is available from the British Library

ISBN   0 7453 2249 2 hardback
ISBN   0 7453 2248 4 paperback

Library of Congress Cataloging in Publication Data applied for

10   9   8   7   6   5   4   3   2   1

Designed and produced for Pluto Press by
Chase Publishing Services, Fortescue, Sidmouth, EX10 9QG, England
Typeset from disk by Stanford DTP Services, Northampton, England
Printed and bound by CPI Group (UK) Ltd, Croydon, CR0 4YY

Contents

List of Tables, Exhibits, and Figures

*To my father whose body died in his birthplace,
but whose spirit lives on among his people.*

*To people of all faiths, who sacrificed so much to
bring us closer to peace and justice in this Holy Land.*

Acknowledgements

To write a book of this nature is really not a project that is done in isolation. As a Palestinian American, I was first and foremost influenced by my upbringing under Israeli occupation, in my undergraduate studies at Jordan University, among Palestinian refugees in Jordan, and in my 24 years in the United States. I am grateful to those people who have touched my life, whether their intent towards me or others was positive or negative. Thus, I am grateful to the Israeli soldier who threw a tear gas bomb into my class, as I am grateful to the Israeli university employee who kindly apologized to me, a young and naive Palestinian student, for her country's actions. I am also grateful to the journalists and editors we tried to educate, with varying degrees of success. These experiences, good and bad, helped shape my life. I feel privileged to have been alive at this moment in world history and I appreciate the opportunity to learn and grow from interactions with so many people of so many varied persuasions, ethnicity, and religions. I am thus grateful to all those whose paths have crossed mine. More specifically, in the last three years, as the idea for this book crystallized and evolved, I received significant help and encouragement from many people – to name a few key ones: Roman Bystrianyk, Justine McCabe, Salman Abu Sitta, David Kirsh, Bob Hartman, Hassan Fouda, Jess Ghannam, Stanley Heller, and members of the Palestine Right to Return Coalition and the Middle East Crisis Committee. I am also grateful to Pluto Press and, in particular, Julie Stoll and Roger van Zwanenberg for their efforts. My wife, Jessie Chang, and son, Dany, have given me significant positive influence, work, and encouragement. To those and many others, I am deeply grateful. I take responsibility for any mistakes, whether of omission or commission. Finally, I am grateful to you the reader for reading this book with an open mind. I would consider it a success if it makes some readers want to find out more, and would consider it an even greater success if the book prompts some to work harder for peace in the troubled land of Canaan.

Esse cuam videri
[To be rather than to seem]

Foreword

Dr Salman Abu Sitta

On the evening of Wednesday, October 31, 1917, Allenby's army, known as the Egyptian Expeditionary Force, encircled Beer Sheba in a surprise move and overcame the small Turkish garrison. The British flag was raised and Palestine lay open to Allenby's conquest. Thus ended 1,400 years of Arab and Muslim rule (with the exception of the brief Crusades period). The British military handed over Palestine to the Civil Administration headed by the Zionist High Commissioner, Herbert Samuel. His mission was to put into effect the Balfour Declaration and plant a Jewish state on Arab soil.

Thus, Palestine came under foreign rule, first British, then Israeli, which has lasted to this day. Palestine entered a century of wars, bloodshed, and suffering; the victims were the national majority of the country.

Why? European colonialism of the nineteenth century found its belated expression among European Jews in colonizing Palestine, for a complexity of historical and financial reasons, first riding on the shoulders of the British Empire, then on its home-grown strength, still supplied generously by Western resources.

One of the little known facts is that Zionism, which took a socialist character, is in fact a capitalist movement aiming to secure a territory from which it would express its ambitions, instead of manipulating European policies and wars. In other words, the Zionist capitalist movement aimed to exercise its power openly and with the recognition of the Western world, not indirectly by proxy.

Some examples to illustrate this will suffice. One of the first colonial settlements in Palestine was established by the French financial tycoon Rothchilde in Caesaria. Affluent bourgeois families became Israel's ruling class. The Hacohen, Ruppin, Shertok, and Elyashar are all related or intermarried. From this 'family' emerged Rosa Cohen, Yitzhak Rabin, Pinchas Sapir, Yigal Yadin, Uzi Narkis, Arthur Ruppin, Asher Yadlin, Eliahu Golomb, Moshe Dayan, Ezer Weitzman, Lord Mund, Ya'akov Meridor, and many others who created and ran the military-financial-industrial complex of Israel.

They have no time for international law or human rights. They forged ahead assured of the support of the British Empire and now of the new US imperial power.

The image conveyed in the West is of a peaceful ingathering of exiles in the 'Promised Land'. To achieve this end, they fabricated a web of myths, all of which have proved to be false, but only after they achieved their purpose: Palestine is a country without a people; the old will die and the young will forget Palestine; the refugees left on Arab orders; the Palestinians are terrorists, ... etc.

Even the specter of coexistence was falsely marketed in the pre-*Nakba*. A Zionist agent would scout for land for sale among Palestinian villagers. He would approach them saying: '*sawa, sawa, ya khabibi'* (together, together, my friend), rubbing his two forefingers vigorously.

That was on the eve of *Al-Nakba* in which 530 towns and villages were depopulated by expulsion and massacres. The expelled inhabitants constituted 85 percent of the Palestinians in the land that became Israel. Their land comprised 92 percent of Israel's area in 1948/49.

Zionist leaders vowed that 'no Arab village or tribe' would remain in the conquered land. As early as February 1948, during the British Mandate and before the creation of Israel, the Zionists planned the settlement of 1.5 million new immigrants on Palestinian land. By June 1948, after the state had been established, Israel made public its long-time policy, still held today, that no Palestinian would be allowed to return to his home. So much for the peaceful exclamation '*sawa, sawa'*.

The pseudo-legal web of laws created to confiscate Palestinian property was soon promulgated and is still in practice today. After 50 years of military victories, financial consolidation, and political recognition, Israel started to shed its socialist skin.

The kibbutzim, the main pillar of Zionism, are dying and on the brink of closure. The land, rented from the state by the kibbutzim, which is the Palestinian refugees' land from which they were expelled, is now offered for sale to any Jew, even if not an Israeli. The labor union, the Histadrut, is being dismantled. In short, Palestine, the land of dispossessed Palestinians, is being privatized. What is left of the old, idealistic Zionism? The answer may lie in the reason for denying the Palestinians' Right of Return.

Serious studies in the last decade have shown that there is no demographic, geographic, legal, water, agricultural, economical, or social reason to prevent the return of the refugees to their homes and live in peace with their neighbors, in accordance with the wording of the famous UN Resolution 194.

There is one major impediment: the ethno-religious-racist laws of Israel. There are at least two dozen laws, unique in the world and condemned by the international community, which discriminate, segregate, and violate decent norms of civilized behavior. As long as these laws are not repealed, bloodshed will continue and peace cannot prevail.

Here comes this book, as a breath of fresh air. The author, a well-known human rights activist, defies all odds and proposes a scheme of coexistence. He envisages a pluralistic society in which human dignity and rights are respected. He eloquently and gently guides you through the maze of obstacles towards the natural and sensible solution of coexistence.

As a Palestinian, whose people have lost 78 percent of Palestine by conquest and 22 percent by occupation and endured countless rounds of wars, raids, oppression, and suffering, his is a remarkable journey in the road to humanity.

It is more genuine than the effected rubbing of forefingers (*sawa, sawa, ya khabibi*). It is, in fact, an expression of Palestinianism. Even to the casual observer, it is known that Palestine was the refuge to Turkomans, Armenians, Circassians, Bosnians, German Templars, and a multitude of Europeans in Palestinian ports or holy cities.

None of these communities attempted to annihilate their hosts. None of them attempted to dominate them. None of them tried to impose their habits or ideology on the national majority of the land or to erase their cultural and physical landscape. The Israelis did all that with various degrees of success. They are still doing this now.

The pluralistic solution articulated by the author is therefore essentially Palestinian. In fact, even the UN Partition Resolution No. 181 of November 29, 1947, which recommended, not decreed because it does not have the right, two sovereign states, stipulated the means for the protection of the Arab and Jewish communities and the preservation of their rights in both states. Such ideas have now become a necessity since brutal naked force used by the Israelis to force the Palestinians into submission has failed. It has earned the Israelis the condemnation of the world and caused the Palestinians agony, for which Israelis will always be accountable.

The Israeli contentions of preserving 'the Jewish character' and demographic supremacy are dangerous dreams, which can, as they have done, cause much bloodshed. These archaic racist ideologies have no place in the twenty-first-century world.

The thesis, advanced by the author, in such a humane and lucid manner, should come naturally to all who seek a genuine and permanent peace. It is not foreign to Palestinians, as their historians, writers, and even politicians have frequently proclaimed.

Of all people, the Israelis should embrace this approach. They first have to shake themselves out of their collective amnesia, in which the Palestinians do not exist, *Al-Nakba* did not happen, ethnic cleansing and war crimes are a myth. Second, they have to educate themselves about the merits of human rights and international law. This should not be difficult to do. The Israeli public must be told what Jews in Europe and the US tell their fellow citizens: be tolerant, have equal rights for all citizens, regardless of race or religion. In other words, they should practice in Israel what they preach abroad.

They would find in this book a well-reasoned and dispassionate formula for a human rights-based peace plan. The author has several qualities to qualify him for advancing this vision: he is a Palestinian whose suffering has not prevented him from being sensitive; his scientific education distances him from fanaticism; he is a human rights advocate, which enables him to see the rights of all, not of some.

Regrettably, that is not the attitude of most Israelis. According to the Israel Democracy Institute (May 2003), most Israelis shun democracy in favor of a 'Jewish' Israel; the majority favor expelling the Palestinian citizens of Israel and oppose giving them full equality. The noted Israeli historian, Benny Morris, laments Ben-Gurion's lack of action to expel the remnants of Palestinians who managed to remain in Israel, and clearly calls for ethnic cleansing by advocating 'them' or 'us'. This is the view of all Israeli governments so far. Tragically, this bodes ill for the future. But we must retain the hope that this will change.

If Israelis embrace human rights, they will win acceptance. If they do not, they will be condemned by the world.

As to the Palestinians who suffered and lost so much, they have no intention of giving up their rights, however long it takes. History teaches us that such people will always prevail.

Salman Abu Sitta
May 2003

About the Author

I was born and raised in Beit Sahour, the biblical Shepherds' Field on the outskirts of Bethlehem. My first-hand experiences as a Palestinian Christian and my educational background in universities in both the Middle East and the US helped shape my evolving worldviews. I was raised under Israeli occupation and my large family still resides in the area.

My memories include vivid recollections of pastoral farm life, urban education, cultural events, and an overall mosaic of people of varied religions and backgrounds. They include a rich international coterie of friends and relatives visiting from Europe, Jordan, Saudi Arabia, and the US. As for Israelis, my interactions with them included not only Israeli soldiers and settlers/colonists, but also average Israelis from all walks of life and all stripes.

My bachelor degree in Jordan included close interaction with the Palestinian refugee community in Jordan (Jordan has over two million Palestinian refugees). I was awarded my Master's degree at the University of Connecticut, a PhD at Texas Tech University and postdoctoral training at St Jude Children's Research Hospital and the University of Tennessee (including a Clinical Fellowship). I was extremely lucky that my research and career have necessitated extensive travel in Jordan, Israel/Palestine, North Africa, East Africa, Europe, and America. The advantage of this scientific work was accompanied by the advantage of meeting people from all walks of life. Thus visiting universities for their scientific collections or to continue my education provided a quite different experience from trapping animals near rural isolated communities in the middle of the Sahara or on the African savannah. This allowed me to gain an understanding of societies not accessible to tourists.

I became active more directly in social and political causes about 15 years ago, but have never been a member of one of the many Palestinian liberation movements. My interests continued to evolve as I read more and had a chance to learn from my interactions with the many people I met during my frequent travels. The educational resources available at the universities to which I was affiliated allowed me to pursue knowledge in new directions.

We also improved abilities to use the internet, Web, and email as tools for activism.

I was co-founder of a number of organizations and groups: The Triangle Middle East Dialogue, the Carolina Middle East Association, the Holy Land Conservation Foundation, the Middle East Genetics Association, the Palestine Right to Return Coalition (http://al-awda.org), Academics For Justice (AcademicsForJustice.org), among others.

I have published more than 120 scientific papers in fields ranging from zoology to genetics. My later training was in genetics and I served as Associate Professor of Genetics and director of cytogenetic services at Duke University and Yale University. I have also published two books: *Mammals of the Holy Land* and *Bats of Egypt*. This book is the first I have written on the Palestine question. However, I have published extensively on Palestinian issues, including over 100 letters to editors and over 30 op-ed pieces. I am also interviewed regularly on TV and radio (local, national, and international). Appearances in national media include the *Washington Post*, *New York Times*, *Boston Globe*, CNBC, C-Span, and ABC, among others.

I share this rather complex background so that you, the reader, can understand more about how I came to appreciate the importance and centrality of a pluralistic solution to the simmering conflict in the land of Canaan.

Glossary

Al-Nakba: Literally, the catastrophe. This is the name given to the dispossession and ethnic cleansing of Palestinians from their homelands between 1947 and 1949.

Apartheid: An official government policy of segregation based on race, ethnicity, or religion. This was officially renounced in 1992 in South Africa.

Arab: Refers to those whose mother tongue is Arabic regardless of their religious or ethnic affiliation.

Ashkenazi, Ashkenazim: Jews who have developed culturally and linguistically starting from areas of the ancient Khazar empire and then into Eastern Europe. Yiddish developed as a unique language of Ashkenazim.

Balfour; Balfour Declaration: Lord Balfour was British Foreign Secretary when he issued a declaration in 1917 addressed to the Zionist movement relaying the support of 'Her Majesty's Government' for the establishment of a 'Jewish homeland in Palestine'.

Bedouin: Semi-nomadic tribes. In Palestine these tribes inhabited discrete geographic areas and subsisted on animal husbandry, trade, and even occasionally agriculture in desert valleys in the Negev. Most Palestinian Bedouins' ancestry is Nabatean.

Canaan, Canaanite: Refers to land and people inhabiting the eastern Mediterranean region. Most spoke Semitic languages and many had flourishing local kingdoms between 2000 BCE and the Roman conquests.

Dunum: Land measurement. A dunum is about a quarter of an acre.

Ethnic cleansing: The violent removal by one ethnic group of another from a particular area. Good examples are what happened in Palestine in 1947–49 and in the former Yugoslavia in the 1990s.

Fellahin: Arabic for farmers. The vast majority of Palestinians in the nineteenth century were farmers. Some were Bedouin (semi-nomadic).

Fertile Crescent: Area stretching from present-day Iraq through Syria and Lebanon to Israel/Palestine. So-called for its rich agricultural land.

Israel: The origin of this word comes from ancient Aramaic YSR (struggle) and EL (the higher God). It is believed to refer to the Biblical story of Jacob struggling with God. After the death of King Solomon, the tribes were separated into two kingdoms: Israel and Judah (see Jew below). The modern state of Israel came about in 1948 as a result of over 100 years of efforts by Christian and Jewish Zionists.

Jew: The root of this word is the ancient Aramaic word Yehudah (Judah), generally accepted as referring to the son of Jacob, who was the son of Isaac, who was the son of Abraham. Originally the concept of Jew (Yehudi) referred to descendants of the tribe/line of Yehudah (Judah) and later to anyone who hailed from the Kingdom of Judah, which contained three tribes. As conversions to newer religions came about and various converts joined, the term started to refer to those who followed a particular religion now called Judaism based on belief in the laws of Moses. This religion continued to evolve with rabbinical Judaism which was dominant in the third century, later branching into reform and conservative ideologies.

Jewish National Fund: 'A non-profit organization founded in 1901 to serve as caretaker of the land of Israel, on behalf of its owners – Jewish People everywhere' (their description).

Knesset: The Israeli parliament or legislative body.

Nabateans: A Canaanite civilization that flourished in southern Canaan (present-day Jordan and Israel/Palestine) and built many wealthy and prosperous cities. Incorporated into the Roman Empire and later resurrected as the Christian Ghassasin Kingdom. Many Palestinians and Jordanians (especially in the southern parts of these countries) trace their ancestry to the Nabateans.

Palestine (Filisteen in Arabic and Aramaic): Falastia is mentioned as a province subdued by a king of Assyria in 800 BCE. For over 2,000 years, beginning with the Roman era, the name Palestine was used as a geographic name for the area currently covered by the modern states of Jordan and Israel/Palestine. While Christian literature mostly refers to Palestine, Muslim literature recognizes it as part of greater Syria (Bilad Al-Sham).

Semitic: Refers to the language group that includes Aramaic, Hebrew, Arabic, Phoenician, and other languages spoken in the eastern Mediterranean region (the land of Canaan).

UNRWA: United Nations Relief and Works Agency for Palestinian Refugees. A UN agency set up for humanitarian aid to the Palestinian refugees following the creation of the state of Israel.

Zionism: A term coined by Nathan Birnbaum to refer to the political ideology or movement concerned with the need to develop a separate national homeland for Jews as a form of self-emancipation. Cultural Zionism believed in development of Hebrew and other cultural national trappings, while political Zionism believed in developing a modern nation-state. See Chapter 6.

1
Introduction

There is no more compelling and dramatic story with more profound international ramifications than that of the conflict raging in the land of Canaan. The movement to gather Jews from across the world to the Holy Land was accompanied by the dispossession of native Palestinian Christians and Muslims. This was followed by decades of conflicts. How did Zionism translate into a nation-state for all Jews? How was such a state established in an already inhabited land? How did religious and geopolitical factors help create one of the most emotional and heated conflicts which remains unresolved to this day? These and other questions have received wide but skewed coverage in the media and in thousands of books published over the past century. This is a story that seems to generate more news internationally and more heated debate than any other.

As in other struggles, the superpowers have attempted to dictate the fate of the indigenous population without consulting them. As in other struggles, individuals have been willing to kill and be killed in the name of nationalism or religion. As in other struggles, this is a story of Cold War rivalries using populations as part of the game of domination. But unlike other struggles, it is a story with unusual twists, involving world religions, and a story that has a global impact. The events of September 11, 2001 and the US invasions first of Afghanistan and more recently of Iraq are but examples of the shock waves of this struggle going beyond its local borders. Yet despite the agony, there are signs of a moral solution involving integration and coexistence.

No other part of the world has had as much of an impact – both positive and negative – on global affairs as the land of Canaan. Here a rich history of innovation, culture, religion, and dominant civilizations evolved. It is here that dramatic and fascinating cave drawings and the stone tools of hunter-gatherers were first discovered. Here hunter-gatherers settled into agriculture, built city-states, and later developed prosperous empires that embraced centers of poetry, agriculture, trade, and science. In an area later known as the Fertile Crescent, in what is now Iraq, Syria, Lebanon, and Israel/Palestine, humans first cultivated wheat and barley and domesticated animals. It is where they first learned to use an alphabet and drafted civil laws. In short, this is where civilization first took root. The series of ancient civilizations was not a clean-cut temporal succession but a mosaic of overlapping cultures, dynasties, languages, and religions. This rich mix included some of the most successful traders (e.g. the Phoenicians), farmers of arid lands (e.g. the Nabatean Arabs), great architects (e.g. the Assyrians, Jebusites), and those who developed influential laws and religions (the Mesopotamians, Hebrews, Arabs). This truly multiethnic and multicultural area oscillated between periods of war and prosperity. In the past 100 years, it has been an era of displacement, violence, and oppression.

While a rich and complex history is reduced to soundbites on television screens, six million Palestinian Christians and Muslims live as refugees or displaced people. A political and economic conflict has on occasion been reduced to simple statements about religion, violence, and ethnic slurs. Some have argued that this is one of the most complicated and difficult conflicts to resolve. They cite the conflict's supposed long history, sometimes claiming it goes back thousands of years. They cite religious involvement and other supposedly complicating factors. They sometimes arrive at the conclusion that the conflict cannot be solved but only 'managed', or at best resolved by an apartheid solution similar to the one already tried and failed in South Africa. This book will review data that suggest a logical way forward.

Britain and France fought many battles including the 100 Years' War. They now share the Channel Tunnel with free movement of people and ideas. The resurgence of conflict between those two great powers is unthinkable today. The Berlin Wall tumbled and apartheid in South Africa was dismantled. Yet the 100 years of conflict in the Middle East remains as a galvanizing force in the twenty-first century. This conflict is simple to understand, yet made complicated by claims and counterclaims, propaganda, power politics, and unimaginable violence and suffering. Israel, established to provide a safe haven for Jews, is ironically the place where Jews are at risk and subject to acts of violence. This is a book intended to provide a vision for peace based on human rights supported by international law. The vision is one of a pluralistic society for all its citizens, with justice and equality as its cornerstones. Such a vision has its detractors. It may seem unrealistic to many, including those uninitiated and those who have acquired their knowledge through mainstream western media. Therefore, I believe it is important to begin with a résumé of the history of the region in order to address some of the myths used to argue against integration and coexistence.

My purpose in this book is to take the reader through the major issues that surround the conflict in order to propose a rational solution to it. There are many books on the conflict that deal in detail with each of the issues I raise: refugees, Jerusalem, terrorism, human rights, etc. I examine the conflict as a whole, giving suggested readings on the different topics for those seeking greater detail. This lays the groundwork, despite the difficulties on all sides, for a solution, which I present in the last chapter. After so much bloodshed, people of different religions and persuasions are only now arriving at this revolutionary yet simple and logical conclusion. Myths prevent what many now know is the fitting solution to this man-made catastrophe, sometimes referred to as the 'Middle East situation'. In this book, we will also examine historical research that helps dispel the myths which have stood in the way of the most obvious and logical conclusion: a durable peace is both possible and inevitable, based on sharing and equality rather than separation and walls.

The citations I provide as sources published in hard copy or on web-sites are those I consider important. I have not tried to reference everything, except in cases where I have directly quoted someone else's work, or when I have thought it useful to do so. However, at the end of each chapter I do provide a brief list of recommended reading for those who want a more in-depth discussion of the issues raised. My aims include exploring forgotten documents and historical facts that relate to how a solution might be found in human rights. Unusual findings in my research include how and why the British Empire pushed for a Jewish settlement in Palestine as early as the 1840s. We will see how and why this Empire's actions included the Balfour Declaration of 1917 and the decades of colonization that followed. We will see how and why Theodor Herzl and other European Jews believed that a Jewish state was the best solution to the 'Jewish problem'. We will see why there was major Jewish opposition to Zionism and will examine various failed solutions, culminating in the Oslo Accords and the so-called road map to peace. We will see why Israel's apartheid wall, snaking through the West Bank, will bring neither security nor peace. We will see why Israeli and Palestinian societies are evolving towards a post-Zionist era both within and outside the cease-fire line of 1949. We will see why this 'Green Line' (or lines), or other lines marked with walls and fences, will never become the border between two sovereign states. We will also see why nihilistic ideas emanating from both sides will succeed only in subjugating the 'other' or tearing the small land of Canaan into pieces.

2
People and the Land

The land of Canaan was never 'a land without a people for a people without a land', as some early Zionists claimed. In order to understand the conflict and thus begin to articulate a solution, we must begin by understanding these people and their origins. Such an understanding helps us to appreciate their interconnectedness, which is intentionally or unintentionally hidden, in order to keep us segregated and thinking tribally. The evolution of these civilizations and their relationships to each other and to outside forces reveal that many perceptions currently expressed for political purposes have no basis in fact. Understanding the history of the people and the land of Canaan is key to shaping a future of peace for all its current and displaced inhabitants. For example, a simple examination of history shows that Canaanitic groups developed the first alphabet and evolved related languages from the original western Semitic languages of Old Aramaic and Syriac, which eventually became the new and flourishing languages of Arabic and Hebrew. This organic connection is easily forgotten and frequently dismissed by those who have a stake in maintaining that the Arabic and Hebrew cultures and civilizations inevitably clash.

ANCIENT PEOPLES AND CULTURE

Archeological evidence from the Fertile Crescent shows that in around 6000–5000 BCE (Before the Common Era) nomadic hunter-gatherers first started to cultivate crops and domesticate animals. This transition happened fairly rapidly and, once established, had a dramatic impact. The presence of a predictable food source allowed small tribes to settle and their populations thereafter increased dramatically. A larger population and human contact in turn led to the need for rules that govern human behavior and leadership; hence city-states evolved. Once humans were dependent on settled land for their sustenance there was the obvious impetus to raid and acquire more land and resources to expand the city-state. Regional conflicts over resources ensued, alliances between

5

different city-states and tribes formed, and finally larger kingdoms and empires coalesced. The Canaanitic civilization emerged as the most dominant for the western part of the Fertile Crescent, while the Sumerian civilization dominated the east.

Canaanites of the eastern Mediterranean region spoke Semitic languages, just as many people in this region still do. One must distinguish here between languages/language groups and ethnicity. English is spoken by people of varied ethnicity, many of whose ancestors may have spoken other languages in the past, even languages not in the same group as English (e.g. people in the Philippines, Australia, or New Zealand). English belongs to the Anglo-Saxon group of languages in the same way as Arabic and Hebrew belong to Semitic group of languages. Strictly speaking, 'Semitic' is not an ethnicity but a language group and thus the term 'Semites' refers to people who speak a Semitic language and not to an ethnic or religious group (see Chapter 6 for discussion of 'anti-Semitism').

The Semitic languages included Phoenician, Aramaic, Arabic (Aramaic modified by Nabatean), Moabite Phoenician, Hebrew (modified Aramaic), Akkadian, Assyrian, and Babylonian. By far the most dominant of the early Semitic languages was Aramaic, which became the most commonly used language in the whole area during the first millennium BCE. The word Aramaic refers to Aram, by tradition the son of Shem (Sam), from which the Aramaic word She-maa-yaa (Semitic) is derived. The land in which the Shem/Semitic people lived, including present-day Syria, Lebanon, Israel/Palestine, and Jordan, is known traditionally as Bilad Al-Sham, or the land of Shem. An inhabitant of this area is referred to in Arabic as 'Shami', or hailing from Bilad Al-Sham.

The original proto-Aramaic language had two major dialectical descendants: western also referred to as Palestinian Aramaic, spoken by people during Jesus' time; and eastern, or Syrian Aramaic, still spoken today by members of the Syriac Orthodox Church in Iraq and Syria. The characters of Aramaic were the precursor of both the Arabic and Hebrew alphabets (see Figure 1). The spoken language continued to expand and had evolved into the classic dominant western Semitic forms by 2000 BCE. Even as new tongues arrived, the area kept its Semitic languages, dominated first by Aramaic, and later by Arabic joined now by a modernized Hebrew.

Abstract or symbolic writing developed from pictorial writing among the Sumerian cultures of Mesopotamia. Stylized cuneiform

	Phoenician	Hebrew	Aramaic (Syriac)		Arabic
Aleph	𐤀	א	܃	܇	ل ا
Beth	𐤁	ב	ܐ	ܒ	بـ بـ
Gimel	𐤂	ג	ܓ	ܔ	جـ جـ
Dalet	𐤃	ד	!	؟	ذ د
He	𐤄	ה	ܗ	ܘ	ه هـ ها
H'et	𐤇	ח	ܚ	ܞ	حـ حـ ح
Waw	𐤅	ו	ο	ο	و
Zayin	𐤆	ז	ܙ	؛	ز
T'ah	𐤈	ט	ܛ	ܞ	ط
Yodh	𐤉	י	ܝ	ܝ	يـ يـ
Kaph	𐤊	ך כ	ܟ	ܠ	كـ كـ ك
Lamedh	𐤋	ל	ܠ	ܠ	لـ لـ ل
Mem	𐤌	ם מ	ܡ	ܡ	مـ مـ م
Nun	𐤍	ן נ	ܢ	ܢ	نـ نـ ن
Ayin	𐤏	ע			عـ عـ ع
Pe	𐤐	ף פ	ܦ	ܦ	فـ فـ ف
Qoph	𐤒	ק	ܩ	ܩ	قـ قـ ق
Resh	𐤓	ר	؟؛	؛	ر
Sin	𐤔	שׂ	ܣ	ܨ	سـ س
Shin		שׁ	ܫ	ܫ	شـ شـ ش
Tau	𐤕	ת	ܬ	ܬ	تـ تـ ت
Samekh	𐤎	שׁ	ܤ	ܤ	صـ صـ ,

Figure 1   Evolution of the Semitic Alphabet

(For an animation, see http://www.wam.umd.edu/~rfradkin/alphapage.html)

was used, based on simplified pictorials of objects or living things (a practice later continued in most other Asian scripts and their evolution). However, more recent studies suggest that the Egyptians may have developed a symbolic script independently. The alphabets we use today (for both European and Semitic languages) were developed by the Phoenician Canaanites shortly after those early successes in Mesopotamia and Egypt. A hybridization of a simplistic design of about two dozen characters arrived at by using the cuneiform structure from Mesopotamia combined with the Sinaitic/Egyptian approach yielded the first alphabet as exemplified by the Ugarit tablets. This Phoenician alphabet formed the basis for all future Semitic and western alphabets (see Figure 1).

The mixture of languages spoken in Canaan 3,000–5,000 years ago and the evolution of the alphabet there clearly indicate that this land lay at the crossroads of ancient civilizations. It is well known that accelerated cultural developments occur with the hybridization of powerful civilizations, languages, inventions, and belief systems. This is the secret to the success not only of the hybrid alphabet of the Phoenicians but also of the philosophies and religions that developed in the area. Each culture and each people had their unique strengths and weaknesses. Great leaps in civilizations occurred with the admixture of languages and cultures. The magnificent peoples of this area left us not only their descendants, but also great achievements and an imprint that shapes all of us today.

The Jebusites are a good example of this Canaanitic cultural blending. In around 3000 BCE they were living in Jebus, which later became known as Ur-Salem (from which Yerushalaym/Jerusalem are derived). Ur-Salem is a Canaanite word meaning the city of Salem, an ancient god-king of the Jebusite clan. The name Salem, or Shalem in some Aramaic dialects, and Ur-Salem thus became Jerusalem/Urhshalem/Yerushalaym. Similarly, while Arabs and Jews say that Bethlehem means house of bread or meat respectively, it is more accurately named after the house of Laham, the Canaanite god of the southern hills.

The temple of Solomon, like the Al-Aqsa mosque, was probably built on a sacred Jebusite site. Historically, religious leaders have built their temples on sacred ground to facilitate the conversion of the local inhabitants to the new religion. Similarly, the Kaaba in Mecca was constructed on the site where pagans once worshipped. Descendants of the Jebusites continued to live in Jerusalem, some accepting the new religions, some intermarrying with immigrants, and some migrating and later returning under new regimes. But the Jebusite imprint on Ur-Salem would be permanent. Without the Jebusites, Jerusalem might not have existed and certainly Jerusalem would be a very different city today without its Jebusite roots.

THE NABATEANS

The Nabateans were another people that flourished in ancient times in the southern parts of Canaan and left an indelible mark on future generations. Few today know about this group and its history seems to have been suppressed. A good summary of their history can be found in Nelson Glueck's *Deities and Dolphins: The Story of the Nabataeans*.[1] The Nabateans prospered on farming and trade. They traded in everything from spices and cloths to animals and minerals. Their kingdom flourished between 400 BCE and 10–150 CE. During the third century BCE, the Nabateans built their first four cities – Abda, Isbeita, El Halus, and Nestan – in Al-Naqab (Negev) along the trade route that crossed the desert to what today is Gaza. The tribes of Saba were the first to settle in what later became Beer Saba' (in Arabic) or Beersheva (in Hebrew) (*beer* means 'well' in both languages). Their capital, Petra, now in southern Jordan, is a marvel of human engineering. At the peak of its power (about 300 BCE), Petra would have accommodated 60,000 people and the area under their control stretched from what is now northern Saudi Arabia to southern Syria (Batsr or Basra was one of their major cities). The port city of Elath (Eilat) in southern Palestine (now Israel) is Arabic Nabatean and its name derives from Al-Latt, a pagan Arabic goddess mentioned in the Qu'ran.

The Nabateans are also mentioned in connection with New Testament events: King Herod spurned the daughter of the Arab-Nabatean king Aretas (al-Harith; Artas is now a locality near Bethlehem), Queen Zenobia (Zannuba, Zaynab in classic Arabic), Odenatus ('Udhayna(t)'), and Vaballatus or Wahbullatt (again from Al-Latt). It is also thought that John the Baptist was Nabatean. Some have gone as far as to suggest that the Romans executed him fearing a Hebrew–Arab anti-Roman alliance.

Nabatean farming techniques were advanced and were critical in establishing trade routes across the deserts. Scholars believe that theirs was the first true farming of desert areas as they constructed dams in dry Wadi systems to capture flash floods. During the Roman period, the Nabateans settled in southern Palestine and 'made the desert bloom'. Their techniques are still practiced by some of their descendants among the current Palestinians around Hebron and Beer Saba' (Beersheva).

The Nabateans had evolved their own Semitic Arabic dialect from proto-Aramaic by the fourth century CE. Their Aramaic script was the first recorded Arabic writing using an adaptation of a version of the Aramaic alphabet and phonetics that was dominant in that era.[2] Its subsequent evolution led to the standard representation of classical Arabic.[3] The Imrulqay's inscription in Nabatean script is the earliest recognizable classic Arabic script. The dots that distinguish the letters b-n-t-y-th, z-r, s-sh, etc. and the strokes for short vowels (damma, kasra, fatha) were added later when Islam was spreading and the Qu'ran was being transcribed.

At Beidha, a few kilometers to the north of Petra, are the excavated remains of a village dated to 6500 BCE when humankind was first making the transition from small bands of hunter-gatherers to settled villagers. Descendants of those inhabitants who still live in the surrounding villages constructed magnificent temples and later the churches and mosques that dot the Jordanian landscape. Nabatea became a prosperous province under Roman rule and then was conquered by the Byzantines, who ruled it for almost four centuries (from 300 to 634 CE). It was in this period that the inhabitants converted to Christianity. They built some of the first churches, including the beautifully decorated ones at Madaba, Siyaghah, Ma'in, Amman Citadel, Jerash, Rihab, Umm el-Jimal, Umm Qais, Tabaqat Fahl, Dhiban, and Umm er-Risas. The artwork in the temples, churches, and later mosques in these areas bears witness to the mixture of ancient symbolism and emphasis on nature in early Nabatean art. Many of the churches were plundered during the Persian invasion, between 614 and 629 CE.

Nabateans were receptive to Judaism, Christianity, and finally Islam in the sixth century. Most converted to Islam, but a Christian population remained especially around Madaba and Karak (now in Jordan) and around Bethlehem, Beit Sahour, and Beit Jala (now in Palestine). The movement of inhabitants between these two areas of Nabatea was recorded as late as the seventeenth century (families in Beit Sahour came from the south and east of Nabatea and families in Karak came from Al-Naqab or southern Palestine). This suggests a cohesiveness within the community even while they practiced Christianity and Islam. To this day, Nabatean farming and trading methods are practiced and include methods to build wells and dams in arid regions, knowledge of local fauna and flora, goat and sheep husbandry, and, even under restriction, moving donkeys and camels across the barren hills from one area to another. Over 40 of their places of residence (housing some 15,000 people) are on the list of 'unrecognized' villages in the state of Israel.

CULTURAL AND RELIGIOUS SYMBIOSIS IN CANAAN

In the north of the land of Canaan, the Phoenician Empire spread throughout the Mediterranean basin.[4] The Phoenicians were the original sea traders, sailing between Mediterranean ports where they bought and sold from many inhabitants, including the Nabateans. Phoenicians spoke an old Semitic tongue closely allied to eastern Semitic (Akkadian, Assyrian, and Babylonian) and the more distant but still related western Semitic (Arabic/Aramaic).

In the land of Canaan the Philistines lived around Gaza and Ashkelon, the Jebusites around Jerusalem, the Hebrews around Hebron and Nablus/Shekhem, the Nabateans in northern Saudi Arabia, southern Jordan and southern Palestine, and the Phoenicians in the north around Galilee, Mount Carmel, and into Lebanon, as well as in established outposts throughout the Mediterranean. All these groups occasionally fought each other, but mostly traded and collaborated; as a result their histories are intertwined.[5] The abundance of food resources and a good climate helped reduce tensions and inter-tribal conflicts. Archeology provides ample evidence of a prosperous and relatively peaceful Canaanitic civilization coexisting with neighboring civilizations.[6]

The Jewish religion and history are covered at length in other books and I could not do justice to this by trying to summarize a rich and influential past. But I do want to make some brief comments. The culture best recognized in the kingdoms of David and Solomon, was, like that of the Nabateans and Jebusites coexisting with them, a culture of native Canaanites who evolved and modified their language and philosophies (religion) as they developed in the context of a rich mixture of civilizations in the Fertile Crescent. This may be hard to glean from some ideologically-derived archeological studies, which seem intent on proving the historicity of the Old Testament. For example, the work of the Israeli general and amateur archeologist Yigal Yadin did not withstand later rigorous archeological research. Other Israeli archeologists, unblinkered by religious dogma, began to examine the history from the physical evidence. Significant archeological discoveries concur with those who suggest that the Old Testament and Torah were not supposed to be taken literally or understood as historically accurate texts, but as lessons and metaphors for our human connection to the spiritual world.[7] For example, documents from Roman and local sources refute the idea of the large-scale removal of Jews from Palestine following the Jewish revolt in CE 70. They argue that the revolt was put down, but there is no evidence of large displaced communities as a result.

Historical reconstruction based on archeological evidence suggests that some western Semitic Canaanites began to identify themselves as belonging to a unique religion worshipping the highest of the Canaanitic gods, El, or, in another case, YHWH. They were among many peoples with other beliefs in this area. El is the high god worshipped by a tribe of Semites called the 'wanderers' or the 'nomads' ('Abiru, Habiru, or later, Hebrews). The root of this word are the letters 'ein, be, ra; roughly 'abr, which relates to crossings over and journeys. These Habirus are mentioned in both Egyptian and Mesopotamian sources. Their worship of El is enshrined in many words, including IsraEl (from Yisra', to struggle with, or Yasra, to persist), IshmaEl/IsmaEl (from yisma'/yishma', heard by god/El), and DaniEl and MichaEl (he who is like El). It is the root of the words for Aramaic (Aalah, Aaloh), later evolving into Hebrew (Eleim, Elohim) and Arabic (Allah). The word Aalah/Allah is a combination of the definite article AL and Ilah or Allah (meaning god, or El in all these languages).

Karen Armstrong has examined the Bible using simple textual analysis and concludes that El was the tribal god of a fairly homogeneous people, the 'Abiru (Habiru), while a more approachable god, Yahweh/YHWH, united many different ethnic groups.[8] These traditions were adopted by some of the tribes of related wanderers or nomadic tribes called 'Arab (the Arabs, also derived from the same language root). These Arabs called God Allah (root El and Elah), the name they used when they adopted first Christianity and later Islam. But even at the height of worship of El/Allah or Yahweh in the millennia before Christianity and Islam, locals who spoke Aramaic and its derived written languages of Hebrew and Arabic maintained Canaanitic religious and social traditions. 'Prophets like Moses preached the lofty religion of Yahweh, but most of the people wanted the older rituals with their holistic vision of unity among the gods, nature and mankind.'[9] But regardless of religious persuasion and its use by all religious leaders to justify their rule, a prosperous community of Canaanitic people continued to exist even as its names and areas of authorities changed (Nabatea, Judea, Samaria, Jebus/Yebus, Filasteen, etc.).

Some argue that fundamentalist followers of any religion or social phenomenon like to emphasize its novelty, freshness, and uniqueness. A closer examination of history shows more of a mosaic and syncretism of cultures, religions, and languages, which makes us feel more optimistic. As stated above, the first Hebrews worshipped only one of the Canaanitic gods, El. Jesus was a practicing Jew who came not to negate but to complement the old scriptures. The Qu'ran clearly states that all its principles were revealed to the prophets before the birth of Mohammed. Many cities under the control of a new religion retained their older names and also their traditions and myths. It is believed that the site of the Church of the Nativity in Bethlehem, where Jesus is said to have been born, sits on ruins of a Canaanitic temple of Lahmu.

A 'MELTING-POT' ORIGIN OF NATIVE PEOPLE

Other peoples settled in the area and married Canaanites. The Egyptians conquered this area frequently, and ruled the land from about 2500 to 1700 BCE, and again between 1550 and 1200 BCE. The Hyksos invaded and ruled from 1710 to 1550 BCE. The Hittites invaded and ruled from 1350 to 1290 BCE. The Philistines (Aegean in origin) ruled from 1250 to 711 BCE. Other peoples lived or ruled in Palestine, including the Edomites, Babylonians, Assyrians, Persians, Greeks, and Armenians.

While variations of ancient philosophical and religious beliefs emerged, tribes and kingdoms variously competed and cooperated. The kingdom of Judah lasted 341 years (927–586 BCE); while Israel lasted 205 years (927–722 BCE). But when the Romans barred some Jews from Jerusalem in the first century CE, these Jewish Canaanites continued to live with other Canaanites elsewhere in Palestine. Some converted to Christianity and later to Islam. Those remaining developed the major rabbinical school which now constitutes the bulk of rabbinical Judaism (developed in Safad in northern Palestine). This Judaism was partially influenced in its philosophy by rabbis being barred from Jerusalem and by the pressures of new religious beliefs and political realities. At the time, this sect of Judaism was in competition with other Jewish religious sects, including the Karaitisites. Karaitism, rabbinical Judaism, cults of Yahweh, and other Canaanitic religions continued to flourish in Palestine. Conversions, intermarriage, and religious plurality were not uncommon. Mulhall comments:

> The Bible states that not only Amorites but other ethnic groups lived in Canaan in Joshua's era. He did not conquer all of them. Judges 1 states that Hebrews enslaved many natives rather than expel or kill them. Judges 3: 5–6 also relates: 'The Israelites lived among the Canaanites and Hittites and Amorites, the Perizzites, Hivites and Jebusites; they married the daughters of these peoples, gave their own daughters in marriage to their sons, and served their gods.' According to this, extensive genetic, religious and cultural blending occurred. Large ethnic groups remained free. Some, including Hittites and Edomites, were noted in David's reign, more than two hundred years later. David vastly extended Hebrew rule by both assimilation and conquest within Canaan. This shows how incomplete Hebrew rule was when he began to reign about 1000 B.C. The Philistines, in Canaan's central and southern coastal area, became David's vassals but kept their identity until the second century B.C. or later.[10]

Similarly, the success of Christianity and Islam did not involve the mass migration of people, but rather religious conversion.[11] Today's Egyptians, for example, are mostly descendants from the Egyptians of the Pharaonic era. A small minority retained the Pharaonic language called Qubti (Coptic) which is still spoken by Egyptian Christians. The predominantly Aramaic- and Hebrew-speaking Canaanitic population of Palestine had become predominantly Christian by the fifth century and predominantly Muslim by the eighth century, but remained ethnically largely western Canaanitic.[12]

PALESTINIANS

The area between the River Jordan and the Mediterranean has enjoyed 6,000 years of civilization. For a large part of its history it formed the southern part of the land of Canaan. For 2,000 years, it was called Palestine. As noted above, native peoples evolved and adapted to new rulers, new political structures, and new or modified religious beliefs. These people, known to the world as Palestinians, absorbed various religions and philosophies and periodically switched their allegiances to survive in an ever-changing world. The latest chapter in their history is now well known. Edward Said summarizes it thus:

> Palestine became a predominately Arab and Islamic country by the end of the seventh century. Almost immediately thereafter its boundaries and its characteristics – including its name in Arabic, Filastin – became known to the entire Islamic world, as much for its fertility and beauty as for its religious significance ... In 1516, Palestine became a province of the Ottoman Empire, but this made it no less fertile, no less Arab or Islamic.[13]

An examination of the folklore and customs of the people of Palestine reveals fascinating stories and facts about the ancient heritage of this society. As one example, we may cite costumes. Each district and town in Palestine has its own traditional fabric and dress designs. Palestinian women's clothes in the Jerusalem area featured grapes; grapes were grown in the area for over 3,000 years and are symbols used in the Jebusite culture to denote abundance and pleasure. Trees and flowers are more common in northern Palestine and are used in designs for bed covers and curtains as well as dresses. These patterns are shared with Syria and Turkey. Cedars are found in the dresses of Palestinians in the Jalil (Galilee) region of northern Palestine and are common Phoenician as well as Lebanese symbols. Schematic motifs interpreted as either palm leaves or ears of wheat are found on dresses from the Ramallah region. One recalls the entrance of Jesus into Jerusalem when the locals placed palm leaves on the road. Easter is celebrated among Christian Palestinians with decorated palm leaves. Stars are common in Palestinian dresses in several districts (stars were objects of worship amongst the Cro-Magnon and Stone Age people in Palestine).

The influence of the twentieth century on Palestinian costumes and traditional clothes has been dramatic. The Palestine Costume Archives put this on its web page:

> At the beginning of the 20th century Palestinian costume could be classified by specific region, tribe or community. Of the three major historical classifications of nomadic Bedouin costume,

Fellahin village dress and urban dress, very little definition remains. Today costume styles are best classified as refugee camp styles, Palestinian Territories styles and Bedouin costume. Only among the Bedouin does costume still retain elements of its traditional pre-1948 role. The styles of clothing worn today in the Palestinian Territories and in the refugee camps include Western dress and Islamic modesty dress as well as various forms of the so-called 'traditional' embroidered dresses. What is now identified as 'traditional' is a much simpler garment in terms of construction and decoration.[14]

The challenge of Zionism was to create a mainly European Jewish-led strong state in a land inhabited by natives of various religions and backgrounds. Early Zionists understood the challenge and, contrary to their public pronouncements about 'a land without a people for a people without a land', came to see that the natives posed an obstacle to their aspirations. As a pioneer of the Zionist movement, Ahad Ha-Am visited the land in 1891 and wrote an essay titled 'Truth from the Land of Palestine' in which he states:

> We abroad are used to believing that Eretz Israel is now almost totally desolate, a desert that is not sowed, and that anyone who wishes to purchase land there may come and purchase as much as he desires. But in truth this is not the case. Throughout the country it is difficult to find fields that are not sowed. Only sand dunes and stony mountains that are not fit to grow anything but fruit trees – and this only after hard labor and great expense of clearing and reclamation – only these are not cultivated.[15]

As we will see in Chapter 4, these natives were dispossessed and became the bulk of the Palestinian refugee population. How to reconcile their basic human rights with the desire for Zionist domination is the subject of discussion in the following chapters.

While use of the terms Israel and Palestine for this piece of land may provoke anxiety and fear among members of one group or another, the use of the term 'land of Canaan' may be more appropriate until these fears subside. The land of Canaan was and is inhabited by Canaanitic people with some intermingling with other groups. Semitic-speaking people continued to live, collaborate, and prosper in this area as pluralistic multiethnic and multi-religious communities with much less violence than many books and publications suggest. This gives us cause for optimism for the future and a vision of peaceful coexistence. For if people were able to live and trade together for thousands of years before the era of international cooperation and a global economy, there is no reason to insist that separation and narrow nationalism in this area will work today.

RECOMMENDED READING

Leila El-Khalidi, *The Art of Palestinian Embroidery* (London: Al Saqi, 1999).

Walter E. Rast, *Through the Ages in Palestinian Archaeology: An Introductory Handbook* (Harrisburg, PA: Trinity Press Intl, 1992).

Arnold J. Toynbee and Ibrahim A. Abu-Lughod (eds.), *The Transformation of Palestine: Essays on the Origin and Development of the Arab-Israeli Conflict*, second edition (Chicago: Northwestern University Press, 1987).

Jonathan N. Tubb, *Canaanites (Peoples of the Past, 2)* (Oklahoma City: University of Oklahoma Press, 1999).

http://www.nabateans.org

3
Biology and Ideology

Zionism was promoted by Eastern European Jews (Ashkenazim) as a means to combat the prejudice of the societies in which they lived. The principal obstacle to creating and maintaining a Jewish state in the land of Canaan was and continues to be the presence of Palestinian natives. Strengthening a claim to the land while denying the rights of the natives is a classic tool of colonial effort. Delegitimizing the Palestinians was and is a strategy to win sympathy from Jews and non-Jews alike for Zionist aspirations. Some have argued that the Palestinians are the descendants of the Arabs who arrived during Islamic rule. As we have seen in Chapter 2 though, the indigenous people adopted a succession of religious beliefs while living in the land. Competing political sovereignty or religions never supersede indigenous peoples' rights. Later chapters will show that the only viable solution is a pluralistic democracy for all inhabitants. But before we get to that, we need to address the argument presented by some that there is a 'right of return' of Jews to lands whose current inhabitants, the Palestinians, were merely squatters on this 'Jewish land'. A rational response is that land can no more be Jewish than a tree or a river can be Christian or Muslim or Jewish. Land belongs to its inhabitants, collectively as natives and individually as humans, regardless of what religion they adopt. In addition to examining the history of Palestinian natives (regardless of their religion), we must re-examine the supposed biological links between Ashkenazi Jews (Eastern European Jews) and the ancient Israelites. This is important because a solution based on human rights can be countered by claims of ancient rights that are retained in perpetuity. And as a geneticist by training and profession (I am Associate Professor of Genetics at Yale University), I have a keen interest in these questions.

Some Ashkenazi Jews argue that assimilation and inter-marriage were never permissible and that Zionism was the 'nationalist' response to anti-Ashkenazi actions in Europe. Ideological and religious constructs sometimes find their way into population genetics and disciplines which we expect to be immune from such biases. Examining the genes of Jews was thus deemed important and a worthwhile venture to many. The Centre for Genetic Anthropology at University College London puts it this way on their web page:

> Another fascinating study is the origins of the Eastern European Jews. You may know that there are at least three main propositions. The first is that they derive in principle from the ancient Israelite population, part of which migrated in Greek, Roman and later times to Eastern France and Western Germany, and early in this millennium to Poland and other areas. Their Yiddish language was a form of Old German with many later Slavic and Hebrew borrowings. A variant of this concept is that the migration was via Italy to Switzerland, Bavaria and Austria, with a postulated later migration east along the Danube valley to Romania and outwards from there. Yiddish shares many words and expressions with the southern form of German. I am not sure for the moment how much inward conversion to Judaism these two hypotheses suppose. The third, and in some ways the most intriguing idea, depending heavily as it does on the syntax and specific vocabulary of Yiddish, is that the Eastern European Jews, in addition to their descent from the ancient Jews population, have a significant part of their ancestry derived from Slavic converts (Sorbs, Balkans and others) plus a minor Turkic input from further east. The proponents of this theory designate Yiddish syntactically as a Slavic language with a mainly German lexicon. This is just the sort of proposition it might be possible to sort out genetically.[1]

However, the information seems to be accepted only when it suits the needs of a certain political perspective (i.e. the relatedness of Jewish populations and justifying Zionist claims to the 'land of Israel'). In articles by those supporting Zionist views, when data conflicted with political constructs, sometimes political ideologies won. Conclusions were not questioned in some cases and in others genetics was used to advocate policy against other people, a concept akin to the misuse of genetics in the first half of the twentieth century. The history of the misuse of science is well exemplified by the eugenics movement.

EUGENICS, POPULATION GENETICS, AND POLITICAL IDEOLOGY

Francis Galton coined the term eugenics in 1883 from the Greek *eu* which means good and *genic* from the word for born. Galton defined it as the science of 'improvement' of the human race germ plasma through better 'breeding'. In the United States between 1907 and 1960 at least 60,000 people were sterilized without their consent pursuant to state laws to prevent those deemed genetically inferior from reproducing. The main victims of this policy were the mentally disabled or those with psychiatric problems. At the peak of these programs in the 1930s, about 5,000 people were being sterilized every year. Building on developments in the United States, especially the works of the American champion of eugenics, Harry Hamilton Laughlin, the Nazis' eugenics program soon eclipsed the Americans' and became even more extreme, culminating in the mass murder of Jews, Romani, and others. How and to what extent the Nazi and Soviet eugenic movements were influenced by the American program is a field of investigation. Today, few people believe it is useful or desirable to limit diversity and enhance racial purity by protecting the gene pool of a given population.

Zionist zealots insist that Jews form not merely a religious community but a national ethnic community and are descendants of the dispersed twelve tribes of Israel. This is used to justify claims to special rights to the land that override those of its current, non-Jewish inhabitants. Biological evidence to the contrary is quickly dismissed. The *Observer* reported on November 25, 2001 the pressure exerted to suppress a research paper:

> A keynote research paper showing that Middle Eastern Jews and Palestinians are genetically almost identical has been pulled from a leading journal. Academics who have already received copies of *Human Immunology* have been urged to rip out the offending pages and throw them away. Such a drastic act of self-censorship is unprecedented in research publishing and has created widespread disquiet, generating fears that it may involve the suppression of scientific work that questions Biblical dogma. British geneticist Sir Walter Bodmer added: 'If the journal didn't like the paper, they shouldn't have published it in the first place. Why wait until it has appeared before acting like this?' The journal's editor, Nicole Sucio-Foca, of Columbia University, New York, claims the article provoked such a welter of complaints

over its extreme political writing that she was forced to repudiate it. The article has been removed from *Human Immunology*'s web site, while letters have been written to libraries and universities throughout the world asking them to ignore or 'preferably to physically remove the relevant pages'. Arnaiz-Villena has been sacked from the journal's editorial board.

In common with earlier studies, the team found no data to support the idea that Jewish people were genetically distinct from other people in the region. In doing so, the team's research challenges claims that Jews are a special, chosen people and that Judaism can only be inherited.

... In the wake of the journal's actions, and claims of mass protests about the article, several scientists have now written to the society to support Arnaiz-Villena and to protest about their heavy-handedness. One of them said: 'If Arnaiz-Villena had found evidence that Jewish people were genetically very special, instead of ordinary, you can be sure no one would have objected to the phrases he used in his article. This is a very sad business.'[2]

The paper in question, 'The Origin of Palestinians and their Genetic Relatedness with other Mediterranean Populations',[3] is one of 13 published in *Human Immunology* by Dr Arnaiz-Villena and colleagues and many published in other journals by that group including over two dozen papers on genetic anthropology. Their work in population genetics is highly respected. The data they presented are consistent with data published in the same journal by Israeli scientists. Amar et al.[4] showed that Palestinians are closer to Sephardic Jews than either population is to Ashkenazi Jews. The data also show that Ethiopian Jews are genetically very distant from all groups studied. Yet contrary to their own data, Amar et al. concluded, 'We have shown that Jews share common features, a fact that points to a common ancestry.' As I discuss below, they failed to include Slavic populations in their study, which would have revealed similarities between Ashkenazi and the populations in the areas around the Black Sea. Arnais-Villena et al. had data, like those of Amar et al., which demonstrate the close affinity of Palestinians and Lebanese to Sephardi but not to Ashkenazi Jews. This makes sense in light of historical evidence (see Chapter 2) that shows the common Canaanitic origins and linguistic affinities between Sephardic Jews and non-Jewish Arabs (both speak Semitic languages derived from proto-Aramaic).

In any case it makes little sense to admit political conclusions for one viewpoint and deny them for the other in the same scientific journal. *Forward* magazine (a Jewish liberal magazine published in New York) picked up the story and concentrated on the fact that Arnaiz-Villena et al. were making political points in a 'scientific paper'.[5] Yet, *Forward* ignored the fact that political commentary and narrative are unchallenged in many published papers (e.g. Amar et al.'s paper, cited at note 4) when they support a certain political agenda.

Succumbing to ideological pressure in scientific work is not uncommon. In my own work on mammals and population genetics, I used the term Palestine to refer to the geographic area that now includes Israel and the occupied Palestinian areas. Journal editors often receive letters complaining that there is no such place as Palestine and that the word Israel should have been used; in at least two of my papers, the change was demanded by the editors. Of course, Israel has never defined its boundaries and has been a political entity only since 1948. The geographic term Palestine was used for the area for 2,000 years, and it is even used by Israeli scientists (e.g. in the series of books titled *Fauna Palestina* and *Flora Palestina* published by the Israeli Academy of Sciences). Many other ideologically-driven Israeli scientists have attempted to enforce their political views via their scientific work. Hence you will see that many scientific papers use the words Israel or Israeli even when it is not needed for the work at hand. A search of 'Current Contents' (the Institute of Scientific Information's database), for example, showed that use of the words 'Israel' and 'Israeli' in the titles of papers from Israeli authors is over 100 times more frequent than in comparable countries with a scientific research program (Greece and Italy were used as comparisons).

In the field of human genetics, there are many diseases that are common in Ashkenazi populations (e.g. Tay Sachs disease, breast cancer, familial dysautonomia, Canavan disease, and Gaucher disease). These diseases are not common among Sephardic Jews or in Arab populations. Yet, genetic counselors in the US, genetic support groups, and others have now adopted the concept that these are 'Jewish genetic diseases'. The 'Mazor Guide to Jewish Genetic Diseases'[6] cites as the 'best resource' Batsheva Bonne-Tamir and Avinoam Adam's *Genetic Diversity among Jews: Diseases and Markers at the DNA Level*,[7] a book that ironically reviews genetic heterogeneity while being littered with generic statements about the supposed historical 'common origin' of Jews. This basic premise seems to be the underlying assumption for which much of the data were 'fitted'.

The National Foundation for Jewish Genetic Diseases, Inc. accurately states in describing their mission: 'The genetic diseases described on this website are disorders which occur more frequently in individuals of Ashkenazi Jewish ancestry, although with the exception of familial dysautonomia they may occur among individuals of other ethnic backgrounds as well.'[8] Although a distinction is drawn between types of Jewish ancestry, the classification is still placed under 'Jewish Genetic Diseases', as if genetic diseases can be related to religion rather than to biological roots.

There is also a concern about the use of the inappropriately all-encompassing term 'Jewish genetic diseases'. There will be those who are Jewish but not Ashkenazi who will be offered unnecessary screening tests and will be subjected to emotional stress when they are at no more risk of those diseases than the general population are. Further, there are genetic diseases found more commonly in Sephardic Jews, as well as Arabs and other Middle Eastern populations, than in Ashkenazi Jews or other populations. These include familial Mediterranean fever, glucose-6-phosphate dehydrogenate deficiency, and Type III glycogen storage disease. In the United States the majority of Jewish Americans are of Ashkenazi heritage. However, with increased immigration of Israeli Jews to the US, many of whom are Sephardic, the risks of such misguided genetic counseling have been increasing.

In the United States, genetic counselors routinely ask individuals if they are 'Jewish' or have 'Jewish relatives'. They justify this by pointing out that there are certain genetic diseases that are more common among people who are 'Jewish' than among other peoples. Jews are in the minority and the questions to all patients in a genetic clinic include 'Are you Jewish?' or 'Do you have any Jewish background?' Few genetic counselors bother to point out the distinction between Ashkenazi, Sephardic, Ethiopian, and Yemenite Jews. The simplicity of asking about 'Jewish' heritage is attractive in talking to individuals who are mostly non-Jewish or, if Jewish, know nothing about the nuances of ethnicity and population genetics. But the result is that all pregnant women in America who are being counseled by a genetic counselor are being told that Jews have certain genetic diseases and the conclusion is thus inevitable that Jews are genetically related. I cannot over-emphasize the significance of this in shaping the mistaken beliefs of many Jews and other Americans about relationships and ethnicity.

GENETICS AND THE BIBLE

An article published in *Science News* states: 'DNA analysis supports the biblical story of the Jewish priesthood. An analysis of Y chromosomes, which pass from father to son, indicates that Jewish priests, or Cohanim, may stem from an ancestor who lived several thousands years ago.'[9] The *New York Times* reported, 'by the yardstick of the Y chromosome, the world's Jewish communities closely resemble not only each other but also Palestinians, Syrians, and Lebanese, suggesting that all are descendants of a common ancestral population that inhabited the Middle East some 4000 years ago'.[10] The former paraphrasing is of work published by Thomas et al. in *Nature* and the latter of a work published by Hammer et al.[11] Misrepresentation of research papers in magazines and newspapers is not unusual, but in this case, the original authors had misled their readership, and the editors reviewing their articles apparently were not doing a good job. The paper by Hammer et al., from the laboratory of Bonne-Tamir, is especially interesting in this regard. Their own data reveal that:

1. North African, Arabian, and Kurdish Jews and other Near Eastern Jews (in other words Sephardic and Mizrachi Jews) are closer genetically to Palestinians and other Arabian populations than either is to Ashkenazi Jews (who are closer to Turks, as shown in their data).
2. Ethiopian Jews are genetically similar to Ethiopians and are very distant from other Jewish populations.
3. The Lemba of South Africa who claim Jewish ancestry are genetically distant from Askenazim, Sephardic Jews, or Arab Muslims and Christians.

Despite this evidence, the authors reach this remarkable conclusion:

The results support the hypothesis that the paternal gene pools of Jewish communities from Europe, North Africa, and the Middle East are descended from a common Middle Eastern ancestral population, and suggest that most Jewish communities have remained relatively isolated from neighboring non-Jewish communities during and after the Diaspora.

Another example is an article by Nebel et al., from Ariella Oppenheim's group, entitled 'The Y Chromosome Pool of Jews as Part of the Genetic Landscape of the Middle East'.[12] The introduction to the article states as its objective: 'We looked for information about how the Y chromosome of Jews fits into the genetic landscape of the Middle East.' This exposed the bias that was clearly evident in the paper. Data were not shared fully and only selective presentation of information was given, which was used to reach unsubstantiated conclusions. For example, the appendix showed the gene data for six of the 14 populations they had studied. The eight populations studied but not included, other than featuring in one figure, included the key group of Turkish people. This omission was not explained, even though the authors state in the methodology that they examined samples from 167 Turks. Other tables, figures, and studies of relationships concentrated on six populations: 'Kurdish Jews', 'Sephardic Jews', 'Ashkenazi Jews', 'Palestinian Arabs', 'Sunni Kurds', and 'Bedouins'. The naming of these groups alone illustrates the bias of these authors as there is no reason to call Kurds of the Jewish religion 'Kurdish Jews' while calling Kurds of the Muslim Sunni religion 'Sunni Kurds'; and Bedouin are certainly Palestinian, speak Arabic, and are hence Arabs. It is not clear why the authors chose these six groups to study in detail (e.g. in their Figure 2 and Table 2, both looking at genetic similarities) and ignored the others. But buried in the paper may be a clue to the answer. The authors mention in one sentence the possibility of a *European* contribution to the Ashkenazi gene pool, stating: 'Alternatively, it is attractive to hypothesize that the Ashkenazim with Eu 19 chromosomes represent descendants of the Khazars.' Had the authors included the Turkish and other populations in the report, readers could have seen that the groupings clearly show evidence that Ashkenazim are genetically closer to Turks than to Palestinians or Sephardic Jews.

Two articles published in the prestigious British journal *Nature* claimed that the Jewish priests known as Cohanim have unique genetic markers not found in other populations. One, by Skorecki et al., was titled 'Y Chromosomes of Jewish Priests';[13] the other, by Thomas et al., was titled 'Origins of Old Testament Priests'.[14] The *New York Times* and other newspapers and media outlets, including CNN, took up the story without questioning it and put it into the vernacular, claiming support for an ancient Jewish lineage. Ironically, the right-wing *Jerusalem Post* (February 28, 2001) revealed an interesting twist to this story:

> Avshalom Zoossmann-Diskin (PhD) of the department of hematology and genetic pathology at the medical school of Flinders University of South Australia in Adelaide, recently published an article in the German-language *Journal of Comparative Human Biology* that attempts to casts doubt on Skorecki's study. Zoossmann-Diskin, who during the 1990s worked in the laboratory of Tel Aviv University geneticist Prof. Batsheva Bonne-Tamir, concludes that studies of kohanim are 'problematic and arrive at conclusions are not supported by all available data.' He maintains that 'Jewish populations around the world descend from a variety of maternal and paternal origins ... preliminary genetic studies of mitochondrial DNA (from maternal ancestries) have already demonstrated the connections between Jewish populations and non-Jewish populations.'[15]

Zoossmann-Diskin questioned the conclusions reached by Skorecki and colleagues:

> Careful examination of their [Skorecki's and Thomas's] works reveals many faults that lead to the inevitable conclusion that their claim has not been proven. The faults are: the definition of the studied communities, significant differences between three samples of Jewish priests, failure to use enough suitable markers to construct the Unique-Event-polymorphism haplotypes, problematic method of calculating coalescence time and under-estimating the mutation rate of Y chromosome microsatellites. The suggestion that the 'Cohen modal haplotype' is a signature haplotype for the ancient Hebrew population is also not supported by data from other populations.[16]

Most interesting is that the modal haplotype (a group of characteristic genetic markers) for the Cohanim is the most common haplotype among Italian, Hungarians, and Iraqi Kurds, and is also found among many Armenians and South African Lembas.

The article, titled 'Jewish and Middle Eastern non-Jewish Populations Share a Common Pool of Y-chromosome Biallelic Haplotypes', was published in the *Proceedings of the National*

Academy of Science in 2000.[17] The article is from the laboratory of Dr Bonne-Tamir in Israel and is co-authored with eleven others. *PNAS* publishes articles based on communications from respected scientists and not by the traditional peer review process (although those communicating the article are encouraged to have them peer-reviewed). The article in question was submitted by Dr Arno G. Motulsky; it is not clear who reviewed it.

The *PNAS* paper indicated that Ashkenazi Jews are more closely genetically related to Arabs than either population is to Europeans. In fact, Ashkenazim are genetically closer to Turkic/Slavic than to Sephardim or Arab populations. These authors failed to study Slavic groups whom other researchers have identified as closely related to the Slavic ancestral populations of modern Ashkenazi communities. The article seems to have avoided discussing this problematic issue and in its conclusion reiterated the contention that Jews today are, by and large, descended from the original Israelites.

On the maternal lineage, there is no question that Jewish communities share little among themselves. Dr Martin Richards writes:

> Studies of human genetic diversity have barely begun. Yet the fashion for genetic ancestry testing is booming ... Buoyed by the hype, the private sector has been moving in. Other groups, such as Jews, are now being targeted. This despite the fact that Jewish communities have little in common on their mitochondrial side – the maternal line down which Judaism is traditionally inherited. It's the male side that shows common ancestry between different Jewish communities – so, of course, that's what the geneticists focus on.[18]

But a more careful examination of the paternal lineage shows a far more revealing diversity than is apparent from limited studies done by groups with an ideological bias. Italian researchers studied many more populations than Hammer et al. did in the *PNAS* paper and included diverse Turkish and Eastern European populations.[19] The study looked at Y chromosome polymorphisms (genetic variations) in 58 populations, including European, Asian, Middle Eastern, and African groups. The study clearly shows that Ashkenazi Jewish samples were distinct from Sephardic Jews and closer to Turkic samples. Overall, the genetic data in the study were congruent with linguistic findings regarding population affinities. The authors concluded that genetic data do not justify a single origin even in the paternal/male line for the currently disparate Jewish sub-populations (Ashkenazi and Sephardi).

GENETICS VERSUS ZIONIST MYTHOLOGY

The claims of a 'single Jewish origin' are not challenged by a substantiated variety of incredibly rich data from historical, archeological, and other sources. The research of Arthur Koestler, an Ashkenazi Jew, demonstrates that most Ashkenazis are convert Khazars with closer ties to Slavic people than to Semitic people.[20] This conclusion is further bolstered by evidence from language development (e.g. the Yiddish origin and history, and an absence of the use of Aramaic in ancient Khazar Jewish sources), and now genetics. But this was not a new claim. On the web-site of the Zionist Organization of America, we find this accurate description from Kevin Brook:

> It is now the accepted opinion among most scholars in the field that the conversion of the Khazars to Judaism was widespread, and not limited merely to the royal house and nobility. Ibn al-Faqih, in fact, wrote 'All of the Khazars are Jews.' Christian of Stavelot wrote in 864 that 'all of them profess the Jewish faith in its entirety.' A Persian work, *Denkart*, represented Judaism as the principal religion of the Khazars. How sincere was their Judaism? Abd al-Jabbar ibn Muhammad al-Hamdani, writing in the early 11th century, pointed out that 'they took upon themselves the difficult obligations enjoined by the law of the Torah, such as circumcision, the ritual ablutions, washing after a discharge of the semen, the prohibition of work on the Sabbath and during the feasts, the prohibition of eating the flesh of forbidden animals according to this religion, and so on' (translation by Shlomo Pines). The common writing system among the Khazars was Hebrew script, according to Muhammad ibn Ishaq an-Nadim, writing in 987 or 988. A large portion of those Khazars who later adopted a script related to the Cyrillic of the Rus were Jews, according to Tárikh-i Fakhr ad-Din Mubarak Shah, a Persian work composed in 1206.[21]

There is ample historical evidence that Levantine people and Eastern European people of all religions share common genetic markers. Greek and Turkish populations migrated throughout the Balkans,

Eastern Europe, Asia Minor, and the Levant (i.e. the Ottoman Empire during the Hellenistic period). Similarly, Slavic populations have migrated into Asia Minor and the Levant. There was thus a tremendous mix of populations, but certain trends and characteristics remain, especially in populations that attempted to maintain ethnic purity and uniqueness. In both Koestler's and Brook's books (see recommended reading), archeological and historical sources are examined, which lead to the conclusion that the origins of the majority of present-day Ashkenazi Jews are Khazar-Turkish rather than Semitic. Their migration from Khazaria into Eastern Europe and Germany and their development of a unique culture and language (Yiddish) have been well documented and analyzed. Genetic data substantiate this conclusion. Most people who identify themselves as Jewish are Ashkenazi. The Sephardic reproductive rate is higher and they constitute 30–40 percent of the Jewish population in Israel/Palestine. Even within the minority 5 percent, there are documented mass conversions (e.g. of Yemenite Arab populations to Judaism and Christianity). Again, the genetic evidence is clear. Thus from a practical point of view, the Zionist concept of 'return' is flawed, at least with respect to Ashkenazi Jews, who are of Khazar ancestry. Return implies that one's ancestors originated from the area in question.

Studies of Eastern European Jews were erroneously claimed to support the idea that Ashkenazi colonization of Palestine represented a return of people to their homeland. There were apparent cases of suppression of evidence that Palestinians (Jews, Christians, and Muslims) are native people who share a genetic pool with others of their Canaanitic cousins. Thus, valid data are questioned and questionable data and conclusions rapidly published and publicized. In any event, the dispossession of the native Palestinians by Ashkenazi immigrants from Europe cannot be justified by population genetics. After all, one would have to be blind to the basic elements of justice to allow the dispossession of people who are native in every sense of the word and whose ancestors farmed the land for hundreds, if not thousands, of years. Further, it is even more unacceptable for natives to be dispossessed to favor members of a particular religion and converts to that religion, but not converts from that religion to other religions. To use genetics, however accurate or deceptive, to justify an ingathering of people of the Jewish faith while denying Palestinian people the right to their homes and lands is a travesty. Genetics and eugenics have been used in many other instances to support unjustifiable acts of oppression and human rights violations. We should learn the lessons of history. On the positive side, the finding of a close genetic affinity between Oriental Jews, Christians, and Muslims suggests the true kinship of these Canaanitic people. Coexistence in the land of Canaan can be aided by knowledge of these relationships. Despite isolationist attempts, this could help unify Israeli (now more mixed Sephardic and Ashkenazi) and Palestinian narratives and cultures. Perhaps our common destiny in the land of Canaan will involve a similar mix of varied cultures as occurred in the past. The Oriental culture indeed has a lot to contribute to the Occident, and vice versa.

RECOMMENDED READING

Kevin Brook, *The Jews of Khazaria*, first edition (Northvale, NJ: Jason Aronson, 1999).

Arthur Koestler, *The Thirteenth Tribe: The Khazar Empire and Its Heritage* (London: Random House, 1976).

4
Palestinian Refugees and Their Right to Return

There is no such thing as a Palestinian people ... It is not as if we came and threw them out and took their country. They didn't exist.

Golda Meir statement to the *Sunday Times*, June 15, 1969

Question: 'I was wondering, would [the Palestinian] dreams about Jaffa and Haifa suddenly disappear?' Peres answered: 'On this issue I recommend to kill and annihilate.'

interview with the Israeli Foreign Minister Shimon Peres,
Yediot Aharonot October 5, 2001

Everyone has the right to leave any country, including his own, and to return to his country.

Universal Declaration of Human Rights, Article 13

Israel's military occupation of Gaza and the West Bank (including East Jerusalem) was the last and longest-lasting military occupation at the end of the twentieth century. But this 36-year occupation is only a small part of the colonization project in the land of Canaan. Its resolution will thus help, but will not be sufficient to bring sustainable peace. The years 1947–49 generated the largest population of refugees still unsettled since the Second World War with the longest displacement in modern history. Resolving this issue is essential if there is to be peace. Until recently, two competing accounts have existed of how and why the refugees came to exist. The first version, advocated by Israeli leaders, holds that the native Palestinians left present-day Israel voluntarily or with the encouragement of their leaders. This version even hints that Israeli leaders wanted the Palestinian people to stay. The second version, reported by the Palestinian refugees themselves, is that they were ethnically cleansed before, during, and after the 1948 war. In their lexicon, the expulsion became known as *Al-Nakba* (the catastrophe) and is

31

the most traumatic event in Palestinian recorded history. Israeli historians, now with access to Israeli declassified material, have debunked the long-running Israeli propaganda of how the Palestinians became refugees. These historians include Ilan Pappe, Benny Morris, Zeev Sternhall, Avi Shlaim, Simha Flapan, and Tom Segev. A detailed analysis of the declassified material is also provided by Nur Masalha.[1] The cumulative research provides a foundation for understanding what transpired before and during the actual transfer of the native Palestinians. This is key to developing a resolution based on truth and justice.

EARLY PROPOSALS FOR POPULATION REMOVAL

The estimated population of Palestine in 1893 was 469,000 (98 percent) 'Arabs', composed of a mixture of Muslims and Christians (M/C), and 10,000 (2 percent) Jews. In 1897, the population of M/C was 563,000 and of Jews 21,500, shifting the population proportions to 96 percent and 4 percent respectively. In 1912, the estimated population of Palestine was 525,000 (93 percent) M/C and 40,000 (6 percent) Jews. By 1920 there were 542,000 (90 percent) Christians and Muslims and 61,000 (10 percent) Jews.[2] Thus in 23 years, only a small number of European Jews had chosen to come live in Palestine. Things changed dramatically in the 1920s as the British occupied the area and proceeded to fulfill their 100-year program to bring Jews to create a colony to support British interests. In the 16 years after 1920, Jewish immigrants flooded into Palestine and, by 1936, 385,400 Jews (28.2 percent of the population) were living among 983,200 M/C.[3] Thus in little more than a generation (40 years), the population of Jews living in Palestine increased from 2 percent to 28 percent due to the synergy of the Zionist program and anti-Jewish policies in Europe. Coupled with continued dispossession of the fellahin (villagers) based on discriminatory land laws (both Ottoman and British), this led to the 1936 revolt by the native Palestinians. The revolt devastated the nascent political organization, but did cause a temporary decline in immigration in 1939. However, dramatic geopolitical changes occurred during and after the Second World War, which led to the partition resolution of 1947 (covered in Chapter 11).

Although Ottoman and British laws caused some Palestinian fellahin to be dispossessed, the bulk of the Palestinian dispossession has its origins in the refugee crisis beginning in 1947.

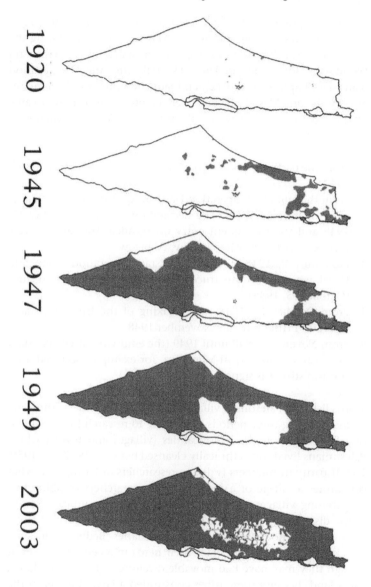

Figure 2   The History of Map Changes in the Land of Canaan for the Past 83 Years.

Jewish and Zionist land ownership in Palestine in 1920; ownership in 1945; UN General Assembly Resolution of 1947 recommending partition; Israeli borders as of 1949 (white areas where later occupied in 1967); Proposed Palestinian 'homeland' based on Israeli government projections (in white).

Contrary to popular belief, the Palestinian refugee problem did not start when Israel was established on May 15, 1948 and during the subsequent war. Preparations began immediately after the Second World War, intensified in late 1947 following the UN partition plan (see Chapters 11 and 12), and launched into a full onslaught months before May 1948 and well before Arab armies became involved.[4] According to Morris, the waves of refugees originated in the following periods:[5]

1. From the partition resolution of November 29, 1947 until March 1948.
2. From the launch of Operation Dalet in April 1948 until the first truce of June 11, 1948. The declaration of statehood May 15, 1948 and the subsequent entry of so-called Arab armies were inconsequential, as will be discussed below.
3. From July 9, 1948 (the start of Israeli Operations Dani and Dekel, which ended the truce) until the end of the second truce (October 15, 1948).
4. From October 15, 1948 (the breaking of the truce by Israel's Operation Hiram) to late November 1948.
5. From November 1948 until 1949 (the emptying of villages such as Al-Faluja and Iraq Al-Manshiya, for example, occurred after the armistice was signed).

Morris lists 369 Palestinian villages and towns (localities) ethnically cleansed during these periods. According to research by Dr Salman Abu Sitta (see note 4), 531 localities (villages and towns) where Palestinians lived were ethnically cleansed between 1947 and 1950. The disparity in numbers is due to researchers differing as to what constitutes a village or a locality. Some researchers combine two neighboring villages into one locality. A more significant source of the discrepancy in numbers is the exclusion by Morris of tribal localities with no definitive village boundaries. Bedouin tribes are well known to reside and graze their herds in a certain area, even though they may have had movable dwellings. Abu Sitta included tribal lands because these tribes constituted a large number of the refugees (about 100,000) and these tribes did have fixed territorial areas well known to travelers to the region. For the purposes of this discussion we will use Abu Sitta's numbers since he lists these localities in detail and with meticulous analysis, with each locality properly charted on a map.

The total number of inhabitants removed from these localities was originally estimated at 750,000, that is to say 80 percent of the Palestinian people living in the land that became Israel. Numbers are easily calculated from village statistics conducted by the British in 1944–45 and adjusting them to 1948–49 numbers by taking into consideration the annual population growth rate (British Mandate measured: 3.8 percent for Muslims, 2 percent for Christians). By including the Bedouins of Beer Sheba, Abu Sitta calculated the actual number of refugees created excluding internal refugees to be 804,767 among a population of about one million that inhabited the area that became Israel by 1949. After the war, the land owned by the Palestinians diminished to 7 percent or 1,474,169 dunums (1 dunum = about 0.25 acre), while Jewish-owned or -controlled lands increased from 8 percent (1,682,000 dunums) to 85 percent. This land, which was allocated to Jews only, made the bulk of the 'land of Israel'.

WHY DID THE PALESTINIANS LEAVE?

Morris has published three books detailing the reasons for the Israeli/Palestinian conflict and the core issue of the displacement of the Palestinians in the creation of Israel:[6] *Israel's Border Wars, 1949–1956: Arab Infiltration, Israeli Retaliation and the Countdown to the Suez War* (1993); *The Birth of the Palestinian Refugee Problem, 1947–1948* (1987); and *Jews and Arabs in Palestine/Israel, 1936–1956* (2000). Based on declassified and newly opened archives from Israeli government and military sources, his books detail the removal of many Palestinian villages to create room for the Jewish state and the intention to allow the immigration of millions of Jews.

According to Morris and other Israeli historians, the reasons Palestinians left these localities were:

1. Expulsion by Zionist/Jewish forces – 122 localities
2. Military assault by Zionist/Jewish forces – 270 localities
3. Fear of Zionist/Jewish attack, or of being caught in the fighting, influence of the fall of a neighboring town, and psychological warfare – 12 localities
4. Abandonment on Arab orders – 6 localities
5. Unknown – 34 localities

While under the 'protection' of the British Mandate, 213 Palestinian villages and towns (population 413,794, or 52 percent of the refugees) were 'cleansed' before the outbreak of the Arab–Israeli war, on May 15, 1948. A further 264 localities (339,272 inhabitants, or 42 percent) were vacated during the 1948 war. After signing the Armistice Agreements, 54 localities were ethnically cleansed (52,000 inhabitants or 6 percent of refugees).

The cleansing (*nikayon*, a word used frequently in Israeli military communications at the time) was usually initiated by massacres. Operation Dalet was launched to conquer the area between Tel Aviv and Jerusalem and commenced in earnest following the massacre of Deir Yassin on April 9, 1948. This was followed by other massacres which terrorized the Palestinians into leaving. There were 33 massacres in 1948 in total:

Mannsurat al Khayt (January 18), Qisarya (February 15), Wadi 'Ara (February 27), Deir Yassin (April 9), Khirbet, Nasir ad Din (April 12), Hawsha (April 15), Al Wa'ra al-Sawda (April 18), Haifa (April 21), Husayniyya (April 21), Balad el-Sheikh (April 25), Ayn az Zaytun (May 2), Al Abbasiyya (May 4), Bayt Daras (May 11), Burayr (May 12), Khubbayza (May 12), Abu Shusha (May 14), Al Kabri (May 21), Al Tantoura (May 21), Qazaza (July 9), Lydda (July 10), Al Tira (July 16), Ijzim (July 24), Beer Sheba (October 21), Isdud (October 28), Al Dawayima (October 29), Eilaboun (October 29), Jish (October 29), Majd al Kurum (October 29), Safsaf (October 29), Arab al Samniyya (October 30), Saliha (October 30), Sa'sa (October 30), Al Khisas (December 18).

Over half of these crimes were committed while the area was still under the protection of the British Mandate. Deir Yassin became the most infamous massacre because of its particular atrocity and the fact that more than 20 villagers were taken to a nearby Jewish settlement, paraded, and then killed to incite panic among the local Palestinians. Menachem Begin, who later became prime minister, gloated about the massacre:

The legend in Deir Yassin helped us in particular in the saving of Tiberia and the conquest of Haifa ... All the Jewish forces proceeded to advance through Haifa like a knife through butter. The Arabs began fleeing in panic, shouting Deir Yassin ... Arabs throughout the country were seized by limitless panic and started to flee for their lives.[7]

These were not acts of horror that occurred in combat (and there were many) but a premeditated plan to cleanse and terrorize the indigenous Palestinian population. In December 20, 1940 Joseph Weitz, responsible for Jewish colonization, a senior official of the Yishuv, and a respected member of David Ben-Gurion's inner circle, wrote in his diary:

it must be clear that there is no room in the country for both peoples ... If the Arabs leave it, the country will become wide and spacious for us ... The only solution is a Land of Israel, at least a western land of Israel [i.e. Palestine since Transjordan is the eastern portion], without Arabs. There is no room here for compromises ... There is no way but to transfer the Arabs from here to the neighboring countries, to transfer all of them, save perhaps for Bethlehem, Nazareth, and the old Jerusalem. Not one village must be left, not one tribe. The transfer must be directed at Iraq, Syria, and even Transjordan. For this goal funds will be found ... And only after this transfer will the country be able to absorb millions of our brothers and the Jewish problem will cease to exist. There is no other solution.[8]

Weitz became chair of the Land and Forest Department of the Jewish National Fund. In 1950 he wrote:

The struggle for the redemption of the land means ... the liberation of the land from the hand of the stranger, from the chains of wilderness; the struggle for its conquest by settlement, and ... the redemption of the settler, both as a human being and as a Jew, through his deep attachment to the soil he tills.[9]

Weitz's mentor and leader was Ben-Gurion, who became Israel's first prime minister. Historians have written extensively about Ben-Gurion's philosophy and statements regarding the non-Jewish residents of the Promised Land. Ben-Gurion encouraged his followers to be circumspect about openly advocating transfer because this could be used as an argument to limit Jewish immigration due to limited space. We find him stating in 1938:

With compulsory transfer we [would] have vast areas ... I support compulsory transfer. I do not see anything immoral in it. But compulsory transfer could only be carried out by England .... Had its implementation been dependent merely on our proposal I would have proposed; but this would be dangerous to propose when the British government has disassociated itself from compulsory transfer. ... But this question should not be removed from the agenda because it is the central question. There are two issues here: 1) sovereignty and 2) the removal of a certain number of Arabs, and we must insist on both of them.[10]

Here is the testimony of an Israeli soldier who participated in the massacre at Al Duwayima, on October 29, 1948:

[they] killed between 80 and 100 Arabs, women and children. To kill the children they fractured their heads with sticks. There was not one house without corpses. The men and women of the villages were pushed into houses without food or water. Then the saboteurs came to dynamite the houses. One commander ordered a soldier to bring two women into a house he was about to blow up ... Another soldier prided himself upon having raped an Arab woman before shooting her to death. Another Arab woman with her newborn baby was made to clean the place for a couple of days, and then they shot her and the baby. Educated and well-mannered commanders who were considered 'good guys' ... became base murderers, and this not in the storm of battle, but as a method of expulsion and extermination. The fewer the Arabs who remained, the better.[11]

Morris quotes similar accounts. A village elder, called Mukhtar in Arabic, is cited as handing a list of 580 killed to the Jordanian Governor of Hebron at the time. Morris details the life of Yosef Nachmani, a high-ranking member of the underground Haganah forces, the precursor to the Israeli Army. Nachmani was also director of the offices of the Jewish National Fund in Tiberias. Nachmani was responsible for settling land throughout Galilee and the Jezreel Valley. At first, he supported the Palestinian transfer, but later underwent a profound change. Morris translates from an entry in Nachmani's journal:

In Salha, which raised a white flag, they carried out a real massacre, killing men and women, about 60 to 70 people. Where did they find such a degree of cruelty like that of the Nazis? They learned from them.[12]

Recently released Red Crescent documents suggest the possible Zionist use of biological warfare for the first time in Palestine in 1948 in Haifa and 'Akka (Acre).[13]

INTENTION, RHETORIC, AND REALITY

Morris, while providing ample evidence on how the removal of natives was accomplished, sometimes with incredible cruelty, nevertheless contends that it was not part of a policy of ethnic cleansing. His critics argue that his conclusion is in direct contradiction to the incredible wealth of data that he presents. Morris defends his thesis thus:

> Certainly Ben-Gurion wanted as few Arabs as possible to remain in Israel. Certainly the majority of the country's political and military leaders were happy to see the Arabs go. Certainly, many officers and officials did what they could to facilitate departure, including occasional expulsions (though, as I pointed out in *Birth*, in most towns and villages the Haganah/IDF had no need to issue expulsion orders as the inhabitants fled before the Jewish troops reached the site; the inhabitants usually fled with the approach of the advancing Jewish column or when the first mortar bombs began to hit their homes). But between what most people want and policy, there is, and was then, a line of demarcation.[14]

More recently, he has written:

> Above all, let me reiterate, the refugee problem was caused by attacks by Jewish forces on Arab villages and towns and by the inhabitants' fear of such attacks, compounded by expulsions, atrocities, and rumors of atrocities – and by the crucial Israeli Cabinet decision in June 1948 to bar a refugee return.[15]

Thus the distinction as to whether a master plan of expulsion existed or not was as lost to the victims as the distinction as to whether Hitler had a master plan for extermination of European Jewry. Irrespective as to whether there was a distinct high-level strategy that was disseminated down, the actions on the ground both before and after the establishment of the state of Israel made it clear as to desired goal and the net outcome. Statements by Zionist leaders are logical though chilling in their correspondence to events on the ground. We read Weitz narrating a conversation with Moshe Shertok (later renamed Sharret, the Israeli foreign minister):

> Transfer-post factum; should we do something so as to transform the exodus of the Arabs from the country into a fact, so that they return no more? ... His [Shertok's] answer: he blesses any initiative in this matter. His opinion is also that we must act in such a way as to transform the exodus of the Arabs into an established fact.[16]

Morris does not deny that massacres were planned to terrify the natives into leaving or that outright expulsions occurred elsewhere as part of Operation Dalet. But his main observation is that the exodus was facilitated by general panic and other issues beyond the deliberate actions of the Zionist forces and did not amount to a master-plan of expulsion. Other historians, including Nur Masalha and Avi Shlaim, argue that the evidence overwhelmingly supports premeditated and coordinated acts of expulsion. Even so, Morris points out that his research has shattered the myth in popular Zionist books like Joan Peters' *From Time Immemorial*.

Gideon Levy, in a review of Morris's most recent work (2000), writes:

> Morris, as calculated as ever, concludes: 'Zionism has always had two faces: a constructive, moral, compromising and considerate aspect; and a destructive, selfish, militant, chauvinistic-racist one ... The simultaneous existence of these two facets was one of the most significant keys to the success of Zionism.'
>
> But, there were also incidents in which they shot – oh, how they shot – and didn't weep at all. And lied. This is the picture that emerges from the chapter about the Israeli press at the time of the Kibiya affair, which expresses the dark side of the then already five-year-old state: no longer a community struggling to establish a country, but an orderly, victorious state, thought of as a democracy, with David Ben-Gurion, who lies, poker-faced, and

its press, which brazenly conceals scandalous information from its readers and even lies knowingly – all for the glory of the State of Israel.[17]

Yitzhak Rabin, the future prime minister and Noble Prize winner, wrote in his diary soon after Lydda's and Ramla's occupation:

> After attacking Lydda and then Ramla ... What would they do with the 50,000 civilians living in the two cities ... Not even Ben-Gurion could offer a solution ... and during the discussion at operation headquarters, he [Ben-Gurion] remained silent, as was his habit in such situations. Clearly, we could not leave hostile and armed populace in our rear, where it could endangered the supply route [to the troops who were] advancing eastward ... Ben-Gurion would repeat the question: What is to be done with the population?, waving his hand in a gesture which said: Drive them out!. 'Driving out' is a term with a harsh ring ... Psychologically, this was one of the most difficult actions we undertook.[18]

THE CONSEQUENCES OF *AL-NAKBA*

Most Israelis acknowledge the history of the Palestinians' expulsion (*Al-Nakba*), but there are those who refuse to address its consequences or the need to redress the injustice. Morris for one recognizes the forced removal of Palestinians but opposes giving the refugees and their descendants the right of return. The right to return was not put forward in peace negotiations even though all segments of the Palestinian people continue to demand it. Understanding this call for the right of return, the origin of the problem and potential viable solutions is thus essential to any lasting peace.

In addition to the myths surrounding the dispossession of the Palestinians, other myths were promulgated between 1947 and 1949. It is now documented that this was not a defensive war on the part of the nascent Jewish state. As previously explained, over half the Palestinian villages were depopulated by operations carried out before the Arab armies intervened. The additional myth of the numerical inferiority of Israeli forces is also easily dispelled. An Israeli historian has calculated the numbers of fighting forces and concluded that: 'indeed, there was never a moment in the 1948

Palestine war that the Jewish forces suffered a numerical inferiority against the Arab forces which they fought'.[19]

But Zionists were not satisfied with the removal of 85 percent of the native people in the areas they occupied. Ben-Gurion wrote: 'If we were an army and not many armies, and if we acted according to [one] strategic plan, we would have been able to "empty" the [Palestinian] population of the upper Galilee, Jerusalem and the road to it, Ramallah, Ludda, South of Palestine in general and the Negev [Al-Naqab] in particular.'[20] The nascent state immediately embarked on a program of plunder and destruction of Palestinian homes, property, and possessions. Dr Don Peretz wrote in 1954:

> nearly half of the new Jewish immigrants live in homes abandoned by the Arabs. They occupy nearly 400 Arab towns and villages ... The Arabs left over 10,000 shops and stores in Jewish hands. The Israel Custodian of Absentee Property took over more than 4,000,000 dunums of former Arab land, or nearly 60 percent of the country's cultivable area. This was nearly two and a half times the total Jewish-owned property at the time the State of Israel was established, and includes most of its olive orchards, a large part of its fruit and vegetable crop land and almost half the citrus groves.[21]

In Lydda from where 60,000 inhabitants were forcibly expelled, the Israeli Army loaded 1,800 trucks worth of looted property.[22] Hadawi estimates Palestinian losses in land and property to be valued at US$562 billion (1988 values).[23] These are only the direct material losses; they do not include loss of life, suffering, injuries, and loss of income.

Meron Benvenisti wrote in his *Sacred Landscape: The Buried History of the Holy Land since 1948*:

> The signing of the armistice agreement did not put an end to the expulsions. In late February 1949, the remaining inhabitants of the township of Faluja and the village of Iraq al-Manshiya ... were expelled. Approximately 3,000 people were ejected from their communities, despite Israel's having guaranteed that they could remain there with full security to themselves, their homes, and all their property.[24]

Following the initial and the largest expulsion of the Palestinians between 1947 and 1949, the state of Israel started a program to 'cleanse' what remained of the Palestinian areas. Thus, an Israeli wrote about Nazareth (the largest remaining Palestinian and mostly Christian Arab town):

> Upper Nazareth, which was created some fifteen years ago, 'in order to create a counterweight to the Arab Nazareth,' constitutes a cornerstone of the 'Judaization of the Galilee' policy. Upper Nazareth was erected upon the hills surrounding Nazareth as a security belt surrounding it almost on all sides. It was built upon thousands of acres of lands which were expropriated high-handedly, purely and simply by force, from the Arab settlements, particularly Nazareth and Rana.[25]

The land acquired by the Jewish National Fund (JNF) from the state of Israel in 1961 was 3,507,000 dunums while the state and development authority controlled 15,205,000 dunums out of a total of 20,323,000 dunums in Israel.[26] The Israel Lands Authority was given control of all lands (whether JNF or state land) and thus controlled most of the land in Israel. This Palestinian land was procured through a variety of mechanisms and then leased only to Jews. This is the land that the kibbutzim were later built on. Still later, with the bankruptcy of the kibbutz movement, Ariel Sharon and other ardent Zionists pushed for the sale of the land to Jews with the proceeds going to the kibbutz leaders.

Israel claimed that it was unifying the city of Jerusalem after its occupation in 1967 and proceeded to settle Jews in the eastern part of the city, including the old Jewish quarter. In this previously Palestinian area many Palestinians had already been evicted from their homes which in 1948 became Jewish West Jerusalem. The reciprocal and fair solution of allowing Palestinians to return to the houses they left in 1948 in West Jerusalem was not contemplated in the process of 'unification' (1967–69). Instead, Israel embarked on a program of further reducing the number of Palestinians in the expanded boundaries of Jerusalem.

CONTINUED ETHNIC CLEANSING
VERSUS JUSTICE AND REPATRIATION

Expulsions were carried out not only between 1947 and 1949 and the years that followed, but also during and following the 1967 war. An estimated 300,000 Palestinians left the West Bank during the Israeli invasion in June 1967, many becoming refugees for a second time. An example of this latter tragedy is the removal of people from Auja refugee camp near Jericho. But this was not the only destructive action perpetrated. All Palestinians who were outside the conquered areas in June 1967 whether as students, on business, or on holiday were prevented from returning and, if they owned property, again this fell to ownership for the Jewish people (via the JNF under absentee property laws).

The Hebrew weekly magazine *Kol Ha'ir* published a letter from the former Israeli Army General Shlomo Lahat, Commander of Eastern Jerusalem immediately after the occupation in 1967, to a Jerusalem council member, in which he wrote: 'In the power of my authority as Military of Jerusalem, immediately after the city was liberated in 1967, I gave orders that Arab inhabitants be evacuated from the Western Wall area and from the Jewish quarter in the Old City. They were given, in agreement, alternative housing in Jerusalem and its environs.'[27]

Like all refugees, Palestinian refugees have an internationally recognized right to repatriation and compensation for their suffering. Article 13 of the Universal Declaration of Human Rights reaffirms the right of every individual to leave and return to his or her country of origin. The Fourth Geneva Convention is also explicit in considering any forced migration or refusal to repatriate people displaced from their homes and lands as a violation of basic human rights.

The refugees themselves have always demanded repatriation and refused resettlement. In the early 1950s the Palestinian refugees themselves steadfastly held to the 'right of return'. UN General Assembly Resolution 194, passed on December 11, 1948, was explicit on the rights of Palestinian refugees. This has been reaffirmed almost every year since by the General Assembly. The resolution states that 'The refugees wishing to return to their homes and live at peace with their neighbors should be permitted to do so at the earliest practicable date.' UN Resolution 181 of November 29, 1947, which recommended the formation of a Jewish state, also forbade population transfer. In fact, Israel's later admission to the UN was conditional on acceptance of relevant UN resolutions, including Resolutions 181 and 194.

Count Folke Bernadotte, former vice chairman of the Swedish Red Cross, successfully challenged the Gestapo chief Heinrich

Himmler's plan to deport 20,000 Swedish Jews to concentration camps during the Second World War. After the war he was appointed Special UN Mediator to the Middle East. Bernadotte stated: 'It would be an offence against the principles of elemental justice if these innocent victims of the conflict were denied the right to return to their homes, while Jewish immigrants flow into Palestine.'[28]

For this outspoken support of basic human rights, Zionists assassinated Bernadotte in Jerusalem on September 17, 1948. An official of the assassination group (Lehi or Stern Gang as it was known to the British), Yitzhak Yizernitzky, later became Israeli prime minister when he was known as Yitzhak Shamir. Nathan Friedman-Yellin was sentenced to five years' imprisonment for the murder, but was pardoned within a few months and, in 1950, elected to the Israeli Knesset. A massive media campaign was then launched to ensure the world did not get the real story about those unfortunate victims of war and repression. The words of Nathan Chofshi from 40 years ago remain true today:

> We came and turned the native Arabs into tragic refugees. And still we have to slander and malign them, to besmirch their name. Instead of being deeply ashamed of what we did and trying to undo some of the evil we committed ... we justify our terrible acts and even attempt to glorify them.[29]

The refugees themselves believed they would eventually return to their homes in what was now Israel and would live in peace with their neighbors. Here is how one refugee captured his feelings:

> Our struggle, as we have proved, has not been merely to live in comfort, to pursue happiness, to acquire purpose, to create, to sing, to make love; it has not been merely to enrich our culture, to contribute to civilization, to leave our imprint in history. But it has been a struggle for the right to do it in Palestine. In the past we were repeatedly offered, were we not, the choice of resettlement elsewhere. More than Palestine, Syria has an abundance of cultivable land to till; Lebanon has more beautiful hills to build on; Australia a more developed economy to benefit from; other parts of the world a more splendid red carpet to welcome us on. But we opted to wait for a return to our homeland, where we had lived, where we danced the dabke, played the oud, where the

men wore their checkered hattas and the women their embroidered shirts, where the sun shone in the winter and the smell of oranges permeated the air and the soul.[30]

In one survey in the West Bank, 74.9 percent of refugees stated that a just solution must include return, 15.6 percent demanded compensation, and 6 percent compensation and return. As for an acceptable solution, 46.2 percent said return, 26.8 percent said compensation, and 18.2 percent improvement in the status of the camps. This is in the West Bank; in Lebanon and Jordan, a higher percentage of people polled wanted to return to their homeland.[31] Another survey showed that 98.7 percent of the refugees (93 percent of all Palestinians) said they would not accept compensation as an alternative to return.[32] Again, the overwhelming majority (96 percent) demanded the right to return to their homes and lands rather than accept a mini-Palestinian state in the West Bank and Gaza. Almost 80 percent of the refugees lack faith in the ability of negotiations to produce positive results for them. Over 85 percent of the general refugee population would return even if it meant living under Israeli sovereignty. Pessimism is higher among the older generation, with 60 percent believing that they will never return to their native land, while in the general population only 23.7 percent believe they will not return.

THE DESIRABILITY AND FEASIBILITY OF RETURN

Many of the refugees live within a short distance of their old homes: Jordan, Syria, Lebanon, the West Bank, and the Gaza Strip. In the Gaza Strip, the population swelled from 80,000 in 1947 to nearly 240,000 at the end of the 1948 war. The population of refugees in Gaza is now approaching a million. This has created a massive humanitarian problem of destitute refugees crowded into a narrow strip of land on Israel's doorstep. Even though fenced in as in a large ghetto, it remains a massive sore on the conscience of many Israelis and their supporters. Is there any logic to having 5,000 individuals per square kilometer in the Gaza Strip while anyone can look over the barbed wire fence and see his land lying practically empty? If all the Gaza refugees returned to their homes in southern Palestine, no more than a tiny fraction of Israeli Jews would be affected. If the refugees of Lebanon returned to their homes in Galilee no more than 1 percent of Israeli Jews would be affected. The total number of refugees from Gaza and Lebanon equals the number of Russian immigrants who came to Israel in the 1990s to occupy the homes of these refugees. What right brings in Russian Jews and what kind of peace deprives Palestinian refugees of the right to return home? Obviously, neither legal nor logistical objections are the reason for withholding the implementation of the right to return. This leaves only one objection and it has to do with racist and apartheid Israeli laws (which we will address in Chapter 7).

One of the main obstacles to offering protection to the Palestinian refugees is that the situation was not only unique in the sense that new people had established a new nation in their homeland, but they were in a legal limbo. When the UN High Commission on Refugees was established, one of its provisions called for the exclusion of refugees who receive protection under another UN agency. The great powers (primarily Britain and the US) protecting Israel's interests interpreted this as excluding Palestinian refugees since they were receiving aid from UNRWA (United Nations Relief and Works Agency for Palestinian Refugees). However, UNRWA, as its name and mandate clearly designate, is a humanitarian organ-ization and its mandate specifically excludes providing protection. Thus Palestinian refugees found themselves in the awkward position of receiving humanitarian aid, but being excluded from UN and international programs to provide protection, resettle-ment, and other political guarantees that UNHCR is able to offer refugees such as those in Afghanistan, Bosnia, and elsewhere. The UN Commission on Human Rights itself recognized this anomaly in a report:

> Such a result [lack of protection] is particularly disturbing as article 1D [of the UN 1951 Convention on Refugees] explicitly recognizes the possibility that alternate forms of protection may fail for one reason or another. The language of article 1D is clear beyond reasonable dispute on this matter: 'When such protection or assistance has ceased for any reason, without the persons being definitively settled in accordance with relevant resolutions adopted by the general Assembly of the United Nations, these persons shall ipso facto be entitled to the benefit of this Convention'. There is no discernible reason to refrain from implementing this inclusionary provision, which should have been done decades ago.[33]

Similarly, the Special Rappoteur to the UN Commission on Human Rights reported finding Israel in violation of the principles and bases of international law in the occupied Palestinian territories. With respect to the plight of the refugees, the report reads:

> The plight of Palestinian refugees in these territories has remained a concern throughout the period of occupation. Most of these refugees were made homeless as a consequence of the war of 1948, as well as the simultaneous and subsequent confiscation of their land, properties and homes, and large-scale demolition of their villages by Israel. Currently, at least 1,353,547 Palestinian registered refugees and other holders of the right of return (as well as to compensation and/or restitution) reside in the territories subject to this mandate [areas occupied by Israel in 1967]. The Special Rapporteur notes that the duty holder, in the case of this right, is also the Occupying Power and bears the main responsibility for the return of persons residing in the occupied Palestinian territories, displaced as a result of the 1948 war, those from the West Bank, the Gaza Strip and Jerusalem displaced in the war of 1967, and refugees from Gaza and elsewhere during and after the hostilities of October 1973. The majority of these refugees still live in 30 camps created after the 1948 war (8 in Gaza and 22 in the West Bank, including Jerusalem).
>
> The continuing violation of the right of return emerged as a special concern during the Special Rapporteur's visit. It is his observation that it is increasingly a subject of both popular and political discourse, including in the form of opinion polls, editorials and petitions, reinforcing the claim to this right. Refugees feel that they are the subjects of continuing violation while kept in limbo for political reasons. Although the international community continues to provide services for Palestinian refugees, they note that there is a lack of adequate protection because they do not fall under the Convention relating to the Status of Refugees of 1951. Israel bears the primary responsibility for the implementation of the right of return, but has not demonstrated willingness to implement it. However, it should be noted that the plight of the Palestinian refugees has become the subject of discourse in certain Israeli political and civil society quarters. For instance, although he did not acknowledge responsibility, in an October 1999 speech to the Knesset Prime Minister

Barak expressed regret for the suffering of the Palestinian people, including refugees.

It is observed, in particular, that the violation of this right grew greater during this review period – as with every passing year – and as the number of right holders grows, the values of their potential compensation and restitution claims increase, and the political and logistical aspects of the task become more complex and difficult.[34]

Indeed, it is getting more complicated, but is not impossible. After all, Palestinians have basic political and human rights that cannot easily be dismissed. Further, research not only shows that the right of the refugees is legal, but also possible. It is a myth that Israelis would have to be displaced to allow for the return of the refugees. A study on the demography of Israel[35] shows that 78 percent of Israelis are living in 14 percent of Israel and that the remaining 86 percent of the land mostly belongs to the refugees on which 22 percent of the Israelis live. However, 20 percent live in city centers, which are mostly Palestinian, such as Beer Al Saba', Ashdod, Majdal, Asqalan, Nazareth, Haifa, Acre, Tiberias, and Safad. Only 2 percent live in kibbutzim. Thus, 154,000 rural Jews control 17,325 square kilometers, which are the home and heritage of five million Palestinian refugees.

An overwhelming body of data clearly demonstrates how and why the catastrophic situation of Palestinian refugees was created and perpetuated by Zionist colonization and expansion. This history is now accepted by most leading Zionist intellectuals. The refusal to remedy the situation remains anchored in racist and suprema-cist insistence on the desire for a homogeneous 'Jewish state' (see Exhibit 1). Research shows that the right of refugees to return is not only legal and moral, but also feasible. A lasting peace cannot be achieved without offering the refugees the choice as sanctioned by basic human rights and international laws and treaties. Of course, choice does not mean every refugee and his or her descendants will return. Depending on the compensation offered, this could vary from a minority to a majority of refugees. The return will advance peace because it will remove the major injustice done in the past 55 years. It may accelerate a positive trend of integration and evolution of Israeli society into a pluralistic and democratic state.

Exhibit 1. Arguments against the Right to Return

Arguments for rejecting refugee return are now well known. They are articulated repeatedly by Israeli leaders (e.g. Shimon Peres in his *The New Middle East*, New York: Henry Holt & Co., Inc. 1993). The three basic arguments are:

1 The Palestinians fled from their villages and towns in 1948 under orders from their leaders.

The allegation surfaced in Zionist discourse directed at new liberal Jewish immigrants who were handed much of the property (lands, homes, belongings) of the Palestinian refugees. According to Sayigh,[36] a pamphlet distributed by Israel's Information Office in New York City after the war also contained this allegation. Many researchers, including Walid Khalidi, Erskine Childers, Benny Morris, Tom Segev, Simha Flapan, and Ilan Pappe, have investigated this and shown it to be without basis. Erskine Childers wrote that 'the charge, Israel claimed, was documented but where were the documents? No dates, names of stations, or texts of messages were ever cited.'[37]

According to Israeli historians such as Benny Morris, a very tiny minority of localities were given notice (not necessarily orders) for residents regarding evacuations. When Arab soldiers were about to retreat from an area they may have warned villagers that they were about to leave, in case the villagers wanted to flee while they still had military protection. According to Sayigh: 'Only in the case of one or two cities, for instance, Haifa, could local Arab authorities be said to have "ordered" flight by organizing evacuation. But in most of the country there was not even this slight degree of organization.'[38]

There is now a consensus that Palestinians became acutely aware of the massacres at Deir Yassin and 33 other localities (some like Tantura actually larger than Deir Yassin). That fear precipitated much of the exodus and was later highly praised by Israeli leaders as making their lives much easier. Arieh Yitzhaqi, for many years a researcher in the history section of the IDF, lists several Arab villages where the Israeli military seemingly followed a policy similar to that carried by Irgun and Stern at Deir Yassin. He cites the attack by the Carmel Brigade on the village of Balad el-Sheikh and the attack by the Third Palmach Battalion on the village of Sa'sa' both resulting in dozens of civilians killed in their homes.[39]

Where these attacks, or the fear of such attacks, did not have the desired 'cleansing' effect, the Israeli Army was forced to take more direct measures. This was the case in Ramle and Lydda, where residents were asked to leave (at gunpoint) after the hostilities ended. Residents on foot, in buses, cars, and trucks were herded east under the watchful eyes of officers and soldiers like Yitzhak Rabin. Further detail from Israeli historians on the cause of the exodus is provided in the chapter main text.

2   There was an exchange of people ('Arab' refugees left Israel while Jewish 'refugees' left the Arab countries) and Arab countries should have resettled those refugees as Israel has resettled Jewish 'refugees'.

There is a rather racist notion implied here that all Arabs are interchangeable and that Palestinians can pay the price for harm done to Jews by others (Arab, Russian, or European governments). While some Jews were expelled from Arab countries, the majority left voluntarily, invited, enticed, or even intimidated into going to Israel to swell the Jewish population as part and parcel of the Zionist program. Most of this happened not between 1947 and 1948 (the years of active violence that resulted in the Palestinian refugees being ethnically cleansed; see http://palestineremembered.com) but in the 20 years after, and was not limited to Arab countries. This was always part of the Zionist plan to gather the Jews regardless of where they lived and settle them on land that belongs to native Palestinians (Christians and Muslims). Israel has never fought for Jews to stay where they are or return to their homelands, whether in Poland or Yemen.

The claim that Palestinian refugees were intentionally not integrated into Arab countries to which they fled is sometimes used to argue for not implementing their basic right to return to their homes and lands. The Universal Declaration of Human Rights, Article 13, states that everyone 'has the right to leave any country, including his own, and to return to his country'. The Geneva Conventions stipulate the right of refugees to return to their homes. UN General Assembly Resolution 194 (adopted in 1948), which specifically applies to Palestinian refugees, states in Paragraph 11, 'the refugees wishing to return to their homes and live at peace with their neighbors should be permitted to do so at the earliest practicable date, and that compensation should be paid for the property of those choosing not to return and for loss of or damage to property which, under principles of international law or in equity, should be made good by the Governments or authorities responsible.' Israel was admitted to the UN in Resolution 273 as a member-state on condition that it abides by Resolution 194. Israel has consistently refused to abide by Resolution 194. It is the will of the Palestinian people that they be repatriated to their homeland. Criticizing neighboring countries because they could not absorb more refugees than they have already is an Israeli attempt to side-step the real issue of the Palestinian right of return.

Covert Israeli operations were carried out to scare Iraqi and Egyptian Jews into fleeing their homes for the 'sanctuary' of Israel.[40] The program to bring them in was motivated more by ideology than by a real interest in their welfare. Tom Segev devoted almost a quarter of his book to documenting the miserable treatment these immigrants received.[41] In any case, the Palestinian refugees did not expel Jews from their homes in Arab countries or any of the other 40 countries from which Jews emigrated to Israel under the banner of Zionism. Palestinian human rights should not be contingent on the actions of other states against their own minorities, action over which Palestinians had no control. We

Palestinians fully support the internationally recognized right to return of Jews to Arab or other countries. The Israeli government, however, has never been willing to fight for their rights, because it knows that by doing so it would implicitly recognize that expulsion and dispossession are wrong, whether the victims are Polish, Russian, Yemenite, or Palestinians. The governments of Morocco, Egypt, Iraq, and Yemen (unlike Israel) have always stated that those who left are welcome to return.

On December 11, 1975, the Iraqi government even took full-page advertisements in newspapers around the world (*New York Times, the Toronto Star, Le Monde*) asking the 140,000 Iraqi-born Jews living in Israel and around the world to return. Egyptian President Sadat extended an invitation to Egyptian Jews to return to Egypt in September 1977, just weeks before his peace trip to Israel.[42] Israel has never extended an invitation to Palestinians to return to their homeland. In either case, Israeli Jews with claims in Arab countries should take them up with those countries and Jews should be treated with respect, dignity, and equality wherever they live. Israel, however, was not interested in discussing this issue when a peace agreement with Egypt was signed (Egypt has a sizeable Jewish presence).

In summary, the immigration of Jews to Palestine under the Zionist banner does not negate Palestinian human rights. One has to remember that Jews from Arab countries as well as Eastern Europe settled in the US and Canada. Their issues and their questions are legitimate areas of exploration (e.g. Jews have a right to be treated equally in their own countries like any other religious group and this must be defended and fought for). Their rights also follow international law and the Universal Declaration of Human Rights (including their right to return to their countries of origin), but certainly do not nullify similar rights for other people, whether Russians or Palestinians. Palestinians who were ethnically cleansed have inalienable right to repatriation. This must be their choice and is enshrined in common logic as well as international law and is not subject to dictates of apartheid and separation envisioned by a colonial settler movement.

3   It is not practical to return refugees and we need to seek a 'reasonable and fair solution' to the refugee problem, i.e. one acceptable to Israelis. Return of refugees is considered a danger to the 'Jewish character of the state'.

This myth needs to be broken down to two constituent parts: the feasibility of return and the issue of the 'Jewish character'. Detailed research had documented that the vast majority of refugees could return to their individual lands without displacing resident Israelis (see note 35). In the case of the urban refugees (in cities like Jaffa and Beersheba), it is possible to consider the natural expansion of cities had Palestinians stayed and thus allow for urban expansion where Palestinians are returned to very near their original locations. The Zionist program acquired land (by confiscation and other means) for the benefit of Jewish people everywhere. Thus, most land now administered as such is not given as private property to Jews or the Jewish communities like the kibbutzim and moshavim. Rather, it is owned by the Israel Lands Authority and transfer to its native Palestinian ownership would not create legal hurdles. As for space, Israel accommodated one million Russians in just one decade, mostly settling them in urban areas. Yet most of the rural Palestinian village lands are empty and population density within the so-called Green Line (1948 occupied Palestine) is at least five times greater than in the areas occupied in 1967. The Israeli government is trying to import as many Jews as possible from all over the world and claims it wants to get most of them into the Holy Land by 2020.

When detailed studies clearly show that feasibility and space are not limiting, the need to 'maintain the Jewish character of the state' is brought up. However, statistical analysis of birth rates shows that even with maximum immigration, Palestinian Muslims and Christians will outnumber Jews in three to four decades even without the return of the refugees. Thus, unless Israel engages in new rounds of ethnic cleansing (as happened in 1947–49 and 1967), the obvious answer is that there can be no ethical or legal justification for maintaining a 'Jewish character' that violates human rights and the basic elements of international law. Further, what is the 'character' of the state and what does it mean for its citizens and how could this be threatened by Palestinians? In Israel, 32 languages are spoken, including Arabic. Palestinians without return constitute 20 percent of the Israeli population and their percentage is expected to continue to grow rapidly due to high birth rates.

To understand the nature of what some claim they want to maintain, one should examine Israeli laws that are clearly discriminatory. Many Jews recognize that Israel needs to evolve a state for all its citizens, and it eventually will, with or without the refugees returning. It is only logical to expect that the 1.2 million Palestinian citizens of Israel and many of their Jewish compatriots do not support the national anthem, which talks about Jewish yearning for a homeland. They are not keen about a state that has no constitution to protect non-Jews but rather has specific laws to discriminate against them. The laws ensure that 'Jewish only' towns and villages continue to flourish while remaining Arab towns are besieged, get fewer or no services, and dwindle. They are not content in a state that has a law of return giving automatic citizenship to any Jew in the world who desires it, while denying citizenship to non-Jewish people who were born and raised there. Many of this latter category are relatives of those Palestinians who remained and many of these people have not seen each other in 55 years. Thus, racist concern over 'diluting the Jewish majority' should not be an acceptable basis for rejecting basic human rights as also supported by an overwhelming body of international law. A more detailed exposé of Israeli laws and practices to maintain the 'Jewish state' is found in Chapter 7.

Table 1   Growth of the Jewish Population of Palestine (000s)

Jews	Population*	Percentage
1893	10	2
1897	21	3.6
1912	40	6
1920	61	10
1936	385	27
1947	530	31
1967	2383	64
1999	5619	68

* After 1947, the percentage is of the remaining population of non-Jews and thus excludes Palestinian (native) refugees. The numbers in 1967 and 1999 exclude Palestinians in the West Bank and Gaza (22 percent of the land, 3.5 million people). Data from Israel Central Bureau of Statistics and Philip Mattar, *Encyclopedia of the Palestinians* (New York: Facts on File, Inc., 2000), pp. 323–34. For total Palestinian population, see Table 2.

Table 2   Christian and Muslim Palestinian Population (000s)

Year	Within Palestine	Israel	West Bank	Gaza	Outside Palestine	Total
1860	411					411
1890	553					553
1914	738					738
1918	689					689
1931	860					860
1940	1,086					1,086
1946	1,308					1,308
1950	1,170	165	765	240	304	1,474
1960	1,340	239	799	302	647	1,987
1970	1,412	367	677	368	1,289	2,701
1980	1,992	531	964	497	2,100	4,092
1990	2,731	687	1,373	671	3,302	6,033
2000	3,787	919	1,836	1,032	4,667	8,454

Source: Justin McCarthy's compilation of data on population, in Philip Mattar, *Encyclopedia of the Palestinians* (New York: Facts on File, Inc., 2000), pp. 323–34.

RECOMMENDED READING

Sami Hadawi, *Bitter Harvest: A Modern History of Palestine*, fourth edition (Northampton, Mass.: Interlink Publishing Group, 1998).
Nur Masalha, *Expulsion of the Palestinians: The Concept of 'Transfer' in Zionist Political Thought, 1882–1948* (Washington, DC: Institute for Palestine Studies, 1992).

Ilan Pappe, *A History of Modern Palestine: One Land, Two Peoples* (Cambridge: Cambridge University Press, 2004).

Tom Segev, *One Palestine, Complete: Jews and Arabs Under the British Mandate*, trans Haim Watzman (New York: Metropolitan Books, 2000).

5
Jerusalem (Ur-Salem, Jebus, Yerushalaym, Al-Qods): A Pluralistic City

Many argue that a settlement of the Palestinian–Israeli conflict hinges on what to do with Jerusalem. Some early European maps placed Jerusalem not only at the center of the map, but at the center of the Earth and Universe. Today many still view Jerusalem as the spiritual center of our world. It is still a center of attention, a center of dispute, and a focal point for wars and religious intolerance. Its history has been variously glorified, exaggerated, diminished, maligned, or distorted for economic, political, and religious ends. Political and religious authorities sometimes hid the history of its inhabitants while emphasizing the history of its rulers. The real history is now being written by native historians and it is a history that is more meaningful and more optimistic than the traditional mythologies advocated by religious extremists. It is a history that has many surprises as well as lessons for those seeking a durable peace. We shall address the history of the city in order to see what can be done in the context of coexistence and sharing.

JEBUSITES AND JERUSALEMITES

A group of western Canaanites called Jebusites built and dwelt in Ur-Salem around 3000 BCE. *Ur* means 'city' in most Semitic languages, including the languages of Akkad, Ashur, Aram, and Phoenicia. Salem or Shalem in the ancient dominant Canaanitic language, Aramaic, is a reference to the ancient god of the place. It is also found in the derived neo-Aramaic, Arabic, and Hebrew languages. In all these Semitic languages Salem or Shalem means in its root (SLM) safety, peace, and protection. Some archeologists argued that Ur-Salem was also recognized as a neutral area and so was not subject to the fierce border clashes of other more powerful economic groups. The city was a small urban center where inhabitants engaged in trade, farming, and small crafts. The city – no more than a small town at the time – could not support a large population because it had only one main spring and few natural resources or assets. This was the beginning of the period of history dominated by city-states, where a city-state is defined as a small state with one large city center.

In the Bible it is stated that the king of the Jebusites was Melchezedek, whose name means 'good king' in Canaanitic languages (Malik Sadeq in Arabic, Melch Tsedeq in Aramaic). He was also recognized as a priest of the High God. The High God, or El in ancient Canaanitic tongues, became Elohim in Hebrew and Allah in Arabic. The early prophets thus recognized and lived alongside the Jebusites as Canaanitic people. King David decided to conquer the Jebusite Ur-Salem and make it his capital in order to unify the various tribes some 3,000 years ago. Ur-Salem was not of religious or political significance to the tribes until David made it so for two reasons. First, Ur-Salem lay halfway between the two holiest sites in Judaism, Shekhem in the north and Hebron in the south. Second, Ur-Salem (Yerushalaym) lay outside the dominion area of the tribes, on the border of the lands assigned to Benjamin and those assigned to Judah. It was under Jebusite rule for over 500 years while other tribes and kingdoms, including the Israelites, surrounded it. This made it more attractive as the site of the capital because it was a neutral area. This situation is analogous to the choice of Washington DC as capital of the 13 states of the budding United States because it was outside of the dominion of each of the states and thus a neutral area.

The temple of Solomon was almost certainly built on the site of a Jebusite temple. Historically, the indigenous population could not be prevented from going to their holy places but it is possible to change what Campbell calls 'the mask of God'.[1] The Bible has contradictory statements about the conquests of the land of Canaan by the Israelites. For example, the Book of Joshua portrays the conquest of Canaan as a single event that took place in one campaign divided into a number of stages, at the end of which the inhabitants of the land were all slaughtered: 'He left not a single survivor' (Joshua 11: 8) and 'the land was now at peace' (Joshua 14: 15) for 'the country now lay subdued at their feet' (Joshua 18: 1). If Joshua annihilated the natives, how does one reconcile this with the Book of Judges, which states that fighting continued after Joshua's death: 'After the death of Joshua the Israelites inquired of YAHWEH, "which tribe should be the first to attack the Canaanites?"' (Judges 1: 1).

We also read that 'Jericho fought against you, as did the Jebusites, but I delivered them into your hands, I drove them out before you' (Joshua 24: 11). Yet in Joshua 10 we read that 'as for the Jebusites the inhabitants of Jerusalem, the children of Judah could not drive them out: but the Jebusites dwell with the children of Judah at Jerusalem unto this day'. Several centuries later, the natives vanquished by Joshua miraculously reappear: 'And the king [David] and his men went to Jerusalem unto the Jebusites, *the inhabitants of the land*: which spoke unto David, saying, Except thou take away the blind and the lame, thou shalt not come in hither: thinking, David cannot come in hither. Nevertheless David took the strong hold of Zion: the same is the city of David ... So David dwelt in the fort, and called it the city of David. And David built round about from Millo and inward' (2 Sam. 5: 6–9).

Can one take the Hebrew Bible with such internal contradictions as a source of historical facts? There is no archeological evidence to support the successful ethnic cleansing of those 'inhabitants of the land', but merely episodic and incomplete triumphs in some areas with the continued existence of many ethnic groups, kingdoms, and tribes. This is similar to the lack of a conclusive victory by the Israelis over the Palestinians and the partial success of the ethnic cleansing of 1947–49. One explanation for the lack of concordance between the Old Testament and the historical record is that stories of battles were written many years after the events and were intended, for the most part, to serve as a means to draw closer together and obey God. They are sometimes exaggerated and sometimes inaccurate in a historical sense. Unfortunately, 'biblical archeology' was and in many ways continues to be greatly influenced by individuals more interested in proving the historicity of the Hebrew Bible than in strict adherence to scientific principles.[2] When archeology is allowed to tell the story, the Bible stories show little correspondence to the events that transpired on the ground.

CHANGING POWERS, ETERNAL PEOPLE

Ur-Salem continued to be inhabited as it came under varying degrees of control from a wide variety of political powers. These included the Assyrians, Egyptians, Israelites, Romans, Islamic Khalifates, Islamic Ottomans, British, Jordanians, and Israeli/Zionists. Jerusalem has always been a center of commerce and activity for the predominantly Jebusite natives of the surrounding hills as Beirut was for the Phoenicians inhabitants of that city's surrounding hills. This was before the modern eras of colonialism and later nationalism. The modern construct of a political capital for a multi-city state is a much more recent historical development. Jerusalem has always been a pluralistic city with a multiethnic and multi-religious community. In the days of King Solomon and King David a flourishing Canaanite population lived around the area and its inhabitants practiced different belief systems and spoke several languages.

When the Romans conquered Jerusalem in 63 BCE, archeological data indicate that much of the population was composed of Aramaic-speaking Nabateans and, to a much lesser degree, Hebrew-speaking Canaanites. The Nabateans were Arab Canaanites who developed Nabatean Aramaic into the first written Arabic script. As before, the area was inhabited by a number of ethnic and religious communities including those who worshipped Ba'al, Yahweh, and other gods, as well as those who spoke other languages. The Romans were very tolerant of religious diversity and allowed autonomy to the local population as long as overall Roman rule was not challenged. A challenge to Roman rule did come about in 70 CE in the form of a rebellion by the Jewish Canaanites led by the Maccabees. The Romans put down this revolt and from that point on prohibited certain religious practices, although Jews continued to live in the surrounding areas. A subsequent revolt in 135 led to even more restrictions and destruction. The Romans rebuilt Jerusalem as a Roman city and named it Alia Capitolina. Gradually, the city became more Romanized and records show that Judaism's influence declined in favor of Christianity as well as the pagan religions of the primarily Canaanitic inhabitants. The Roman Empire adopted Christianity in the fourth century and ushered in a new era of 'state religion'. During this period other religions were oppressed while Christianity and with it Jerusalem grew in importance.

The Persian takeover of Jerusalem in 614 was a significant blow to the local communities. Jews sided with the Persians and exacted violent revenge on the local Christian communities and remaining Romans for their years of oppression. The Christian Byzantine Empire conquered Jerusalem in 628 banning Hebrews and many other natives from the city. But this was to be a very short and brutal nine-year rule because Jerusalem was brought under Islamic control in 637, ushering an era of stability.

JERUSALEM UNDER ISLAMIC RULE

Karen Armstrong, in her respected book *Jerusalem: One City Three Faiths*, wrote that Khalif Umar Ibn Al-Khattab, the Islamic leader at the time:

> expressed the monotheistic ideal of compassion more than any previous conqueror of Jerusalem, with the possible exception of King David. He presided over the most peaceful and bloodless conquest that the city had seen in its long and often tragic history. Once the Christians had surrendered, there was no killing, no destruction of property, no burning of rival religious symbols, no expulsions or expropriations, and no attempt to force the inhabitants to embrace Islam. If a respect for the previous occupants of the city is the sign of the integrity of a monotheistic power, Islam began its long tenure in Jerusalem very well indeed.[3]

Upon taking the city, Umar lifted the ban on Jews worshipping in Jerusalem. Umar was not happy that Temple Mount had been allowed to deteriorate and set about clearing and restoring it. According to Armstrong, 'Both the Jewish and Muslim sources make it clear that Jews took part in the reclamation of the [Temple] Mount.'[4]

Mecca and Jerusalem are each mentioned only once in the Qu'ran and Medina only twice. Yet, the fact that they are mentioned so few times certainly does not diminish their status in the eyes of Muslims. The Qu'ran is not a history book but is mainly concerned with giving guidance to believers on how they can best serve God. Jerusalem was the original Qibla, or direction of prayer, for Muslims. Muslims believe that Prophet Muhammad made a miraculous journey from Mecca to the Al-Aqsa mosque in Jerusalem in 621, where he ascended to heaven and conversed with God. The event is central to Islamic belief, and is mentioned in the Qu'ran (Al-Isra, 17): 'Glory to Him Who did take his servant for a journey by night from the Sacred Mosque [in Mecca] to Al-Aqsa Mosque [in Jerusalem] Whose precincts We did bless in order that We might show him some of Our signs.'

Islamic texts are not only comprised of the Qu'ran, but of the Hadith of the Prophet and the Shariah. The Hadith (sayings) state that a prayer offered at the Haram area in Jerusalem is worth 500 prayers elsewhere. This is the reason why many devout Palestinian Muslims risk so much to get through blockades and checkpoints for

Friday prayers in Jerusalem. Further, much of the land in and around the city of Jerusalem is Waqf land – that is, a religious endowment set aside so that no private or state ownership is allowed.

Islamic rule was interrupted briefly by the brutal conquest of the city during the Crusades. Crusaders persecuted and many banished from Jerusalem not only Muslims but also Jews and Orthodox Christians. It was not until Islamic forces under the leadership of Salah Ed Din (Saladin) retook the city that all were invited back to the city they held sacred.

TWENTIETH-CENTURY NATIONALISM

In the twentieth century, inhabitants of many areas of the world fought for independence from colonial rule. Over 70 percent of the countries in Asia and Africa regained independence between 1940 and 1965. Western Jerusalem and dozens of villages around it were ethnically cleansed well before the Arab armies came in, ostensibly to create stability. Natives of villages west of Jerusalem were terrorized to leave or massacred outright (e.g. in Deir Yassin). The activities of Ben-Gurion and his troops around Jerusalem are now well documented.[5]

The Zionist leadership was involved in a tacit agreement with King Abdullah of Jordan. According to this agreement, Abdullah would take the area of Palestine allotted to the Arabs west of the Jordan Valley according to UN Resolution 181 (II) of November 29, 1947. This region later became known as the West Bank. The rest of Palestine was to be left for the 'Exclusive Jewish State'. Intriguing details of this agreement are reported in Avi Shlaim's *The Politics of Partition: King Abdullah, the Zionist Movement, and the Partition of Palestine*.[6]

Britain was aware and highly supportive of this agreement. Abdullah was Britain's agent in the area, and expanding his emirate west of the Jordan would be consistent with Britain's interests. On February 7, 1948, the British Foreign Office received Tawfiq Abul Huda and Glubb Pasha for discussions on the future of Palestine. Glubb, who was the 'Arab legion' leader, was also British. Glubb took troops into the areas designated for the Palestinian state, areas which later were called the West Bank. Intense fighting occurred only around Jerusalem. This was due partially to a lack of communications and agreement between Abdullah and the Hagannah on the fate of the city designated as an international area by the UN General Assembly Resolution 181.[7]

The history of the Israeli conquest of the western part of the district of Jerusalem is well known. The last population surveys undertaken by the British revealed that the area around Jerusalem had slightly more than a quarter of a million inhabitants, of whom 40.4 percent were Jews, predominantly new immigrants who had arrived in the previous 15–20 years under the Zionist banner. Palestinian Christians and Muslims owned 91.8 percent (231,446 dunums) of the western part that was conquered by Israel in 1948; 2.7 percent of the western part was Jewish-owned, and the rest (6 percent) was public land. This area was emptied of its native inhabitants and their lands handed over to the Jewish Agency (Jewish National Fund) for Jewish settlement. Villages like Deir Yassin were emptied by massacres, others by fear of attack, and yet others by straightforward expulsion. In total, 30,000 Jerusalem inhabitants were driven out of Lifta, Shaikh Badr, Ein Kerem, Deir Yassin, Talbiya, and Al-Maliha. Israel declared Jerusalem its capital in 1950 and in the same year Jordan annexed the West Bank. Both moves were illegal according to international law.

UN General Assembly Resolution 181, on which the legality of the Israeli state is sometimes premised, insisted that Jerusalem (including West Jerusalem) be designated an international city and thus should not fall under the sovereignty of Israel or the Arab state. General Assembly Resolution 303, 'Palestine: The question of an international regime for the Jerusalem area and the protection of the Holy Places', was adopted on December 9, 1949. It reiterated the intention of Resolutions 181 and 194 regarding Jerusalem being international. The Security Council implicitly accepted all three resolutions and has never recognized Israeli rule over West Jerusalem. The Security Council was more explicit in rejecting the administrative actions of Israel in East Jerusalem as violating UN Security Council Resolution 242. In this resolution, Israel was asked to withdraw from the areas occupied in 1967, based on the premise of 'inadmissibility of acquisition of territory by force'. No subsequent international treaty recognized West or East Jerusalem as part of Israel. No government has been willing to relocate its embassy to Jerusalem until the final status is resolved.

Israel has intentionally never defined its borders due to its expansionist character. On a practical level, this has resulted in a process that has led to the physical, economic, and psychological separation of Jerusalem into two cities. West Jerusalem developed a European character with new buildings in the demolished Palestinian neighborhoods and more of an ethnocentric and mono-religious character. East Jerusalem became even more Arabic, but retained Christians, Muslims, and peoples of other religious backgrounds. The two halves of Jerusalem truly became separate and unequal, while remaining contested and unstable.

Between 1948 and 1967, citizens from each side of the divided Jerusalem could not visit the other side because officially a state of war existed and laws in force prevented freedom of movement. This does not mean that Jews were barred from the old city, only that Israelis could not go to Jordanian-controlled areas and Palestinians and Jordanians could not enter Israeli-controlled areas. Many local Jews such as the Samaritans in Nablus and European and American Jews could visit freely.

REUNIFICATION OR APARTHEID AND EXCLUSION

In 1967, Israel launched a war that resulted in the occupation of the remaining 22 percent of geographic Palestine, including East Jerusalem, as well as the Egyptian Sinai and the Syrian Golan Heights. Israel carried out a general census of the newly occupied territory on July 25, 1967. All residents who were outside the area for any reason – working, studying, visiting relatives or on holiday – were considered absentees and thus denied the right to reside in Jerusalem or in the occupied areas. Their lands were acquired by the Jewish Agency as 'absentee property'. This was thus a repeat of the 1948 displacement, but on a smaller scale (in 1947–49 over 800,000 were made refugees, while in 1967 the number was some 300,000). Israeli laws and actions continued the removal of native Palestinians and acquisition of their lands: in 1948 in West Jerusalem and after 1967 in East Jerusalem. The government did not try to make a secret of its plan to make Jerusalem a Jewish metropolis while keeping the non-Jewish population at less than 30 percent. This was deemed to have the added advantage of preventing the establishment of a sovereign Palestinian state with Jerusalem as its capital.

How did the Israeli conquest of Jerusalem fare in comparison to conquests by previous rulers? Armstrong writes:

On the night of Saturday 10 June [1967], after the armistice had been signed, the 619 inhabitants of the Maghribi Quarter were

given three hours to evacuate their homes. Then the bulldozers
came in and reduced this historic district – one of the earliest of
the Jerusalem Al-Waqf [Islamic trusts] – to rubble. This act, which
contravened the Geneva Conventions, was supervised by [then
Israeli Jerusalem mayor Teddy] Kollek in order to create a plaza
big enough to accommodate the thousands of Jewish pilgrims
who were expected to flock to the Western Wall. This was only
the first act in a long and continuing process of 'urban renewal'
– a renewal based on the dismantling of historic Arab Jerusalem
– that would entirely transform the appearance and character of
the city.[8]

The assault on Jerusalem's Arab inhabitants is well documented in
such books as *Separate and Unequal: The Inside Story of Israeli Rule
in East Jerusalem*, written by no lesser authorities than three Israeli
Jews, two of whom were former advisers on Arab Affairs to Mayors
Teddy Kollek and Ehud Olmert, and the third a former senior
reporter for the *Jerusalem Post*.[9] The Knesset adopted three legislative acts on June 27, 28 and 29, 1967, extending Israeli law to the
occupied eastern sector of the city and enlarging the municipal
boundaries of 'united' Jerusalem. The 'new city' thus expanded
from 44,000 dunums to 108,000 dunums (approximately 29,000
acres). These laws defy UN resolutions and basic international law,
which prohibit countries from acquiring territory by force.

The local Muslim Waqf had had ownership of the Haram Al-
Sharif area for hundreds of years. Claiming the site of an ancient
Jewish temple provides a poor legal argument for sovereignty to
be given to the modern state of Israel established as a Jewish state
some 2,000 years later. Jews consider the Western Wall as holy and
their right to visit it and worship there should be acknowledged. It
should be noted that the Western Wall is a retaining wall to the hill
and thus directly supports the compound of the Haram Al Sharif.
Under the British Mandate an international team of investigation
was dispatched to the city to resolve the issue of the right of worship
and ownership of the holy places. On June 8, 1931, the results of
the investigations were enshrined in law. Regarding the Western
Wall and the adjacent Moghrabi Quarters, the report stated:

To the Muslims belongs the sole ownership and the sole propri-
etary right to the Western Wall, seeing fit that it forms an integral
part of the Haram Al Sharif area. To the Muslims there also

belongs the ownership of the pavement in front of the Moghrabi
(Moroccan) Quarter opposite the Wall.

Despite this, Palestinians now acknowledge the historic and
religious Jewish rights to the Western Wall. Yet, Palestinians judge
Israel's rule not just by its conduct in Jerusalem's holy sites, but
by its history of removing them and repressing them throughout
the city and indeed the whole country. Palestinians remember that
after dozens of Muslims were massacred at the Ibrahimi mosque
in Hebron, Israel divided the mosque in two and gave one part
to Jewish settlers, including the place where Abraham's tomb is
believed to be located. More than 100,000 Palestinians in Hebron
live under extreme duress to guarantee the 'religious' rights of a
few hundred Jewish settlers there. Palestinians see how Israel seized
Rachel's Tomb and Joseph's Tomb in Bethlehem and Nablus, which
had both existed unmolested for millennia, and turned them into
armed camps from which non-Jews are banned, and from which
Israeli soldiers control access to and from these cities.

THE FUTURE: A CITY OF PEACE

The 'compromise' offered by Prime Minister Ehud Barak at Camp
David in July 2000 would have handed over the remaining Palestinian villages in the Jerusalem area to Palestinian control, but would
have maintained Israel's sovereignty. Air control, security, and
all other aspects of authority would have remained under Israeli
dominion. Palestinians would be allowed to establish their capital
not in Jerusalem, but in the village of Abu-Dis. When Sharon,
authorized by Barak, 'visited' the Muslim holy site with 1,000
security forces to drive home Israel's intention to exercise its rule,
the uprising began. The message of the Palestinian demonstrators
was that no peace will come with illegal and discriminatory rule in
Jerusalem.

Jerusalem has been and remains, as it was for thousands of years,
a multiethnic and multi-religious community. Its major inhabitants
were and continue to be Canaanites of various religions. Jebusites,
Hebrews, Nabateans, and other Canaanites lived together in relative
harmony, except for short periods of strife. Wars were glorified and
history exaggerated by descendants of the conquerors. There were
political struggles to control power and borders with few conflicts
arising over other issues. But no large ethnic cleansing occurred

until recently. After the large-scale ethnic cleansing in West Jerusalem in 1948 and since 1967 there has been a slow thinning of Palestinian residents in East Jerusalem. This, coupled with massive immigration of primarily Ashkenazi Jews into the vacated and confiscated areas, is changing the multiethnic, multi-religious character of this great city. Considering its history and current composition, the envisaged solutions are now limited. The city cannot remain under Israeli rule with its current discriminatory laws (see Chapter 7). Few are revisiting UN Resolution 181 recommending UN custodianship of the city. Later UN resolutions and international law require Israel to withdraw from the old city and the expanded eastern half (conquered in 1967). But why not make Jerusalem the capital of a pluralistic unitary country for all its citizens? Clearly, considering the mixed neighborhoods of the city, and its status among the three main monotheistic religions, the only viable and durable solution is this option. Jerusalem will then become the unifying capital it once was for the people of the land of Canaan. Jerusalem will then become a true golden city of coexistence, setting an example to all humanity.

RECOMMENDED READING

Karen Armstrong, *Jerusalem: One City Three Faiths* (New York: Knopf, 1996).

6
Zionism

Promised Land, Promised Land
I was taken to a foreign land.
A land believed to be full of promise.
I was told it bore fruits with the sweetest of nectar.
Its soil so rich with olive branches of peace.
Where the streets were paved with golden orange groves.
The nectar though sweet to my tongue
Brought tears to my bowels.
The peace-bearing olives were pressed
To make oil of bullfights. *Ole!*

Ahlam Shalhout

Zionism is variously looked at as a salvation or as a catastrophic power. Yet all agree that Zionism was and is at the center of the conflict that has now raged for over 100 years in the land of Canaan. No lasting solution can be approached without an honest examination of the origin and consequences of this phenomenon, which continues to shape events, not only in Palestine/Israel, but in the region and the entire world. The origins of Zionism are often said to have been initiated in the nineteenth century by European Ashkenazi Jews. But this political movement has an earlier and more dramatic history, some of it distinctly un-Jewish in origin. In dealing with the problems plaguing the land of Canaan today, we must have a clear handle on Zionist history and the forces that have challenged or promoted it.

CHRISTIAN ZIONISM AND COLONIALISM

Napoleon Bonaparte was the first to attempt to construct a network of Jews loyal to the French Empire throughout Europe. More concrete planning and action from the British Empire quickly replaced this early initiative.[1] At the time very few Jews were living in Britain or France. With the loss of the American Colonies, British colonialism focused on India, 'the Jewel in the Crown', and perhaps as importantly on the road to India.[2] In the words of a *Times* correspondent in 1840, 'the proposition to plant the Jewish people in the land of their fathers, under the protection of the five Powers, is no longer a mere matter of speculation, but a serious political consideration'.[3] The following extract from the *Quarterly Review* of 1838 shows that British, non-Jewish Zionist plans were being instituted primarily for the benefit of the British Empire:

> The growing interest manifested for these regions, the larger investment of British capital, and the confluence of British travelers and strangers from all parts of the world, have recently induced the Secretary of State for Foreign Affairs to station there a representative of our Sovereign, in the person of a Vice-Consul. This gentleman set sail for Alexandria at the end of last September – his residence will be fixed at Jerusalem, but his jurisdiction will extend to the whole country within the ancient limits of the Holy Land; he is thus accredited, as it were, to the former kingdom of David and the Twelve Tribes. The soil and climate of Palestine are singularly adapted to the growth of produce required for the exigencies of Great Britain; the finest cotton may be obtained in almost unlimited abundance; silk and madder are the staple of the country, and oil-olive is now, as it ever was, the very fatness of the land. Capital and skill are alone required: the presence of a British officer, and the increased security of property which his presence will confer, may invite them [the Jews] from these islands to the cultivation of Palestine; and the Jews, who will betake themselves to agriculture in no other land, having found, in the English Consul, a mediator between their people and the Pasha, will probably return in yet greater numbers, and become once more the husbandmen of Judæa and Galilee ... Napoleon knew well the value of an Hebrew alliance; and endeavoured to reproduce, in the capital of France, the spectacle of the ancient Sanhedrim, which, basking in the might of imperial favour, might give laws to the whole body of the Jews throughout the habitable world, and aid him, no doubt, in his audacious plans against Poland and the East That which Napoleon designed in his violence and ambition, thinking 'to destroy nations not a few,' we may wisely and legitimately undertake for the maintenance of our Empire.[4]

British diplomacy with the Ottoman Sultan starting in the 1830s included explicit requests to encourage and facilitate the settlements of Jews in Palestine. Many Jews were understandably wary of schemes by European Gentiles and in the nineteenth century Zionism failed to convince much of European Jewry. The few Jews who were interested in living in Palestine made the move for a variety of reasons: religious individuals relocated near Safed and other centers of religious Judaism in Palestine; some were enticed by financed relocation; and some were idealistic socialist Zionists who felt that assimilation had failed and that enlightenment was best developed separately until the rest of the world caught up. These early converts to Zionism were vastly outnumbered by non-Zionist and anti-Zionist Jews. Many were even fearful that Zionism was yet another scheme on the part of Gentiles to expel them from their countries. Yet, Zionism as a colonial venture could not succeed without the Jews taking it up as a cause in much larger numbers. The first attempt was the formation in early 1809 of a new organization, the London Society for Promoting Christianity among the Jews. Its aims included educating Jews in their own history and promoting Eastern European immigration to Palestine as a fulfillment of Christian theology. These early attempts were the true antecedents of the Christian Zionist movement, which remains influential in Britain and the United States to this day. Colonel Charles Henry Churchill, the British Consul in Syria, stated in 1841 that success of Zionism depended on 'Firstly[,] that the Jews themselves will take up the matter, universally and unanimously. Secondly[,] that the European powers will aid them in their views.'[5]

To achieve such goals, the British Empire employed the services of Lieutenant Colonel George Gawler (1796–1869). (Gawler was a colonization expert who founded a penal colony in Australia and after whom a major city and state in Australia are named.) In 1845, Gawler published his vision of how this might be accomplished in *Tranquilization of Syria and the East: Observations and Practical Suggestions, in Furtherance of the Establishment of Jewish Colonies in Palestine, the Most Sober and Sensible Remedy for the Miseries of Asiatic Turkey*.[6] In 1852, the Association for Promoting Jewish Settlement in Palestine was founded by Gawler and other British officials and later evolved it into the Palestine Fund.[7] Winston Churchill wrote in 1920 immediately following his assertion that Bolshevism was being led and initiated mostly by Jews:

But if, as may well happen, there should be created in our life time by the banks of the Jordan a Jewish State under the protection of the British Crown, which might comprise three or four millions of Jews, an event would have occurred in the history of the world which would, from every point of view be beneficial, *and would be especially in harmony with the truest interests of the British Empire.*[8]

ZIONISM TAKING ROOT AMONG EUROPEAN JEWISH COMMUNITIES

There is much to be learned about the transition of Zionism in the nineteenth century from a movement sponsored and promoted by non-Jews to a Jewish-led movement that then took the initiative to change the course of history. The number of Jews who looked with favor on Zionism varied according to their country of residence and the political and economic situation in which they found themselves. Nineteenth-century nationalism gave Zionism a more racial and nationalistic tone. Yet, Jewish advocates of Zionism remained in the minority throughout the nineteenth century and early into the twentieth century. The movement clearly continued to depend on imperial interests for its very survival and this need for greater cooperation with British colonial interests grew. The movement's strength in the Ashkenazi communities was largely related to levels of anti-Ashkenazi feelings. Thus, Moses Hess (1812–1875) argued that there was no cure for the 'illness' of Jewish hatred other than to establish a Jewish state in Palestine. A man with similar views, Judah Leib (Leon) Pinsker (1821–1891), became a co-founder, with Moses Lilienblum, of Hibbat Zion, an early Zionist movement. In 1882, he published anonymously a pamphlet titled 'Auto-Emancipation: An appeal to his people by a Russian Jew' in which he argued that anti-Ashkenazim (known in Europe as anti-Semitism) was a pathological phenomenon beyond the reach of any future triumphs of 'humanity and enlightenment'. This is why he believed in Zionism:

This is the kernel of the problem, as we see it: the Jews comprise a distinctive element among the nations under which they dwell, and as such can neither assimilate nor be readily digested by any nation. Hence the solution lies in finding a means of so readjusting this exclusive element to the family of nations, that the basis of the Jewish question will be permanently removed.

Having analyzed Judeophobia as a hereditary form of demon-opathy, peculiar to the human race, and having represented Anti-Semitism as proceeding from an inherited aberration of the human mind, we must draw the important conclusion that we must give up contending against these hostile impulses as we must against every other inherited predisposition.

Our future will remain insecure and precarious unless a radical change in our position is made. This change cannot be brought about by the civil emancipation of the Jews in this or that state, but only by the auto-emancipation of the Jewish people as a nation, the foundation of a colonial community belonging to the Jews, which is some day to become our inalienable home, our country.

The international Jewish question must have a national solution. Of course, our national regeneration can only proceed slowly. We must take the first step. Our descendants must follow us at a measured and not over-precipitant speed.[9]

Pinsker became a leader of the movement and, with funds from the wealthy British philanthropist Baron Edmond de Rothschild, developed the first Jewish agricultural settlements in Palestine: Rishon LeZiyyon south of Tel Aviv, and Zikhron Yaaqov, south of Haifa. By 1891, about 10,000 Jews had relocated to these settlements (then in the Ottoman Empire). Yet, in the period of Jewish emigration from Europe, 1882–1903, it was only a tiny fraction that left for Palestine; most went to North or South America.

Nathan Birnbaum (also known as Mathias Ascher) coined the term 'Zionism', based on the ideas of Hess and Pinsker, to describe a political movement for Jewish 'self-emancipation' and nation-alism. In 1893, he published a brochure entitled 'Die Nationale Wiedergeburtder Juedischen Volkes in seinem Lande als Mittel zur Loesung der Judenfrage' ('The National Rebirth of the Jewish People in Its Homeland as a Means of Solving the Jewish Problem'). Later, Theodore Herzl's work formed the ideological underpinnings for the movement. Similar to his intellectual fathers, he recognized that anti-Semitism would be harnessed to his own – Zionist – purposes.[10] Thus, proponents of Zionism, non-Jews and Jews alike, built their popular base on Jewish fears of anti-Jewish sentiments and actions. Zionism, they were told, is the best solution to the 'Jewish problem'.

ZIONISM AFTER 1948

While Zionism as a political program was supposed to 'emancipate the Jewish people' by giving them their own state, once that state was established and native people largely removed, new roles and arguments were to be presented to sustain and reinvent Zionism. The 'protection' of the 'Jewish people' from the 'outside' remained the essential philosophical argument underpinning Zionism. But more was needed. The Jerusalem Program for Zionism adopted in 1951 and revised by the World Zionist Congress in 1968 took this as a definition of the goals of Zionism:

- Encourage immigration, absorption and integration of immigrants;
- Intensive work for pioneering and training for pioneering;
- Concerted effort to harness funds to carry out the tasks of Zionism;
- Encouragement of private capital investment;
- Fostering of Jewish consciousness by propagating the Zionist idea ...;
- Mobilization of world public opinion for Israel and Zionism;
- Participation in efforts to organize and intensify Jewish life on democratic foundations ... defense of Jewish rights.

In June 1968, the Zionist Congress, held in Jerusalem, redefined the aims of Zionism in the 'Jerusalem Program' more broadly:

1. Unity of the Jewish People and the Centrality of Israel in Jewish life;
2. The ingathering of the Jewish people in its historic homeland Eretz Yisrael through Aliyah from all countries.
3. The strengthening of the State of Israel, which is based on the prophetic vision of justice and peace;
4. The preservation of the identity of the Jewish people through the fostering of Jewish, Zionist and Hebrew education and of Jewish spiritual and cultural values;
5. The protection of Jewish rights everywhere.

Note the wide mandate dictated by the key words power, strength, and protection against any perceived threat to Jews. One need only substitute Jew/Jewish with Christian or white to see the unfairness and racism in both the 1951 and 1968 programs. After all, what does the ingathering of Jewish 'people' mean? What does it mean when many Jews have converted to Christianity and many to Islam? What does it mean for the majority of Jews who are converts from Christianity, paganism, etc.? How does the 'ingathering' and seizing of land from natives via the 'strengthening' of the state of Israel in the name of the 'unity of the Jewish people' help in the 'protection of Jewish rights everywhere'?

The government of Israel still mindlessly talks about Zionism as the solution to 'anti-Semitic' (anti-Jewish) hatred rather than working to advance equality for Jews and non-Jews everywhere:

> The Zionist movement aimed to solve the 'Jewish problem,' the problem of a perennial minority, a people subjected to repeated pogroms and persecution, a homeless community whose alienism was underscored by discrimination wherever Jews settled. Zionism aspired to deal with this situation by affecting a return to the historical homeland of the Jews – Land of Israel ... The Zionist national solution was the establishment of a Jewish national state with a Jewish majority in the historical homeland, thus realizing the Jewish people's right to self-determination.[11]

Note the sweeping generalizations and sense of perpetual victimization, which reflect the theology of Hess, Pinsker, and Herzl, which argue that discrimination against Jews is a pathological condition for which there is no cure other than a powerful state with a majority Jewish population. Amnon Rubinstein wrote in *Haaretz* on March 13, 2002:

> the new secular Jewish nationalism, which was the foundation on which Israel was built, is a nationalism of no choice. It is true that on the basis of the lack of choice were piled on additional traditional national elements: the memory of the biblical past, the impact of the revival of Hebrew, the concept of a return to Zion, and the characteristic accoutrements of other national movements. But the major strength of Zionism stemmed from its sense that there was no other choice, from this inability to be like everyone else. Without the locked gate, the Zionist gate would not have opened very wide and the longing for Zion would have stayed in the prayer book.[12]

So do Jews really have no choice other than Zionism if they are to prosper? Has Zionism helped or hindered the case for tolerance (Jews towards non-Jews and vice versa)? Jews have grappled with such questions for decades and arrived at different conclusions, with anti-Zionist Jews reaching opposite conclusions to those reached by Herzl, Pinsker, Hess, and their followers. As history would prove, the critics were right. Today, after over 150 years of Zionism, there is only one place where Jews are threatened with annihilation and that is in the self-declared 'Jewish state'. In Israel, one finds a government that is preparing public parks as sites for possible mass graves in the event of biological or chemical attacks. In Israel, one finds unrealistic attempts to reassure the public that they can survive such attacks. Why are Jews safer in America or France than in Israel? Are anti-Jewish sentiments around the world fueled or diminished by the Zionist program and its effect on the native Palestinians?

The answers to these questions are making many Jews reconsider the deceptions of the militaristic Zionist program. Political Zionism was catastrophic for the indigenous Palestinians (Christians and Muslims alike). In published articles and books, Herzl was careful to describe what Zionism meant in practice and how it was to be implemented in an already inhabited Palestine. But, as we saw in Chapter 4, Herzl's diaries and the diaries of other early Zionists are now available and shed light on the colonial nature of Zionism and its true intentions.

Herzl understood the need for a concrete program to realize the goals he was articulating. For this, others were needed for the practical application of Zionism. This included Nachman Syrkin and Ber Borochov, who developed Labor Zionism as a dominant force in Zionist quarters. This brand of practical Zionism exists in a form represented by the Labor Party and some of the minor parties in Israel today. Labor Zionists criticized the Rothschild-supported settlements on purely capitalist terms (e.g. hiring Arab labor). They called for Jewish settlements based on socialist modes of organization: the accumulation of capital managed by a central Jewish organization and employment of Jewish laborers only. A key pillar of this was the need for 'Jewish power' (physical, material) which could translate into state and political power undiluted by non-Jews.

Labor Zionists knew that power was necessary, but they also knew that the achievement of their goals required skillful political maneuvering around existing powers in the region of their settlement.

For many ardent Zionists, this smacked of a compromise they were unwilling to accept. This set the stage for the evolution of other methods to achieve the goals of Zionism. Some argued that strong economic and military power was all that mattered for the realization of Zionist dreams. Vladimir Jabotinsky was the founder of this ideology of 'revisionist Zionism', which Menachem Begin, Binyamin Netanyahu, Ariel Sharon and other Israeli leaders identify as their ideological underpinning (now represented by the Likud Party and other right-wing parties in Israel). Jabotinsky's 1923 writings clearly demonstrate his mode of thinking:

Every reader has some idea of the early history of other countries which have been settled. I suggest that he recall all known instances. If he should attempt to seek but one instance of a country settled with the consent of those born there he will not succeed. The inhabitants (no matter whether they are civilized or savages) have always put up a stubborn fight. Furthermore, how the settler acted had no effect whatsoever. The Spaniards who conquered Mexico and Peru, or our own ancestors in the days of Joshua ben Nun behaved, one might say, like plunderers.

... Compromisers in our midst attempt to convince us that the Arabs are some kind of fools who can be tricked by a softened formulation of our goals, or a tribe of money grubbers who will abandon their birth right to Palestine for cultural and economic gains. I flatly reject this assessment of the Palestinian Arabs. Culturally they are 500 years behind us, spiritually they do not have our endurance or our strength of will, but this exhausts all of the internal differences. We can talk as much as we want about our good intentions; but they understand as well as we what is not good for them. They look upon Palestine with the same instinctive love and true fervor that any Aztec looked upon his Mexico or any Sioux looked upon his prairie.

... It is of no importance whether we quote Herzl or Herbert Samuel to justify our activities. Colonization itself has its own explanation, integral and inescapable, and understood by every Arab and every Jew with his wits about him. Colonization can have only one goal. For the Palestinian Arabs this goal is inadmissible. This is in the nature of things. To change that nature is impossible.

... *Zionist colonization, even the most restricted, must either be terminated or carried out in defiance of the will of the native population.*

This colonization can, therefore, continue and develop only under the protection of a force independent of the local population – an iron wall which the native population cannot break through. This is, in toto, our policy towards the Arabs. To formulate it any other way would only be hypocrisy. Not only must this be so, it is so whether we admit it or not. What does the Balfour Declaration and the Mandate mean for us? It is the fact that a disinterested power committed itself to create such security conditions that the local population would be deterred from interfering with our efforts.

All of us, without exception, are constantly demanding that this power strictly fulfill its obligations. In this sense, there are no meaningful differences between our 'militarists' and our 'vegetarians'. One prefers an iron wall of Jewish bayonets, the other proposes an iron wall of British bayonets, the third proposes an agreement with Baghdad, and appears to be satisfied with Baghdad's bayonets – a strange and somewhat risky taste – but we all applaud, day and night, the iron wall. We would destroy our cause if we proclaimed the necessity of an agreement, and fill the minds of the Mandatory with the belief that we do not need an iron wall, but rather endless talks. Such a proclamation can only harm us. Therefore it is our sacred duty to expose such talk and prove that it is a snare and a delusion.[13]

This is essential reading for those who want to understand the nature of Zionist designs unencumbered by soothing words or skillful maneuvering. The 'wall' refers to the wall of bayonets, British and/or Zionist, necessarily required to establish a colonial Jewish state. The author persuasively argues why Arabs will not accept a Jewish state in Palestine. His vision, as articulated in this article, is prophetic in what was to transpire in Palestine over the next 80 years.

IS ZIONISM THE MIRROR IMAGE OF ANTI-SEMITISM?

Zionism in essence was a project that accommodated slightly varied modes of operations, such as using Arab labor or not, working with existing political systems to achieve its goals, or using only military means. The essence of it was and remains the creation and maintenance of a Jewish state with a clear and unambiguous Jewish majority (as long as this Jewish majority support Zionism). In a land already occupied by other people, its tactics were viewed as a traumatic, but necessary, loss. The main means towards the realization of this dream was 'anti-Semitism'. This form of racism was well intertwined with and is also explained by deep psychological phenomena.

The term anti-Semite was coined in 1879 by the anti-Jewish bigot Wilhelm Marr. According to the Yahoo encyclopedia, Marr's 1862 pamphlet titled 'Der Judenspiegel' ('The Jewish Mirror') was followed by the influential 'The Victory of Judaism over Germandom, Considered from a Non-Religious point of View'. Marr did not want to use the word 'Jew' as it connotes a religion, but wanted a term that refers to ethnicity. He was probably unfamiliar with the word Ashkenazi and assumed Ashkenazi/European Jews were 'Semitic'. Marr thus introduced the word 'anti-Semite' into the political vocabulary by founding the League of anti-Semites, which organized lectures and published a short-lived monthly. The League failed as an organization, but was historically important for it was the first attempt to create a popular political movement based on hatred of Ashkenazim. As we saw in Chapter 2, Semites refer to all people who speak a Semitic language (Arabic, Hebrew, Aramaic). Ashkenazi Jews technically were not Semitic as they spoke Yiddish. The fact that this term, developed by a racist, was adopted by many Jews and Zionists is astonishing, yet fits well within the context of development of Zionist thought as discussed above (i.e. a solution to the 'Jewish problem' being relocation to a 'Jewish state').

That Zionism and Judeophobia are intimately connected is evidenced by the writings of early Zionists. Here is Jabotinsky, writing in 1904 about the 'Jewish problem':

It is inconceivable from a physical point of view, that a Jew born to a family of pure Jewish blood over several generations can become adapted to the spiritual outlook of a German or a Frenchman. A Jew brought up among Germans may assume German customs, German words. He may be wholly imbued with that German fluid but the nucleus of his spiritual structure will always remain Jewish, because his blood, his body, his physical-racial type are Jewish ... And a man whose body is Jewish can not possibly mold within himself the spirit of a Frenchman ... It is impossible for a man to become assimilated with people whose blood is different than his own.[14]

Perhaps this parallel quote from Adolf Hitler's *Mein Kampf* needs to be pondered and analyzed:

Yet I could no longer very well doubt that the objects of my study were not Germans of a special religion, but a people in themselves; for once I had begun to concern myself with this question and to take cognizance of the Jews, Vienna appeared to me in a different light than before. Wherever I went, I began to see Jews, and the more I saw, the more sharply they became distinguished in my eyes from the rest of humanity. Particularly the Inner City and the districts north of the Danube Canal swarmed with a people, which even outwardly had lost all resemblance to Germans. And whatever doubts I may still have nourished were finally dispelled by the attitude of a portion of the Jews themselves. Among them there was a great movement, quite extensive in Vienna, which came out sharply in confirmation of the national character of the Jews: this was the *Zionists*. [emphasis in original][15]

Hitler's book is the most horrific denigration of Jews and other people – the most racist book one could imagine. For him to state that whatever 'lingering doubts' he had about his anti-Semitism were dispelled because Zionists agreed with him about the national character of Jews is amazing and historically has been almost completely ignored. It is an important notion because Zionists not only agreed with Hitler that Jews should leave Europe, but they actually worked towards that goal. Here is what the Zionist Federation of Germany wrote in a letter to the new Nazi regime:

Zionism believes that a rebirth of national life, such as is occurring in German life through adhesion to Christian and national values, must also take place in the Jewish national group.[16]

Zionists and Nazis agreed that Jews could not be Germans. They both believed that Jews could not function in other societies as equal citizens. Zionists in fact were clearly putting a primary goal of colonial Jewish presence in a majority in Palestine ahead of any other issues, even when this goal contradicted the welfare of European Jews. This is why they collaborated with the Nazis and thwarted efforts to rescue Jews.

The Zionists cooperated with the Nazis in the mid-1930s to facilitate Jewish emigration to Palestine. The details of this agreement are given by Edwin Black.[17] After attacks on Jews under German control started, the British, in the hope of easing the pressure for increased immigration to Palestine, proposed that thousands of

Jewish children be admitted to Britain. Ben-Gurion, the recognized leader of Labor Zionism at the time, was opposed to the plan, telling a meeting of Labor Zionist leaders on December 7, 1938:

> If I knew that it would be possible to save all the children in Germany by bringing them over to England, and only half of them by transporting them to Eretz Yisrael, then I would opt for the second alternative. For we must weigh not only the life of these children, but also the history of the People of Israel.[18]

Rabbi Shonfeld quotes the Zionist leader Yitzhak Greenbaum, as stating after the war:

> When they asked me, couldn't you give money out of the United Jewish Appeal funds for the rescue of Jews in Europe, I said, 'NO!' and I say again 'NO!' ... one should resist this wave which pushes the Zionist activities to secondary importance.[19]

Most Jews in the nineteenth and early twentieth centuries criticized Zionist methodologies and even the whole concept of Zionism. They saw the movement as a cynical use of religion to establish state power. Perhaps the most interesting were the views of highly intelligent and humanistic Jews like Albert Einstein and Sigmund Freud, who, while not openly opposed to Zionism, refused to take part in it. They reflected the majority Jewish opinion before the establishment of the state of Israel.

Freud, the father of psychoanalysis, when asked to sign a petition to condemn the Arab riots in Palestine and support the settlement of Jews in Israel, sent a polite letter of decline:

> Dear Sir,
>
> I cannot do as you wish. I am unable to overcome my aversion to burdening the public with my name, and even the present critical time does not seem to me to warrant it. Whoever wants to influence the masses must give them something rousing and inflammatory and my sober judgment of Zionism does not permit this. I certainly sympathize with its goals, am proud of our University in Jerusalem and am delighted with our settlement's prosperity. But, on the other hand, I do not think that Palestine could ever become a Jewish state, nor that the Christian and Islamic worlds would ever be prepared to have their holy places

under Jewish care. It would have seemed more sensible to me to establish a Jewish homeland on a less historically-burdened land. But I know that such a rational viewpoint would never have gained the enthusiasm of the masses and the financial support of the wealthy. I concede with sorrow that the baseless fanaticism of our people is in part to be blamed for the awakening of Arab distrust. I can raise no sympathy at all for the misdirected piety which transforms a piece of a Herodian wall into a national relic, thereby offending the feelings of the natives.

Now judge for yourself whether I, with such a critical point of view, am the right person to come forward as the solace of a people deluded by unjustified hope.[20]

Freud was referring to the methods of Zionists of the day to assert sovereignty in areas of Palestine and to confront and show the natives that their interests were incompatible. Zionism desired a state of the Jews and not a democratic state for a variety of people. As Freud pointed out, it is born of a preference for a tribal affiliation that haunts us to this day. Hillel Halkin wrote in the *Jerusalem Post* in 2002:

You would like me to look at it objectively. Objectively, I agree: we are only breeding more hatred and violence. You want me to imagine how I would feel if I were a Palestinian. I suppose that if I were, I might want to kill Israelis myself. But I am not objective and I am not a Palestinian. It's not that the lives of Palestinians don't matter to me. But Israeli lives matter more.

I know this doesn't sound terribly enlightened. And it certainly doesn't lead to any of the political solutions that we both know are necessary if this horror is going to end. But being objective would not make me more human. It would make me less.

I can try to be objective about Russians and Chechnyans, or about Hindus and Muslims in Kashmir, without drying up the milk of human kindness in me, just as you can try to be objective about us here, but that is only because I am not a Russian or a Chechnyan. If I were, and if I didn't put my own people first, I would simply be an emotional monster. Nothing good could come of that.[21]

Thus, Zionism's victims were not only the intended native displacements but also, it could be argued, humane Jewish values. In his book *Ben-Gurion's Scandals*, Naeim Giladi, an Iraqi Jew and ex-Zionist, discusses Zionist tactics in trying to move Jews from Iraq to Israel in the 1950s. He emigrated to the US and recently published an article in *The Link*, the publication of the Americans for Middle East Understanding, in which he wrote: 'about 125,000 Jews left Iraq for Israel in the late 1940s and into 1952, mostly because they had been lied to and put into a panic by what I came to learn were Zionist bombs [referring to the bombings at synagogues and other areas of Jewish public concentration]. But my mother and father were among the 6,000 who did not go to Israel.'[22] Other books discuss Zionist discourse and its relationship to anti-Ashkenazim and Judeophobia. Some of these are cited in the recommended reading below.

A POST-ZIONIST DISCOURSE

The Zionist program tried but failed to make its ideology the ideology of 'the Jewish people'. Many even argued that Zionists were trying to replace Judaism with Zionism, or at least trying to ensure that Zionism is a dominant feature of mainstream Jewish thought. Hence, one understands the need to label anti-Zionists or even non-Zionists as 'anti-Semitic' or, if they are Jewish, as 'self-hating Jews'. In the first 80 years of apartheid South Africa, the leaders of white South Africans called apartheid a national movement for the protection of the white population and all opposition from blacks as anti-white racism. Jewish intellectuals and many others opposed Zionism simply because they knew it was not workable for Jewish self-determination or freedom.

When Palestinians return to their lands and form a pluralistic society for all, will the descendants of those expelled Palestinians remember the words and actions of Herzl, Ben-Gurion, Barak, and Sharon, or will they remember the words and actions of Martin Buber, Israel Shahak, Uri Avneri, and Norman Finkelstein? Will those memories teach us to be more tolerant of each other or will they instill in us the kind of self-righteous, know it all, 'we were the perpetual victim' mentality that has been characteristic of many Zionists. Victims of the Holocaust learnt different lessons from it. Some, perhaps goaded or misled by the simplistic and rather unrealistic notion of separation/apartheid, thought 'never again' but meant never again for the Jews, who thus must separate themselves from the rest of humanity. To make sure the Holocaust did not happen again, they would build a very strong state, backed by Jewish power. A logical place was Palestine, the ancient homeland of the Jews. Of course, the problem was that Palestine was already inhabited and the native population was simply not going to consent to having sovereignty of their land transferred to an extra-national entity. Other Holocaust survivors and their children, like Finkelstein, Shahak, and tens of thousands like them, understood that 'never again' meant that they would never allow hatred or racism to be perpetrated against anyone. Others rejected the notion of a secular 'Jewish state' on the grounds of theological arguments. (This was true of essentially all Orthodox Jews until 1967 and is still common among the ultra-orthodox, such as the Naturei Karta.)

I am confident that an exclusionary Palestinian movement analogous to Zionism will not gain widespread support or be allowed to gain a foothold analogous to Zionism among the Jewish masses. I believe this because I have witnessed it among natives in other parts of the world. In South Africa, the blacks won their freedom but did not expel the whites, as was feared. Palestinians will not push out the Jews. Yet the reverse happened in 1948 when Palestinians were literally pushed into the sea at Jaffa and loaded into boats to end up in the Gaza Strip. It is also something that the world would never tolerate in the twenty-first century, as witnessed in Bosnia.

Jewish voices against Zionism and Israeli actions are gaining momentum, but it is true that the dominant feature in at least the organized Jewish community is Zionism. However, one must realize that the majority of Jews in all surveys state that they are not Zionists and even today the majority of Jews live outside Israel. Further, the growth of the Jewish anti-Zionist and post-Zionist movements has been dramatic. What are some of the good things about these movements?

1. Jewish opponents to Zionism make it impossible for Zionists and other racists to make generalizations about 'the Jews'. This is important, but the most important is that generalizations can lead to racism and attacks on the whole community. It is an ironic twist that the Jews whom Zionists vilify as 'self-hating' or as traitors to their religion do a lot of good for their religion and enhance protection for their co-religionists while Zionists who perpetuate brutalities and claim they represent all Jews increase anti-Jewish paranoia. The lesson to all, including Palestinians,

is never to vilify those who stand up for justice and freedom for all.

2. Jewish opponents of Zionism take a moral stance on issues regardless of the victim or the perpetrator. They provide the highest of human ideals in rejecting tribalism and the philosophies of 'us' and 'them'. They assess each event on its merits and are thus free of the hypocrisy of ideological adherence. Zionists must continuously play a game of moral relativism and hypocritical support of human rights in some cases, while opposing them on others (depending on whether the tribe is affected or not). This is not a healthy way to live and creates many sleepless nights among Zionists I know. The lesson to all, including Palestinians, is never to think or act tribally; think and act as a human being.

Those Jews who oppose Zionism are not doing so to set an example; nor are they doing so because they think they can change history. They do so for a very simple reason – because it is right. In fact, the more of us who think like that, the less likely will be wars, tribal conflicts, nationalism, and the more likely there will be peace and prosperity for all.

The questions asked by those skeptical of Zionist aspirations are still relevant today. Were Jews really able to survive only because of the creation of the Jewish state of Israel and the continuing dispossession of the native Palestinians? What price have natives paid for a Jewish state? Does Zionism really resolve the lingering feeling of being oppressed or discriminated against? Do Zionism and anti-Jewish feelings ('anti-Semitism') feed on each other in order to prosper? In the US, Jews, Christians, Muslims, and others are well adapted as members of a society that protects their rights. During the zenith of Arabic/Islamic civilization, Jews, Christians, and Muslims similarly prospered and built a great economic, architectural, intellectual, and cultural heritage. The best example of this is the pluralistic society developed in Al-Andalus (Spain). My grandfather frequently spoke of the amicable relationships he, as a Palestinian Christian, observed among all communities in Palestine well before the disasters imposed by the British Zionist project unfolded. Jewish colleagues agree with my grandfather's statement. It is not true what Zionism preached to us that we could not live together. It is a shame that instead of building a pluralistic country for all, some chose to build a country for one and dispossess the other.

The record indeed shows that Zionism and anti-Jewish feelings (anti-Semitism) have a symbiotic relationship. Victims of Zionist ideology were not limited to the Palestinians (the native inhabitants) but extended to Jews and many others. They included Sephardic Jews who were forced to flee their homes and lives in Arab countries as Israel pushed to undermine their presence there and as anti-Jewish feelings increased due to the repression of the Palestinians by self-declared Jewish representatives. Even today, the policies of the state of Israel are increasing and certainly are not decreasing the threats and danger to Jews around the world. So strictly judged even from its own stated goals of providing normality and safety for Jews, Zionism has been a failure. But perhaps these stated goals were not truly genuine and that Zionism, like so many other -isms, has been mainly about power and control. Declassified documents are shedding light on these issues and raising very troubling questions.

Questions about the relationship of Zionism to anti-Judaic feelings and Jewish reactions to it are worth exploring. But the story with regard to the native Palestinian inhabitants is much simpler and much less controversial. In practice, to fulfill the dreams of Zionist leaders, ethnic cleansing was and continues to be practiced. After taking 78 percent of the land from its native people and expelling more than three-quarters of them, Zionism was still not satisfied and Israeli leaders are aggressively and violently insisting on partitioning the remaining 22 percent (apartheid) while insisting on no return of Palestinian refugees and on maintaining racist laws that discriminate against non-Jews. The idea is to keep the Jewish character of the state. These laws and beliefs are the topic of the next chapter.

RECOMMENDED READING

Edwin Black, *The Transfer Agreement: The Dramatic Story of the Pact Between the Third Reich and Jewish Palestine* (New York: Carroll & Graf, 2001).

Lenni Brenner, *The Iron Wall: Zionist Revisionism from Jabotinsky to Shamir* (London: Zed Books, 1984).

Marc H. Ellis, *Israel and Palestine: Out of the Ashes* (London: Pluto Press, 2003).

Naeim Giladi, *Ben-Gurion's Scandals* (Flushing: Glilit, 1995).

Tom Segev with Haim Watzman (trans.), *The Seventh Million: The Israelis and the Holocaust* (New York: Owl Books, 2000).

7
Is Israel a Democracy?

The Jewish State cannot exist without a special ideological content. We cannot exist for long like any other state whose main interest is to ensure the welfare of its citizens.

Prime Minister Yitzhak Shamir, *New York Times*, July 14, 1992

Woe to those who devise iniquity and work evil upon their beds! When the morning dawns, they perform it, because it is in the power of their hand. They covet fields, and seize them; and houses, and take them away; they oppress a man and his house, a man and his inheritance.

Micah 2: 1–2

Examining the nature of individual and state relation is crucial to peace. Regardless of the solution advocated, any state or states in the region have to relate to their internal minorities. Since we should all agree that human rights are a cornerstone, it is important to consider the nature of state government. There are now great pressures on the Palestinians to ensure that any future governing body is democratic and transparent. As we will show later, the prospect of a separate and truly sovereign Palestinian state in the West Bank and Gaza are remote. That leaves the other governing body now with great power and sovereignty over the areas: Israel. Many Israelis describe Israel as the only democracy in the area. Many Palestinians describe Israel as an ethnocentric racist state built on their destruction as a society. To arrive at a mutually agreed solution, such varied interpretations need to be reconciled by a serious examination of Israeli basic laws and what they are intended to accomplish. If some laws are discriminatory and/or racist, then perhaps addressing them is the key to a durable peace.

A BASIC ANALYSIS OF THE 'BASIC LAWS'

Amnesty International, in a report on 'Racism and the Administration of Justice', reported:

In Israel for example, several laws are explicitly discriminatory. These can be traced back to Israel's foundation in 1948 which, driven primarily by the racist genocide suffered by Jews in Europe during the Second World War, was based on the notion of a Jewish state for Jewish people. Some of Israel's laws reflect this principle and as a result discriminate against non-Jews, particularly Palestinians who had lived on the lands for generations. Various areas of Israeli law discriminate against Palestinians. The Law of Return for instance provides automatic Israeli citizenship for Jewish immigrants, whereas Palestinian refugees who were born and raised in what is now Israel are denied even the right to return home. Other statutes explicitly grant preferential treatment to Jewish citizens in areas such as education, public housing, health, and employment.[1]

My analysis in this chapter is not intended to be comprehensive because, in addition to such human rights resources, there are many books and other resources available on this issue.[2] Israeli law is a vast subject well beyond the scope of this work, but we need at least to address some key concepts and basic laws in order to articulate what needs to be done to achieve a durable solution based on equality. Let us start at the beginning of Israel's ambition and genesis of its laws with an excerpt from Israel's Declaration of Independence (May 15, 1948):

We declare that, with effect from the moment of the termination of the Mandate being tonight, the eve of Sabbath, the 6th Iyar, 5708 (15th May, 1948), *until the establishment of the elected, regular authorities of the State in accordance with the Constitution which shall be adopted by the Elected Constituent Assembly not later than the 1st October 1948*, the People's Council shall act as a Provisional Council of State, and its executive organ, the People's Administration, shall be the Provisional Government of the Jewish State, to be called Israel.

Needless to say, the constitution was never written. Reasons given for not promulgating a constitution have ranged from instability and war to the issue of religion and Halachic law. The Knesset's web-site states:

Since the Constituent Assembly and the first Knesset were unable to put a constitution together, the Knesset started to legislate basic laws on various subjects. After all the basic laws will be enacted, they will constitute together, with an appropriate introduction and several general rulings, the constitution of the State of Israel.[3]

The basic laws of the state of Israel can be found on the web-site of the Ministry of Foreign Affairs in both Hebrew and English,[4] although they are mistranslated in English to obfuscate the separation in the Hebrew text between *ezrahut* (citizenship) and membership of Am Yisrael (the people of Israel, referring to all Jews anywhere). Gentiles cannot be part of the nation of Israel or Am Yisrael, even if they are citizens of the state. This is an important point. Under Israeli law, every Jew, regardless of culture, genetics, or citizenship, is considered a national of Israel, a member of Am Yisrael, and is entitled to the benefits of residency and life in the self-declared Jewish state. According to the so-called 'law of return':

> Every Jew has the right to come to this country as an oleh ... An oleh's visa shall be granted to every Jew who has expressed his desire to settle in Israel, unless the Minister of Immigration is satisfied that the applicant (1) is engaged in an activity directed against the Jewish people; or (2) is likely to endanger public health or the security of the State.

Under this law, no Jew emigrates to Israel; Jews (including converts) 'return' (hence the name of the law). You have to reject this *oleh* (this alludes to going to a higher level when 'returning' to Israel) if you are Jewish and happen to have any form of residency in Israel but do not wish to become a citizen. The law is thus not an immigration law *per se*, because all non-Jews who wish to live in Israel on a permanent basis are subject to an entirely different set of laws, which are analogous to immigration laws in other countries. Also, it is only Jews who are given financial and logistical support once they 'return'/make *aliyah*.

In the Hebrew version of what in the English version is called the 'Nationality Law', the word used is *ezrahut*, which means citizenship. There is no 'nationality' status apart from 'Jewish nationality' in Israeli law (all Jews are considered Jewish nationals and part of

Am Yisrael). In Hebrew the word is *'le'om'* not *ezrahut*. The ezrahut law states:

> The ezrahut law relates to persons born in Israel or resident therein, as well as to those wishing to settle in the country, regardless of race, religion, creed, sex or political belief. Citizenship [again *ezrahut* not *le'ot* status] may be acquired by:
> Birth
> The law of return
> Residence
> Naturalization
> Acquisition of ezrahut by birth is granted to:
> 1. Persons who were born in Israel to a mother or a father who are Israeli citizens.
> 2. Persons born outside Israel, if their father or mother holds Israeli citizenship, acquired either by birth in Israel, according to the Law of Return, by residence, or by naturalization.
> 3. Persons born after the death of one of their parents, if the late parent was an Israeli citizen by virtue of the conditions enumerated in 1. and 2. above at the time of death.
> 4. Persons born in Israel, who have never had any nationality and subject to limitations specified in the law, if they: Apply for it in the period between their 18th and 25th birthday and have been residents of Israel for five consecutive years, immediately preceding the day of the filing of their application.

According to this basic law, you acquire Israeli citizenship by: birth, the (Jewish) 'law of return', residence, or naturalization. For each of these categories, a Palestinian born in a village in Galilee and expelled in 1948 does not qualify because of the language used in the law. Thus, while specifically not stating so, the law is directed against native Palestinians. Its sophistry cannot hide its intentions. Further, being a citizen means you are either a citizen national or a citizen non-national. Those who are citizens but not nationals (such as the Palestinians who remained after the expulsions of 1947–49) cannot benefit from any of the institutions or privileges reserved to nationals. These include services of the supra-state groups which wield significant power over Israeli lands and resources. These include the Jewish National Fund, World Zionist Organization, and the Jewish Agency. JNF controls a third of the water resources, for example. The Israel Land Authority (ILA) controls 90 percent of the land in Israel.

THE 'ABSENTEE LAW'

Palestinians who could not become citizens had their property allocated to Jews based on the 'absentee law' enacted in 1950. This law states that all absentees' property is under the care of the 'Custodian of Absentee Properties'. Under this law, absentees are defined as anyone who was away from his home, either within the borders of Israel or in a neighboring state, on or after November 29, 1947. This legislation gave rise to a paradoxical category: 'present absentees', that is, Palestinians who remained inside the borders of the state after November 29, 1947, but who were outside their village. These citizens, also known as 'internal refugees', account for at least a quarter of all Palestinian citizens in Israel. In 1958, the Knesset passed the Israel Lands Law, a basic law that prohibits transfer of land ownership: 'The ownership of Israel lands, being the lands in Israel of the State, the Development Authority or the Keren Kayemet Le-Israel, shall not be transferred either by sale or in any other manner.' In 1960, a new state body, the Israel Lands Authority, was established as the governmental office responsible for the administration of all Israeli lands, including the lands of the 'absentees'; the law became applicable to this body. Thus, the land is administered for Jewish development, but can never be transferred or owned by others.

In 1958, the Law of Return was amended to exclude those born as Jews who converted to other religious faiths. The law was upheld despite a challenge in 1962 by Oswald Rufeisen. Rufeisen was a member of a Zionist youth movement in Poland. A Holocaust survivor who saved fellow Jews, he later converted to Christianity and became a priest. In the 1950s, he moved to Israel. The state denied his application for citizenship under the Law of Return. The High Court of Justice rejected his claim even though the Chief Rabbinate had ruled in his favor on the grounds that he was 'Jewish' according to Halacha rules. In 1970, the guidelines of immigration eligibility were more clearly defined and now state that anyone who is the child or grandchild of a Jew can immigrate and bring their families with them. But the 1958 law barring Jews who have converted to other faiths is still in force.

Until recently, the Israel Interior Ministry issued identity cards to citizens which state their 'nationality': Jewish, Arab, Druze,

Assyrian. The full list was kept confidential, but the Ministry refused requests by a group calling itself 'I am Israeli' to list their nationality as 'Israeli'. The Ministry instead dropped the designation on the cards all together. Legally, the category of 'Israeli nationality' does not exist. Israel's Supreme Court decision of 1970 in *George Tamarin* v *The State of Israel* ruled that there is no Israeli nationality apart from Jewish nationality (Le'om, Am Yisrael). The President of the High Court, Justice Shimon, explained that recognizing an Israeli nationality 'would negate the very foundation upon which the State of Israel was formed'.[5]

The minority of Palestinians who managed to remain in the newly formed state of Israel (a quarter of the original Palestinian population) are those most directly impacted by Israeli law. The absentee law allows the Israeli government to declare that non-Jews who left (refugees) or who remained and became 'equal' Israeli citizens be declared absent in order that their property can be confiscated as 'abandoned'. Their property is then turned over to the Jewish Agency for the exclusive use of Jews. The law does not use the word 'Jews', but the words 'those who benefit from the law of return', which means Jews. In fact, there have been Palestinians, who are nominally Israeli citizens, who tried to lease their own land and were prevented from doing so because they were not Jews (see below).

Here is what Tom Segev has written about the absentee law:

The definition in the law was changed to embrace all who had abandoned their 'usual place of residence', even if they were still living in [and 'equal' residents of] Israel ... the law defined them as absentees, even if they had only left their homes for a few days and stayed with relatives in a nearby village or town, waiting for the fighting to end. Later they came to be referred to as 'present absentees' (in Hebrew, *nochihim nifkadim*). The majority of them were not allowed to return to their homes. Those refugees who were permitted to return to Israel after the war were also formally absentees and their property was not restored to them and quoting M. Porath in a secret report to the Minister of Finance:

"... the fact that we are holding the property of legal residents of the country, who otherwise enjoy all the normal rights of citizenship, is a source of great bitterness and constant agitation among the Arabs who are affected by it. Most of the complaints made by Arabs against our department are made by 'absentees' who see their property in the hands of others and can't bear it. These absentees try by every means to get their lands back, and offer to lease them even at exorbitant rents. In accordance with the general rule originally established, our office does not lease the lands expropriated by the government to the present absentees [i.e. non-Jews], so as not to weaken our control over the properties" ... The number of 'present absentees' runs into the thousands, most of them owners of real estate. There are already new people [Jews] living on some of these properties ... Any attempt to return the properties to these absentees would, therefore, adversely affect thousands, or tens of thousands, of settlers ...[6]

Thus, inside the Green Line (Israel's borders before 1967), legislation forms the basis for justifying government land acquisition and transfer from native people (Gentiles) to Jewish settlers. After adapting the British Mandate property laws to absorb the lands and properties already claimed as public, the Knesset enacted its own laws. The first in a tactical series of basic laws, the absentee property law, authorized the state to confiscate any property if, between the end of November 1947 and May 19, 1948, the legal owner or owners were absent from the property for even one day. The law, passed in 1950, was retroactive and had a sweeping effect on the Arab population. This new law created a basic premise for future land confiscation.

A basic law passed in 1985 ensures the official exclusion from political participation of any party that does not assent to the primacy of Israel's Jewish identity and *raison d'être*. The law came as a response to two tendencies: racism against non-Jewish citizens as expressed in Rabbi Kahane's Kach Party; and a challenge, posed by the Progressive List for Peace, a joint Arab–Jewish party, to the state's identification as 'Jewish'. The law states that:

A list of candidates shall not participate in the elections for the Knesset if its aims or actions, expressly or by implication, point to one of the following:
1. Denial of the existence of Israel as a state of the Jewish people.
2. Denial of the democratic nature of the state.
3. Incitement to racism.

Clearly, it is illegal under this law to call for changes in the law challenging the concept of a state for a religious community around the world, a state 'of the Jewish people', or to make Israel a state of its citizens.

INSTITUTIONALIZED DISCRIMINATION

Israel's treatment of the Palestinians who remained within its borders following the ethnic cleansing of 1947–49 (detailed in Chapter 4) is particularly telling. Palestinians were placed under martial law from 1948 to 1966 while Jewish immigrants consolidated their control, built settlements on confiscated Palestinian land, and built an infrastructure and a working country from the infrastructure of Palestine. In 1966, martial law was lifted, after which Palestinians were supposed to be 'equal citizens'. The reality was far from equal, as the discussion of Israeli laws above illustrates. Palestinians were now in the minority with voting rights, and they were also excluded from all aspects of a society that defined itself as a Jewish culture and state. Details of these issues can be found on the web pages of Israeli Palestinians and human rights organizations in Israel trying to preserve some semblance of human rights.

According to the Arab Association for Human Rights there are about 100 Palestinian Arab villages in Israel that the government does not recognize officially:

Over 70,000 Palestinian Arab citizens live in villages that are threatened with destruction, prevented from development and are not shown on any map. Despite the fact that most of the 'unrecognized villages' existed before the establishment of Israel, state policy considers their inhabitants as lawbreakers. It prevents them from repairing existing homes or building new ones; withholds basic rights, such as drinking water and health clinics; and in certain cases even fences off whole villages. These measures coincide with a wider policy of concentrating Palestinian Arabs and 'redeeming' their lands for new Jewish mitzpim [the *mitzpim* 'lookout' settlements were established as part of the Judaization of the Galilee program to change the demographic balance of Arab areas] settlements. Many of these settlements are built next to their unrecognized neighbors, often illegally, yet with a complete provision of services.

The villages were delegalized by the enactment of the (1965) Planning and Construction Law. This law set down a framework of regulations and a national outline plan for the country's future development. It zoned land for residential, agricultural and industrial use, and forbade any form of unlicensed construction or construction on agricultural lands. The unrecognized villages were not incorporated into the planning schemes, and their lands were reclassified as agricultural. Villagers were not consulted on either the law or its plans.[7]

Living conditions in these areas became horrific: no public schools, sewerage, water supply, electricity, or medical services. The poor in these villages are not even counted in the statistics that determine poverty levels in the country. Many live in conditions analogous to refugee camps in the Gaza Strip or Lebanon even though they are supposedly Israeli citizens. While civil rights groups have tried to effect a change in the law, these have been largely ineffective or have achieved superficial, cosmetic changes only.

Over 130,000 Bedouins are descendants of the few thousand who remained after the ethnic cleansing of 1947–49. They are considered Israeli citizens and many have even served in the Israeli Army. The Bedouins and the Druz are the only non-Jewish communities who regularly serve in the Israeli Army. Moshe Shohat, the Israeli government official in charge of Bedouin affairs, spoke about 'blood-thirsty Bedouins who commit polygamy, have 30 children and continue to expand their illegal settlements, taking over state land'. As for providing schools with indoor plumbing, he added, 'in their culture they take care of their needs outdoors ... They don't even know how to flush a toilet.'

On August 17, 2001, *Jewish Week* wrote that the government's inquiry into these remarks via a committee headed by Doron Mor is questionable. Mor did not even want to look at Shohat's book, which contained racist slurs against Bedouins. *Jewish Week* candidly stated this at the end of their article titled 'Bedouin Probe Seen as a "farce"':

While being questioned by Mor as part of his probe, a reporter was told no less than three times that 'if you are truly an Orthodox Jewish Zionist you will write another article talking about how much the government and Mr. Shohat have done for the Bedouins'.[8]

At the time, Shohat was still in charge of Bedouin affairs. Bedouins and Palestinians who are Israeli citizens ask rightly why their interests are represented in the government not by their own members but by Jews, and worse yet by Jews who are racist and bigoted Zionists. Shohat is not the first and perhaps will not be the last Israeli official to adhere to the classic Zionist philosophy which concerns itself only with the fate of Zionist Jews at the expense of the native Palestinians.

The contradiction between democracy and the Jewish character of the state is best illustrated by these comments from *Haaretz*:

> Our right to Eretz Israel and our right to establish a sovereign national entity on it does not depend on our numbers, and on whether we are a majority or a minority. This land was our country when we were a small, isolated minority.
>
> Five hundred or a thousand years ago, a few thousand Jews lived in the country. In 1919, the League of Nations recognized the Jewish people's right to the land, without any connection to their number in it (tens of thousands). In 1948, 600,000 Jews lived in the country. The numerical issue was never brought up as an element determining the Jewish people's connection to or belonging in the country.
>
> Hence, for us it doesn't matter whether there are more Jews or Arabs here. Of course, we would prefer it if there are a majority of Jews here. But no matter, the Jewish people will retain their right to the country.
>
> By definition the state of Israel was founded as a Jewish state. The regime constituted in it is democratic in character, but its essence is Jewish. And if there is a contradiction between this essence and the character of the government, it is clear that the essence takes precedence, and that steps are to be taken to prevent damage or changes to this Jewish essence. Democracy cannot be exploited to destroy the Jewish state.
>
> Legislators should settle this point in clear, categorical terms, without any qualms of conscience or moral compunction. Absolute justice holds that the state of Israel is, and has always been, the only Jewish state, and this country has been solely that of the Jewish people. That's how things have been defined, and that's how they will remain. Whoever wants a different state should look for it somewhere else.[9]

The Jewish Agency, a supra-national entity, says of the law of return:

In 1950, Israel's Knesset passed a remarkable law, beginning with a few simple words that defined Israel's central purpose: 'Every Jew has the right to immigrate to this country ...' Two thousand years of wandering were officially over. Since then, Jews have been entitled to simply show up and declare themselves to be Israeli citizens, assuming they posed no imminent danger to public health, state security, or the Jewish people as a whole. Essentially, all Jews everywhere are Israeli citizens by right.[10]

Zionist philosophy is thus built on the concept that Eretz Yisrael is a 'birthright' conferred on all Jews (defined to include anyone who has not acquired another religion, even though he/she might not be a practicing Jew). It is no accident that the latest Zionist venture in the US, which offers free trips to Israel for young Jewish Americans, is called 'Birthright Israel'. The land belongs to the Jewish people and not to the citizens of the state or the native people displaced. The justification for this Jewish 'right' is that God himself made a 'promise' to give the land to Abraham's descendants as an 'everlasting covenant'. Many religious Jews argue that only if they kept God's commandments would they keep the land and the fact of their dispersion is testament to God's will. Christianity is based on the concept that the arrival of the Messiah extended God's promise to all humanity and fulfilled the promise of the Old Testament. A tiny minority of Christians (so-called 'Christian Zionists') justify Zionism on religious grounds. But in either case, this religious 'justification', no matter how flawed theologically, would have to be reconciled with the evidence that many of the Zionist Jews trace their ancestry to European Khazars and not Semitic people (see Chapter 3). Further, the basic laws do not give a right to 'return' to a Christian family, even if their ancestors were original Hebrews. They do give a right to converts to Judaism to 'return'.

The Law of Return clearly applies to members of a particular religion and gives them an automatic right of citizenship in a country they have never even visited. Non-Jews are not eligible for this 'right', regardless of their birth, ancestry, or other factors. Jews who do not identify with Zionist ideologies can be excluded at the discretion of the Interior Ministry under the section that covers threats to the Jewish nation. Thus, Palestinian refugees can be excluded even if they convert to Judaism. Israel is the only country that nationalizes any person regardless of where they live only by virtue of a religious identification.

All citizens of Israel can vote for the Knesset, the prime minister, parties, unions, and in municipal elections. In this sense they have citizenship rights. However, Israel is the only country in which there is also a set of rights reserved for 'nationals' which is denied to non-Jewish citizens. The nationals are defined as Am Yisrael. Other privileges enshrined in law are for those who serve in the Israeli Army but they also are granted to 'nationals' who do not serve in the army (orthodox Jews). Again, Palestinians are denied these benefits or basic rights. Nationals have benefits beyond automatic citizenship, which include land rights, and economic, cultural, and political benefits. These rights are denied to non-Jews.

Without addressing Israeli laws, the prospects for a lasting peace remain remote. Israel defines itself and shapes its laws on the premise that it is not a country of its citizens but a state for and by Jews throughout the world. The land of Israel (Eretz Yisrael) is held 'in trust' for Am Yisrael. Land leasing and other laws are intended to ensure transfer of land ownership from Palestinian Christians and Muslims to Jews. This has resulted in wholesale ethnic cleansing, discrimination, and racism against non-Jewish natives of the land. This Zionist discourse could not have been achieved without mass violence, a topic that will be addressed in the next chapter.

RECOMMENDED READING

Marwan Bishara, *Palestine/Israel: Peace or Apartheid: Occupation, Terrorism, and the Future* (London: Zed Books, 2003).
Israel Shahak and Norton Mezvinsky, *Jewish Fundamentalism in Israel* (London: Pluto Press, 1999).

8
Violence and Terrorism

Those who make peaceful revolution impossible will make violent revolution inevitable.

John F. Kennedy, March 12, 1962

Terrorism and violence are thought by some to be the main if not the sole issues to consider in formulating a solution to the Israel/Palestine conflict. The following pages address terrorism and violence as symptoms of an underlying disease. I believe this perspective is more logical and more hopeful since it deals with violence not as an inevitable or unanalyzable phenomenon. It will become apparent that the only way to tackle violence is not only to deal with its roots, but to dissect the seeds from which the whole originates. Put another way, treating a patient by treating the symptoms is far less effective than finding and dealing with the etiology of the disease.

THE SEEDS AND ROOTS OF TERRORISM

First, it is important to apply a uniform definition of such inflammatory words as terrorism, genocide, and murder. Further, significant violence against civilians, including war crimes, is sometimes ignored by applying a label to it other than terrorism. Conversely, there are many groups that engage in legitimate resistance but are labeled terrorist by their adversaries. Since the word terrorism is in vogue, let us begin by dissecting it and understanding what it means.

Although the English term terror dates back to the fourteenth century, the noun terrorism, meaning the systematic use of terror especially as a means of coercion, was not used until the last decade of eighteenth-century France. Maximilien Robespierre, a leader of the French Revolution, justified the Reign of Terror with these words: 'In times of peace, the springs of popular government are in virtue, but in times of revolution, they are both in virtue and terror.'[1] Terrorism as used by some governments, such as Israel and the United States, is deliberately not well defined and as such acts of terror can be considered as self-defense in some situations and as collateral damage in others.

President George W. Bush signed Executive Order 13224 'Blocking property and prohibiting transactions with persons who commit, threaten to commit, or support terrorism' (September 23, 2001, with an expanded list in November 7, 2001). Under this Order, the president designated as 'terrorist' several resistance movements, including the Kurdistan Workers' Party, the Democratic Front for the Liberation of Palestine, the Popular Front for the Liberation of Palestine, the Islamic Movement of Uzbekistan, Islamic Resistance Movement (Hamas), Lebanese Resistance Movement (Hizballah), and the Colombian Leftist insurgents.

Here is how the US government defined terrorism under this order:

> The term 'terrorism' means an activity that –
> (i)   involves a violent act or an act dangerous to human life, property, or infrastructure; and
> (ii) appears to be intended –
>   (A) to intimidate or coerce a civilian population;
>   (B) to influence the policy of a government by intimidation or coercion; or
>   (C) to affect the conduct of a government by mass destruction, assassination, kidnapping, or hostage taking.

If taken literally, under this law we would classify as terrorism the US nuclear attacks on Hiroshima and Nagasaki. We would also classify as terrorism the US-led sanctions that killed over one million Iraqis in eleven years according to the United Nations, as well as the bombing campaign in 1991 that decimated the infrastructure in Iraq. We would describe as terrorism the siege of Palestinian towns and villages by the Israeli Army and its shelling of infrastructure and neighborhoods.

The neo-conservatives in the Bush administration characterized the events of September 11, 2001 as so unique and world transforming as to warrant putting into action the plans (hatched earlier) of a perpetual 'war on terrorism'. Yet, many questioned whether the events of September 11, 2001 were qualitatively or quantitatively an historically unique violent occurrence. Even if we limit this to the North American continent, the greatest number of people killed were the millions of native Americans by the European invaders.

Native Americans used to be called savages and barbarians before the word terrorist came into widespread use. This carnage on the North American continent was followed by the countless tens of thousands killed in the slave trade and in the American civil war. This massive death toll was far more horrific as man-made catastrophes than anything since in North America. Serious and honest introspection on the ramifications of these events has yet to occur, as evidenced by the strong movement against reparations for slavery while accepting as natural reparations for Nazi atrocities.

Outside the United States, there are many more examples of mass carnage that belong to the category of mass terror. As many as 20 million civilians perished in the Second World War. Algeria lost a million of its citizens to French colonial rule. Rwanda had hundreds of thousands of civilians killed just a few years ago while the majority of the world kept silent. Proxies of the West massacred millions of Philippinos, Koreans, and Vietnamese, either directly or indirectly. Congress still refuses to acknowledge the Armenian genocide by the Turks at the beginning of the twentieth century. Many still consider as legitimate acts of war the bombings of Dresden, Hiroshima, and Nagasaki in which hundreds of thousands were killed. Hundreds of thousands of African slaves perished at the hands of their European and American white masters. So while not minimizing terror on America, we need to keep the tragedy of 9/11 in perspective in relation to what the rest of the world has experienced.

An estimated 100,000–200,000 Iraqis were killed during and in the immediate aftermath of the first Gulf War in 1991. In addition, according to the United Nations, at least a million Iraqi civilians, the majority of them children, have died since then as a result of the embargo imposed by the United States and Britain. In May 1996, Lesley Stahl of 60 Minutes asked then US Secretary of State Madeleine Albright: 'We have heard that a half million children have died [because of sanctions against Iraq]. I mean, that's more children than died in Hiroshima and you know, is the price worth it?' Albright looked straight at the camera and said: 'I think this is a very hard choice, but the price – we think the price is worth it.'

For many years now, the US has had a policy of helping Kurds in northern Iraq fighting against Saddam Hussein while helping Turkey with weapons, armaments, and support to crush the same Kurdish people fighting for independence in eastern and southern Turkey. The hypocrisy and lack of principle are not lost on the Kurds, the Turks, or the Iraqis. In Vietnam, the dispossession, maiming, and poisoning of an entire nation was an apocalyptic manifestation of US power. CIA Operation Phoenix alone resulted in the deaths of around 50,000 people. The ethnic cleansing of Palestine and the illegal Israeli occupation and violence against the native Palestinians could not continue without US backing. Israel, which represents about 0.1 percent of the world's population, receives 30 percent of US foreign aid.

FEAR

Fear is the most powerful tool governments can use. Fear caused good Germans to support the Nazis in 1934 and surrender their liberty for supposed protection from 'terrorism' and domination by the communists who, some capitalists believed at the time, were dominated by 'Jewish elements'. It causes many good Jews to support Israeli atrocities and it causes good Americans, Canadians, and British today to support the curtailment of civil liberties, and profiling and other acts that are undemocratic in nature. Fear is the most potent political propaganda because it destroys all rational capacity for logical thought.

While invading other countries, the Nazi government always argued that they were defending Germany from others and not fighting a war of aggression. They often claimed that they were 'invited' by their allies or were fighting a 'defensive' war. The onslaught by Israel against Arab countries in 1967 was also thought of as a 'defensive war' and 'pre-emptive' in nature. Many Americans were similarly duped into believing that the invasion of Iraq in 2003 was not an act of aggression but rather an action taken in self-defense. Even though US troops have bombed over 30 countries since 1946 and US troops and 'advisers' are now stationed in over 140 countries, many still believe that they are defending 'freedom'. Yet, not one Iraqi, Korean, Nicaraguan, Vietnamese, Dominican, Grenadian, Panamanian, or Lebanese soldier has ever set foot on American soil. In each case, fear spread by those in power has led the population of the aggressor nations to accept the absurd propaganda of their governments and to acquiesce in the victimization of other people.

The esteemed psychologist Dr William Sargant has argued that governments use fear to create temporary impaired judgement and heighten individual and mass suggestibility, creating a 'herd instinct' most noticeable during times of conflict.[2] A good example of this psychological effect is the public sentiments in the crisis atmosphere following the attacks on the United States on September 11, 2001. It is now well documented how the administration in Washington used the atmosphere of fear to promote its own agenda of hegemony and control, ranging from the so-called PATRIOT Act to the invasion of Iraq.

TERRORISM IN THE LAND OF CANAAN

The violence between settlers and the natives began early (history covered elsewhere). However, Zionists were the first to use modern terror tools in Palestine. On July 22, 1946, a Zionist truck bomb blew up the King David hotel in Jerusalem (where the British civil administration was housed) killing 28 British, 41 Arab, 17 Jewish, and five others, and injuring more than 200. This was the first use of a car bomb in the Middle East. Irgun, a Jewish underground movement led by Menachem Begin, claimed responsibility. However, later evidence showed involvement of the Haganah (the forerunner of the regular Israeli Army). In July 1938 alone, Irgun killed 76 Palestinians in terrorist attacks.[3]

The first letter bombs used by groups operating in the Middle East were made by Zionists and sent to British Cabinet ministers in June 1947. On September 3, 1947 a postal bomb addressed to the British War Office exploded in a Post Office sorting room in London, injuring two.[4]

The Zionists were also the first to introduce economic sabotage. In 1939, the Haganah blew up the Iraqi oil pipeline near Haifa. Moshe Dayan (the famed Israeli Minister of Defense) was one of the participants in this act. The first plane hijacking was sanctioned by the state. On December 12, 1954, Israelis hijacked a civilian Syrian airliner shortly after take-off. In 1973, Israel shot down a Libyan civil aircraft, which strayed over Sinai in a sandstorm, killing all 106 civilian passengers.

Political assassinations were first introduced in the Middle East by Zionists, ironically against the British not the Palestinians. On November 6, 1944, Zionist members of the Stern underground movement (the forerunner of right-wing political parties in Israel) ambushed and assassinated Lord Moyne, the British Minister Resident in the Middle East, in Cairo.

The first attack on a ship by terrorists was on November 25, 1940 when the SS *Patria* carrying illegal Jewish immigrants was attacked with explosives in Haifa harbor. The attack was meant to embarrass the British and was also a result of rivalry among Zionist groups. In that incident 268 Jewish immigrants drowned.

On December 11, 1947, underground Zionist groups tossed bombs at Arab buses in Haifa. Six Palestinians were killed and 30 wounded. On January 5, 1948, Haganah forces planted bombs in the Palestinian-owned Semiramis Hotel in Jerusalem, killing 20, among them Viscount de Tapia, the Spanish Consul. Between December 13, 1947 and February 10, 1948, seven incidents of bomb tossing at innocent Palestinian civilians in cafés and markets were reported. This resulted in the killing of 138 and wounding of 271. Zionist underground forces mined passenger trains killing 93 and wounding 161 in less than ten months. On March 3, 1948, Stern members drove a truck loaded with 400 lb of explosives into the Palestinian-owned building Salam (translated as 'peace') in Haifa. The seven-storey building sustained considerable damage killing 14 civilians (including three Armenians) and injuring 23. Both Menachem Begin and Yitzhak Shamir, as well as the current Likud leader Ariel Sharon, were terrorist commanders responsible for atrocities, including acts against Jews.[5]

Before the Arab countries engaged in the Palestine/Israel conflict, Zionist forces had already committed a number of massacres, including the infamous one at Deir Yassin on April 9, 1948. On December 30, 1947, the Palmach, the strike forces of Haganah, attacked and massacred 60 Palestinian villagers in Balad el-Sheikh. More than half of the 531 Palestinian villages and towns were depopulated by Israeli military actions before Israel was established in May 15, 1948. All this occurred before the beginning of the first major Arab–Israeli war, according to Israeli historians (see Chapter 4). Israel also continued to terrorize the natives into leaving even after the hostilities ended and cease-fires were signed. According to Israeli historians, this postwar ethnic cleansing occurred in 64 of the 500+ Palestinian localities depopulated.

More massacres and terror ensued after Israeli independence. Under the command of a young ambitious officer, Ariel Sharon, 700 regular Israeli troops of Unit 101 attacked the border village of Qibya on October 14, 1953. Forty-two houses were blown up, as well as local schools and the mosque. Every man, woman, and child found was murdered, resulting in a death toll of between 53 and 75, according to independent estimates. In response to world outrage, Ben-Gurion initially claimed that the action was carried out by 'Jewish terrorists' and not by the IDF, but later admitted government involvement. However, Qibya was only a minor massacre compared to those committed by Israel in Lebanon (e.g. at Qana) or by Israeli-paid cronies (at Sabra and Shatila, etc.). Israeli actions were responsible in total for the killing of perhaps as many as 50,000 Palestinian and Lebanese civilians. Historians also now acknowledge that Israeli forces executed hundreds of prisoners of war in the Sinai in 1967. Between September 2000 and April 2003, over 2,300 Palestinians were killed and over 40,000 injured. Most of the victims were civilians. Israeli forces uprooted 112,900 olive trees from Palestinian land and are building an apartheid wall to isolate Palestinians in ghettos.

RESISTANCE VERSUS TERRORISM

Generally, occupying or colonial powers call resistance to their occupation terrorism. Some examples of resistance/terrorism include the French resistance to German occupation, the Algerian resistance to French occupation, the Palestinian resistance to British occupation, the South African black resistance to apartheid, the Afghan resistance to Soviet occupation, and the Palestinian resistance to Israeli occupation. One must distinguish between legitimate resistance to oppression and colonization, as approved in the UN Charter, and terrorism. In the context of the Palestinian struggle for self-determination the Zionists and the western media have intentionally obfuscated this distinction. Terror indeed occasionally is resorted to in acts of native populations against colonial powers. Examples are too numerous to cite, but include ANC 'necklacing' of collaborators, native American attacks on civilians, the bombing of British and Arab civilian areas by Jewish groups in Palestine in the 1930s, Palestinian airplane hijacking, and attacks on civilians in Hebron from 1929 until today.

Any native people subject to repressive colonialism develop a bell-shaped curve of responses ranging from all non-violent forms at one end of the curve to horrible crimes, usually termed terrorism, at the other. The majority in the middle of this curve will always have an element of resistance that is neither terrorism nor completely non-violent. Historical examination will reveal examples of wide-ranging tactics adopted by different segments of society, even when all are living under the same degree of occupation or repression. Differences in tactics between individuals in their responses can be, but are not necessarily, related to the external pressures faced by that individual. Examples of the full range of this bell-shaped curve were evident among the Irish, black South Africans, African American blacks, and Native Americans. In each of these groups, segments within the same society expressed their emotions and their aspirations by acts ranging from writing, to peaceful demonstrations, to civil disobedience, to terrorism.

The Jewish resistance to the Romans at the time of Jesus also involved acts of terror. The Sakkari sect of resisters to the Roman occupation became legendary among extremist Zionists in their struggle against Palestinians. Sakkaris were reputed to conceal a knife in their clothes and attack unwary victims in a characteristic way. Victims included those perceived to have collaborated with the Romans and their families, and all Roman citizens.

Palestinians also resorted to terrorism in their struggle against colonial Zionism, as did other groups, such as native Americans, the IRA in Northern Ireland, the ANC in South Africa, and many other anti-colonial movements. However, the amount and extent of Palestinian terrorism was minuscule compared to Israel's. Israeli terrorist acts were both qualitatively and quantitatively far greater than those of the Palestinians. The number of civilians killed by Zionist actions, both before the state was created and since, is more than ten times the number killed by Palestinian groups. These numbers are documented in reports from the Red Cross and human rights organizations.

Terror and extremism are known to have increased following the 1967 attack by Israel, which resulted in Israel's acquisition of more Arab lands. Academic circles attribute the dramatic effect of the 1967 war to the immediate realization by people in the streets that secular and democratic Arab movements and other forms of resistance had failed to restore Palestinian rights, including the rights of refugees to go home.

It would be meaningless to try to compare individual acts of terrorism (whether committed by Palestinians or Israelis) and set them on a 'morality' scale. Terrorism by definition is immoral and falls outside the scope of what the majority of people would consider acceptable. It makes little difference to the civilian victims whether Israeli public transport is used by soldiers and civilians, or whether Israeli bombing of civilian neighborhoods or demolishing entire olive groves was supposed to thwart native attacks. How much difference is there in how civilians die, whether by a burning tire ('necklacing', in South Africa), the shelling of villages and towns (US in Vietnam or Israeli forces in Palestine today), dying at a checkpoint waiting to go to a hospital, the bombing of a café or bus (Northern Ireland and Palestine), or dying as the result of an external siege (as in Iraq and now likely in Palestine). A quantitative gradient or even a discontinuous spectrum of different levels of immorality or inhumanity is meaningless to its victims and thus should be meaningless to the rest of humanity.

There are questions about who a civilian is. Does the definition include Palestinian policemen or Jewish settlers/colonialists or even Israelis who serve three years in the military and then one month a year for 40 years? But whether we use the strictest or the most liberal of criteria to define civilian, we still find that Israelis have killed many more Palestinian civilians than Israeli civilians have been killed by Palestinians. But a head count does not provide a measure of morality to either 'group'. It also fails to address the core issues beyond a grizzly count of the dead. The killing in the case of Israel/Palestine is done in the context of subduing a native people by a colonizing society and that is the etiology of the underlying disease, whose symptoms include acts of violence. Failing to investigate the disease at its core is not conducive to diagnosis or treatment.

The motivational issues with regards to terrorists are often misunderstood. From a psycho-social standpoint, some individuals identify more with the perceived suffering or injustice done to others in their community because they have a strong group 'instinct' or tribalism. They can develop extreme forms of violence even when individually they are not personally affected by the situation. In other words, the individuals most oppressed are not necessarily the most violent. But societies that are most oppressed or have a perceived oppression will express a level of violence among some of their elements that reflects this oppression. Some of the worst acts of terrorism were not committed by individuals who themselves were victims of oppression, but where that individual identified with a presumed or actual oppression of 'their' people. Hundreds of examples can be cited, ranging from such groups as Irgun, the Stern Gang, and Kakh (Jewish terrorist groups operating in Palestine), to the Ku Klux Klan (a Christian terrorist group), and Al-Qaeda (a Muslim terrorist group). A Kach member, Baruch Goldman (Goldstein), an immigrant from New York who massacred over 29 Muslim civilians while they were at prayer, left a comfortable life in America and was in no physical danger or under duress himself.[6] Osama Bin Laden and Ariel Sharon similarly come from privileged backgrounds, but 'feel the pain' of their people. These violent few believe they have to take matters into their own hands to rectify a real or perceived injustice. Some may think there is a need to create a balance of terror since they cannot create a balance of power. Hence the Zionist terror against the far more superior British forces in Palestine in the 1930s and 1940s. Their effect is further increased by exaggeration and due to the unpredictability of their next target. Hence they create terror and fear among the target population. They become more dangerous when:

1. a large segment of the society, while not willing to engage in similar tactics, 'understands' their actions and provides excuses for them; and
2. the media exaggerate their actions creating fear and panic among the target population (terror).

Dissecting and understanding the motivation in a population is not to condone terrorism by a segment of that population. Between 1947 and 1949, over 33 massacres of Palestinian civilians occurred in a process that is now understood, even by Israeli historians, to have been intended to 'cleanse' non-Jews from the areas that were to become part of a Jewish state. A media frenzy resulted in even more panic and fear among the hapless Palestinian peasant population. This resulted in the largest and now most persistent refugee problem in the world. It is these refugee camps, abandoned by the whole world, that are now called centers of terror.

Nearly six of the nine million Palestinians in the world are refugees or displaced people. Their feelings were captured over 30 years ago in the personal account of Fawaz Turki:

The private terrors that shadow the everyday life of the exile, the refugee, the occupied, the stateless would have forever remained private were it not for the fact that from these terrors an occasional outcry of fathomless anger is emitted, spilling over to the outside world. This outside world, standing with its back to the human passions housed within the confines of the ghetto, the refugee camp, the occupied city, and the colonized town, does not understand these occasional outcries, simply because their idiom and their metaphor, their cause and effect stem from a reality alien to the outside world. Yet those of us who have known no other reality, driven by it as if by the terrors of a primal pain, also share our humanity with other men and women, denying them monopoly of this humanity.

Such is the matrix of logic of the outside world in this day that the onus always falls on the oppressed to explain his position, to prove his sincerity, to justify his platform, to articulate his vision of the future and to truly, truly convince his oppressor (whose napalm and military occupation, whose racist excesses and sadistic regressions have crushed his very soul and reduced him to a fragment) that he is motivated by love and not hate. Above all, he is called upon to believe in the notion that the violence of the oppressor to subdue him with sophisticated weapons and keys to the dungeons, is moral. His own violence which he uses to break his chains is immoral. And so on.[7]

JUSTICE BRINGS PEACE, INJUSTICE PERPETUATES VIOLENCE

During the many years of the Oslo 'peace process', many of us warned that what Israel is doing (land confiscation, settlement building, home demolitions, torture, a slow process of ethnic cleansing, and other human rights violations) will not lead to peace. We have argued that a just peace cannot be achieved between a strong, colonial, and belligerent Israeli government and weak Palestinians under occupation or dispersed as refugees. We have argued that violence and military power do not solve problems but exacerbate them. We have argued for international intervention to defend human rights. The involvement of the international community, we have argued, is similar to what materialized in South Africa. Many in the US media choose to ignore our voices and instead listen to Israeli government officials who believe they have figured out how to deal with the Palestinian 'problem' and 'violence'.

For Labor Zionists, the Oslo agreements were intended to maintain the Zionist program and land acquisition while giving Palestinians autonomy. This autonomy could be called a Palestinian 'state' but without real sovereignty and would have consisted of only 16 percent of the original land of Palestine or 80 percent of the lands of the occupied areas of Gaza and the West Bank. Israel would then maintain control of the natural resources, borders, land, and most areas of true sovereignty. For Likud Zionists, the arrangements were to maintain the Zionist program by giving Palestinians autonomy, but not statehood, in a smaller area (10 percent of the original land of Palestine or 42 percent of the lands of the occupied areas of Gaza and the West Bank), and maintain control of the natural resources, borders, and land. Both groups denied basic international law on the right of refugees to return to their homes and lands.

Intoxicated with the power of being the fifth strongest army in the world and with backing from the only remaining superpower, both brands of Zionism were emboldened to continue to think in the tradition of earlier Zionists: that Palestinians will either cease to exist or acquiesce to Israeli domination. But despite all the oppression and ethnic cleansing over 55 years, half the Palestinian natives continue to exist in Palestine and all Palestinians still demand self-determination, true sovereignty, and basic human rights. Violence will continue until this basic injustice is remedied.

In deciding how to deal with terrorism, we would be remiss if we did not learn from history. But even if governments are short-sighted enough to address it in its most proximal dimension (i.e. targeting those who commit the acts and their supporters and financiers), we must address this within existing international criminal laws rather than a clash of civilization or a war. Francis A. Boyle, Professor of International Law, refers to the power of the 1971 Montreal Sabotage Convention as the international law dealing with terrorism. The US and 173 other states are signatories and are obliged to resolve disputes according to provisions of the convention and UN Charter Articles 2(3) and 33 as well as the Kellogg–Briand Pact of 1928.

The Declaration on Principles of International Law of 1970 emphasized that all states are under a duty to refrain from any forcible action that deprives people of their right to self-determination. The Declaration also notes that 'in their actions against, and resistance to, such forcible action' such peoples could receive support in accordance with the purpose and principles of the UN Charter. Various UN resolutions have reaffirmed the legitimacy of the struggle of peoples for liberation from colonial domination and alien subjection, 'by all available means including armed struggle' (e.g. UN General Assembly Resolutions 3070, 3103, 3246, 3328, 3481, 31/91, 32/42 and 32/154). Article 1, section 4, of Protocol I (additional to the Geneva Conventions) considers self-determination struggles as international armed conflict situations. The principle of self-determination itself provides that where forcible action has been taken to suppress the right, force may be used in order to counter this and achieve self-determination. The right of resistance is internationally recognized, but not the right of indiscriminate use of violence.

The majority of the 600,000 Jews in Palestine at the time of the founding of the state of Israel saw the massacres of thousands and expulsion of hundreds of thousands of Palestinians as justifiable and part and parcel of the Zionist program to create the 'Jewish state'. The Knesset passed laws by an overwhelming majority to prevent the return of the 800,000 Palestinian refugees. Laws were enacted to acquire the land of both the fleeing refugees and the remaining Palestinians. Few Jews complained about this large-scale ethnic cleansing. Many Palestinians in the refugee camps today see terror attacks against Israelis as so much less than what they themselves have suffered at the hands of Israel over the past 55 years. The difference of course is that the Israeli state has victimized Palestinians who had nothing to do with Nazi atrocities, while the Palestinian militants respond to the same society that victimized them.

Group responsibility for violence is a topic far beyond the scope of this work. One has to realize though that the majority of Germans did not engage in the creation and running of the concentration camps but acquiesced to them. The majority of the Israeli Jews did not participate in the ethnic cleansing of the Palestinians from 1947 to 1949 but acquiesced to them. The majority of Israelis do not participate in occupying or oppressing Palestinians but acquiesce to it. The majority of Americans did not participate in starving the Iraqi people but acquiesced to it. The majority of Palestinians do not engage in terrorism but acquiesce to it. In none of those situations is one justified in labeling entire societies 'guilty', but it does not prevent attempts to redress the injustice to the victims. I strongly believe that humans are not only capable of making war but are also capable of achieving justice and peace. Most of all, humans are capable of influencing each other to recognize the need to remedy injustice. In the age of the Internet, this is becoming more possible.

One segment of society does and should criticize other segments and sometimes these internal divisions succeed in halting atrocities or at least ameliorating their intensity. Those at the center and those farther to the left do denounce terrorism and violence and can and do work to promote better societal systems. Those who engage in terrorism may see non-violent resistance as passive acceptance of evil and may try to influence others to engage in violence. But history is not ambiguous or neutral in this equation. History reveals that violence breeds violence. This fact is usually lost to those in the dominant culture or power at the time. This is precisely because, having arrived at dominance by military means, they believe it to be economically and logistically acceptable to engage in violence. They merely relabel such actions as just wars, security, or self-defense. Being lulled into thinking that power can be maintained through more violence and more military spending, these powers lose sight of the long-term effects. They may then disintegrate both from within and from without, to be replaced by other, similarly foolish empires. That was the fate of the Roman Empire, the Persian Empire, the British Empire and the Soviet Empire. Will it be the fate of the US and Israel? That is up to us who care to try and avert this by insisting that these governments act in a humane and peaceful way.

The insistence of some that terrorism is a phenomenon of certain cultures or religions is false and cannot lead to any rational diagnosis and treatment of this blemish on human heritage. At best it is a corrupt and cowardly intellectual exercise to say that certain people and cultures are 'not like us'; at worst it is pure racism.

Violence is not a mystical or elusive force. Rather, its causes and effects are easy to discern and understand in the context of power politics. It is also not an inevitable phenomenon nor is it a phenomenon directly related to religious beliefs or a particular geography or culture. Terrorism in the Arab world was introduced well before Islam. Modern-day violence against civilians is practiced by both states and individuals. Violence as practiced by individuals acting outside of state control may be related to (but is not excused by) disenfranchised and oppressed status. State violence against civilians is usually related to (and also is not excused by) mainte- nance of the power and privileges of the few. The two phenomena (state and individual 'terrorism') are intimately linked and grow by feeding on each other in a cycle that can be broken only by justice and equality.

Violence is not an incidental by-product of occupation or oppression or dispossession; it is their chosen tool and consequence. Tackling violence means tackling it at its roots. But it is an illusion to fight violence with violence. What is needed is to follow the lead of the hundreds of Israeli reserve soldiers and officers who are refusing to serve in the occupied areas and to follow the lead of the 1,000 generals and army personnel who have called on their government to withdraw from the occupied areas and vacate the Israeli settle- ments. The US is funding this occupation with its tax dollars and is thus complicit in perpetuating the misery of both Palestinians and

Israelis. Apartheid and colonial rule have failed in South Africa and cannot and will not succeed in Israel/Palestine. It is time to say: end the occupation which is killing all of us, respect human rights, and grant dignity and equality to all.

A brief examination of history reveals two related facts: 1) that those in power use fear to rally the people, who will then give them greater powers to carry on with their ambitions and wars; 2) that the biggest dangers to great powers are when they overextend themselves, take on more than they can handle, and become too self-centered and arrogant to see the world around them changing. The collapse of the Roman, Ottoman, Spanish, Soviet, and British Empires provide many lessons. Will Israel and the US learn these lessons in time?

In our search for answers to the violence in this world we should remember history to learn from all the good that people have done as well as the evil lest we repeat the mistakes and generate more violence. To truly 'drain the swamp' that breeds terror we must and will positively tackle the forces and powers filling the swamp: propaganda, economic deprivation, injustice perpetuated on native people, the widening gap between rich and poor, and other social and environmental ills that plague this earth. The basic condition for shaping a better world is thus advancing human rights, an issue we address in the next chapter. We must become positive agents of change rather than support violence as a means of enhancing 'our security'. We should join those who worry about the security of this small planet. Only by being aware of history and working for justice and non-violence can we hope to 'fight terrorism' effectively, but, more importantly, create a liveable world.

To be hopeful in bad times is not just foolishly romantic. It is based on the fact that human history is a history not only of cruelty, but also of compassion, sacrifice, courage, [and] kindness. What we choose to emphasize in this complex history will determine our lives. If we see only the worst, it destroys our capacity to do something. If we remember those times and places – and there are so many – where people have behaved magnificently, this gives us the energy to act, and at least the possibility of sending this spinning top of a world in a different direction. And if we do act, in however small a way, we don't have to wait for some grand utopian future. The future is an infinite succession of presents, and to live now as we think human beings should live, in defiance of all that is bad around us, is itself a marvelous victory.[8]

RECOMMENDED READING

Joseph L. Heller, *The Stern Gang: Ideology, Politics, and Terror, 1940–1949* (London: Frank Cass & Co., 1995).

David Hirst, *The Gun and the Olive Branch* (New York: Thunder's Mouth Press, 2nd ed., 2003).

9
Human Rights

Amnesty International has proposed a ten-point agenda for a durable peace based on human rights. These ten points (see Exhibit 2) are a well thought out and articulate vision for peace. It is in fact impossible to envision a peace that would work without human rights. A peace agreement was attempted via the agreements signed by Israel and the PLO in Oslo which disregarded basic rights enshrined in the Fourth Geneva Convention (refugees rights, illegal settlement activities, collective punishment) and the Universal Declaration of Human Rights. It is becoming clear that future peace agreements will similarly fail if they do not encompass respect for human rights. Amnesty International issued a press release on March 26, 2001 entitled 'Developing a Human Rights Agenda for Peace'. It stated:

> Recognition of the inherent dignity and of the equal and inalienable rights of all members of the human family is the foundation of freedom, justice and peace in the world [Preamble of the Universal Declaration of Human Rights]. Amnesty International calls unreservedly for the full enjoyment of the human rights in the Universal Declaration of Human Rights for all people. A major flaw of the process that began with the Oslo Agreement of 1993 was that peace was not founded on ensuring respect and protection for human rights. The past months have shown more clearly than ever that if human rights are sacrificed in the search for peace and security there will be no peace and no security. Even if the human rights agenda is not the only answer, it must be part of the solution.[1]

THE UNIVERSAL DECLARATION OF HUMAN RIGHTS

Inalienable human rights include two interrelated and indivisible categories: civil and political rights; and economic, social and cultural rights.[2] Some self-interested parties want to limit human rights to those that they consider non-threatening to their own economic or social powers. Members of society not only have rights, but also responsibilities to uphold these rights for others. To the extent that these rights and responsibilities are honored, societies function. The misunderstanding concerning concepts of social Darwinism fails to appreciate that even under Darwin's theory of evolution, selection can operate not only at the individual level but at the group level (what is called group selection). In other words, these rights are a given whether one believes they are given by our creator or are advantageous to societies that enjoy them (by creating less friction and allowing development in a sustainable manner).

The Universal Declaration of Human Rights (UDHR; see Exhibit 3) is a unique document outlining civil, political, social, economic and cultural rights. This has become the consensus of nations and people, although many choose to emphasize only parts of this remarkable document. The UDHR actually lays out what it would take to bring peace to the land of Canaan. No agreement can be valid without recognition of basic human rights. Like Amnesty International, the UN Commission on Human Rights stated on March 15, 2000:

> A final consideration seems to be in order with reference to the fact that any agreement between the Occupying Power and a body representing the occupied civilian population is null and void if it violates the terms of the Fourth Geneva Convention. In other words, while protection of human rights and humanitarian law should never become an obstacle in the way of a peace process, an ultimate solution should not be achieved to the detriment of human rights. Indeed, respect for human rights and fundamental freedoms must be considered part and parcel of any viable peace process as they are a condition sine qua non of any enduring peace.[3]

Thus, the Universal Declaration of Human Rights has become the benchmark of human rights organizations, and has been ratified by most countries, including Israel and the US.

In reading the Declaration, one is struck by the incredible number of provisions that have been violated by Israel. Let us allow the statements from human rights organizations themselves address some of the issues, beginning first with the issue of civilian killings. Palestinian attacks by sub-national groups on Israeli civilians are addressed in Chapter 8 on 'Violence and Terrorism'. We will not address here the massive human rights violations involving ethnic cleansing that occurred between 1947 and 1949 and again in 1967 (these are addressed in Chapter 4). In this chapter we address the killing of civilians and other violations by the state of Israel, as these remain an obstacle to a peace based on international law and human rights.

In an open letter addressed to leaders of the US, EU, Israel, Palestinian Authority, and UN Secretary-General Kofi Annan (June 6, 2001), Amnesty International and Human Rights Watch called for the dispatch of international human rights monitors, despite Israeli objections. They stated:

the clashes between Israelis and Palestinians since October 2000 have been marked by systematic violations of international human rights and humanitarian law. Civilians have been the main victims of the violence, and an immediate priority must be to bring such violations to an end. At least 470 Palestinians have been killed, most of them unlawfully by Israeli security forces when their lives and the lives of others were not in danger. More than 120 Israelis have been killed, most of them civilians deliberately targeted by armed groups and individuals. The death toll includes more than 130 children.[4]

The letter goes on to document abuses of human rights by the Israeli government and the settlers as well as by individuals and groups of Palestinians. The letter stated that the joint Israeli–Palestinian Authority security committees have not been able to address repeated human rights and humanitarian law violations on their own.

TORTURE

The use of torture by the Israeli authorities has been well documented by human rights organizations. In fact, torture as a method to obtain confessions was considered legal in Israel for 52 years until an Israeli High Court ruling of September 6, 1999. Israel's High Court of Justice issued a unanimous decision that ruled that the violent interrogation techniques used by the Israeli General Security Service (GSS) against Palestinian detainees were illegal. Yet, the Court refrained from defining these as torture and advised that such practices might be acceptable if specifically authorized by new legislation. In February 2000, the head of the GSS withdrew his request for legislation of 'special' interrogation methods. Yet, the Israeli Attorney General reiterated the promise to grant legal protection to any interrogator who uses 'special means' in individual cases. The UN Committee Against Torture, while noting an improvement in the situation following the 1999 High Court decision, stated that a further improvement, in light of continuing allegations by human rights organizations and individuals of situations amounting to torture, would be to amend Israeli law to remove 'necessity as a possible justification to the crime of torture'.[5] The 1999 High Court decision has not brought Israel to compliance with basic international human rights law. The Associated Press reported that the Danes were incensed at the appointment of Carmi Gilon, former director of Israel's Shin Bet (the secret service that engaged in torture) as Ambassador to Denmark. He continued to defend torture and boasted that he had 'authorized about 100 cases of torture while heading Shin Bet'.[6]

Amnesty International has written in regard to the issue:

> Amnesty International's briefing to the Committee [UN Committee Against Torture] stated that, since the September 1999 High Court of Justice judgment which banned interrogation methods constituting torture, there has been strong evidence that these methods – including sleep deprivation often seated in painful positions; prolonged squatting on haunches; painful handcuffing – are now being used again.
>
> We regret that notwithstanding the High Court of Justice's 1999 ruling and the Committee Against Torture's clear statement in 1997 that these methods constitute torture, the State of Israel, in its report to the Committee, continues to deny this.
>
> Amnesty International also called on the Committee Against Torture to declare that the demolition of Palestinian homes constitutes cruel, inhuman or degrading treatment under Article 16 of the Convention Against Torture. The European Court of Human Rights has deemed Turkish demolition of houses to constitute inhuman treatment in breach of Article 3 of the European Convention of Human Rights ... Amnesty International also considers that other forms of collective punishment carried out by the Israeli authorities, including the prolonged closures of towns, villages and whole areas, denying freedom of movement to Palestinians, and prolonged curfews might also fall under Article 16 of the Convention.[7]

TARGETING CIVILIANS

Contrary to propaganda about accidental shootings, all human rights organizations have concluded that Israeli forces target non-combatants (civilians) and intentionally shoot children even when Israeli lives are not threatened.

In a press release B'Tselem stated:

In every city and refugee camp that they have entered, IDF soldiers have repeated the same pattern: indiscriminate firing and the killing of innocent civilians, intentional harm to water, electricity and telephone infrastructure, taking over civilian houses, extensive damage to civilian property, shooting at ambulances and prevention of medical care to the injured.[8]

Physicians for Human Rights USA have investigated the high number of Palestinian deaths and injuries in the first months of the Intifada and blamed both Israelis and Palestinians for these unnecessary deaths. It concluded that: 'the pattern of injuries seen in many victims did not reflect IDF [Israel Defense Forces] use of firearms in life-threatening situations but rather indicated targeting solely for the purpose of wounding or killing'.[9]

The same group sent forensics experts and an orthopedic surgeon in one investigation and concluded that the Israeli Army 'has used live ammunition and rubber bullets excessively and inappropriately to control demonstrators, and that based on the high number of documented injuries to the head and thighs, soldiers appear to be shooting to inflict harm, rather than solely in self-defense'.[10]

Amnesty International stated that it is 'gravely concerned at recent reports of random shelling and shootings by the Israeli Defense Force in Palestinian residential areas, among them Jenin, Ramallah, Tulkarm, Bethlehem, and Beit Jala, which has left at least 25 Palestinians killed, among them several children, and scores of others injured, in retaliation for the killing of the Israeli Minister of Tourism, Rehavam Zeevi on 17 October'.[11]

Human Rights Watch issued a report on Israeli atrocities in Jenin, stating:

civilians were killed willfully or unlawfully [by the Israeli military]. ... [which] used Palestinian civilians as 'human shields' and used indiscriminate and excessive force ... The abuses we documented in Jenin are extremely serious, and in some cases appear to be war crimes. Criminal investigations are needed to ascertain individual responsibility for the most serious violations.[12]

Besides human rights organizations, occasional news items in Israeli and US media have reported on what Palestinians have been experiencing.

In an interview with *Haaretz* reporter Amira Hass, an Israeli sniper described the commands he receives from his superiors as '[age] twelve and up, you're allowed to shoot. That's what they tell us.'[13]

Yediot Aharonot quoted Tal Etlinger, a 'border guard' trained to quell demonstrations, as stating that riots at Um Al Fahm (where scores of unarmed Palestinian citizens of Israel were shot and many killed by snipers) were much less violent than Jewish riots (such as in Tiberias), which were 'much worse ... but we handle Jewish riots differently ... [t]o a demonstration like this we know in advance to come without weapons ... These are the orders from above, and we use only gas.'[14]

The *Washington Post* had this to say: 'Iyad was shot because he ran too fast. Nshat was shot because he missed his ride. Ronny was shot for throwing a stone. And Abdel Kareem was shot where his two friends died. Iyad, Nshat, Ronny and Abdel Kareem had never met before. But these four young Palestinians now see one another daily, as patients at the Abu Raya Rehabilitation Center.'[15]

HUMAN RIGHTS AS THE CORNERSTONE FOR PEACE

Amnesty and Human Rights Watch have issued press releases asking the international community to act to end the daily violations of human rights in the occupied Palestinian areas. They have called for an end to Israel's policy of closures and house demolitions, which punish entire populations and devastate their livelihoods. According to an Amnesty International report of December 1999, 2,650 Palestinian houses have been destroyed since 1987 in the West Bank, including East Jerusalem, on the pretext of not having building permission. Further thousands of acres owned by Palestinians have been confiscated to build settlements in the occupied territories in contravention of the Fourth Geneva Convention, which states, in Article 49, that the 'Occupying Power shall not transfer parts of its own civilian population into the territory it occupies'.[16] A colonization project based on Zionism and the creation of a

Jewish state has resulted in the removal of over 70 percent of Palestinians from their homes and lands. This project has resulted in direct violations of basic human rights. The latest and most visible (literally and figuratively) manifestation of this and the violation of the Universal Declaration of Human Rights is the so-called 'security barrier' that Israel is currently building inside the West Bank and surrounding Palestinian cities and towns.

The barrier is not a security fence built along the Green Line. Rather, it is a huge engineering project of walls, ditches, electrified fences, towers, and exclusion zones snaking through the most fertile Palestinian areas in the West Bank. Its length is some 650 km and has cost about US$1.2 billion. It is leaving shrunken Palestinian areas isolated in ghettos; its primary objective is the expansion of the illegal Israeli settlements.[17]

The UN Commission on Human Rights reported its findings with respect to Israeli violation of the principles and bases of international law in the occupied Palestinian territories:

> The Occupying Power's confiscation of land and properties belonging privately and collectively to the Palestinians in the occupied Palestinian territories is a dominant feature of the occupation and an essential component of population transfer carried out by Israel. This practice violates the long-established international law principle of the unacceptability of the acquisition of territory by force, as well as specific resolutions concerning Israel's confiscation of land and settlement activities. Since 1967, Israel has confiscated land for public, semi-public and private use in order to create Israeli military zones, settlements, industrial areas, elaborate 'by-pass' roads, and quarries, as well as to hold 'State land' for exclusive Israeli use. Estimates place the proportion of Palestinian land confiscated by Israel at some 60 per cent of the West Bank, 33 per cent of the Gaza Strip, and at least 32.5 km[2], or approximately 33 per cent of the Palestinian land area in Jerusalem.[18]

Despite international opposition and a UN resolution adopted by the overwhelming majority of members (only the US, Israel, Micronesia, and Marshal Islands voted against), Israel is building what it calls its 'security fence' in the occupied Palestinian areas. Palestinians and human right advocates call Israel's separation barrier the 'apartheid wall'. Over 300 cities held events on November 9, 2003 to protest against this project (the date is the anniversary of the dismantling of the Berlin Wall).

The barrier is a 650 km system of fortifications consisting of very high concrete walls in some areas and trenches, rows of barbed wires, and high steel fencing in other areas. Where the wall is not constructed of 10 meter concrete sections, it involves ditches, fences (barbed wire or high steel wires), with security roads along both sides of the fence for army patrols, and yet more ditches and barriers. It is a very expensive venture costing an estimated $1.2 billion. US taxpayers gave Israel $5 billion in direct aid in 2003 and many more billions in indirect aid. So perhaps we should learn a little more about this project.

The first striking feature is where the wall is being built: the route is amazing (see maps at http://stopthewall.org). If you are building a wall or a fence for security purposes and want to patrol both sides you would build it 3 km inside your own territory. In this case it would be inside the 1949 armistice border. Instead, the wall in some places snakes its way 15–30 km inside the Palestinian areas, leaving them disjointed and *de facto* annexes 50 percent of the West Bank to Israel. The colonies/settlements are where they are for 'a good reason', as an Israeli prime minister once said: because of Israeli rulers' need to control the Jordan valley (to the east; some 20 percent of the West Bank), the water resources (to the west), Arab East Jerusalem (at the centre), and connections between these. Palestinians (including refugees) would be left with just 12 percent of historic Palestine and would live in five disjointed cantons. To understand better the genesis of this project, some history is appropriate.

Before the war of 1948 the Palestinian area of Al-Majdal was thriving, home to thousands of Palestinians. Most of the inhabitants were driven out during the war. In early 1950, well after the war ended, Israeli forces started to apply all sorts of restrictions on the remaining 1,500 residents. They were prevented from using their lands, restricted to one part of the remaining city (now renamed Ashkelon), and encircled with fences. They were forced to choose between economic and even literal starvation in this prison or 'voluntary' transfer. By November 1950 all had left to join the hundreds of thousands of refugees. This method was used elsewhere and is just one of many other tools used. In Ramla and Lydda (now Lod), outright expulsions at the point of the gun were carried out. Israel immediately introduced laws to confiscate the land and prevent refugees from returning (regardless of how they were forced out). The Israeli Army was ordered to shoot to kill any Palestinian found in those areas. As a result, hundreds of 'infiltrators' (villagers attempting to return) were killed.

Ashkelon now has a large prison in which many Israeli Jews are employed to guard hundreds of Palestinians. Some of the prisoners are the children or grandchildren of the Al-Majdal refugees. Tens of thousands of Al-Majdal refugees live in the Gaza Strip. Gaza is effectively an open air prison and is one of the most densely populated and poorest areas in the world. Many have had their shacks and homes demolished as part of a collective punishment or to seize land for the Jewish-only settlements in the Gaza Strip.

The barrier is thus aptly described as an apartheid wall the intention of which is to complete the process of ethnic cleansing and conquest of the 1947–50 era. Amnesty International stated on November 7, 2003:

'This fence/wall is having devastating economic and social consequences on the daily lives of hundreds of thousands of Palestinians, separating families and communities from each other and from their land and water – their most crucial assets,' the London-based group said ... The construction of this fence/wall in its current location must be halted immediately. As it continues to snake through Palestinian land, more and more Palestinians find themselves trapped into enclaves and cantons, unable to have any semblance of a normal life.[19]

When completed, the wall will become the *de facto* border of the so-called 'Palestinian state', which will exist in at least four cantons (Northern West Bank, Southern West Bank, Jericho, and the Gaza Strip). These cantons will be surrounded by confiscated lands under Israeli control and will be dependent on the goodwill of Israeli leaders for water, access, and most other elements of national sovereignty. Palestinian refugees and displaced people will be told to accept that might equals right and that as such they will have to accept the forfeiture of their inalienable right to return to their homes and lands. This is an untenable situation, one that cannot last long. It is a recipe for continued bloodshed and injustice. As Amnesty International and other human rights organizations have pointed out, the only durable solution will respect human rights. Towards this, a re-reading of Amnesty's ten-point agenda for peace and the Universal Declaration of Human Rights should become the cornerstone of any peace agreement. Pretending that human rights can be shelved while getting security or peace is the worst form of self-delusion or outright deception.

Exhibit 2. Ten Principles that Amnesty International Articulated for a Durable Peace Based on Human Rights (press release, March 26, 2001)

1. Everybody has the right to life, liberty and security of person. Extra-judicial executions, suicide bombings or other attacks against civilians, excessive lethal force and targeting of residential areas have violated the right to life of hundreds. The life of each individual must be protected. The authorities must prohibit unlawful killings. Opposition groups must equally not carry out unlawful killings. Every killing must be investigated and the perpetrators of any unlawful killing should be brought to justice in fair trials. The Palestinian Authority should abolish the death penalty.

2. No one should be subjected to torture or to cruel, inhuman or degrading treatment or punishment. Torture and police brutality has been frequent both in Israel and under the jurisdiction of the Palestinian Authority. Torture, brutality by the security forces, and all other cruel treatment or punishment should be eradicated; any cases of torture or ill treatment should be immediately independently and thoroughly investigated and the perpetrators brought to justice in fair trials. Incommunicado detention should be ended and all detainees should have prompt access to lawyers and family.

3. No one should be subjected to arbitrary arrest and detention. In Israel detainees have been held without charge or fair trial in administrative detention; under the Palestinian Authority hundreds have been held without charge or trial even after the Palestinian High Court of Justice has ordered their release. Such arbitrary detention has often been carried out in the name of the fight against 'terrorism'. All political prisoners held without charge or trial should be tried in fair trials or immediately released.

4. Everyone has the right to a fair trial. In Israel the trials of Palestinians in military courts have diminished defendants' rights to fair trials. Under the Palestinian Authority the State Security Court hands down sentences in summary trials in flagrant violation of fair trial rights. Palestinian military courts have also held unfair trials. Laws and practice in Israel, the Occupied Territories and the Palestinian Authority must ensure respect for the right to fair trial as enshrined in international human rights standards.

5. All persons are free and equal in dignity and rights. There should be no distinction or discrimination against anyone on the grounds of ethnic origin, religion, sex or other status in the enjoyment of human rights and freedoms.

Discriminatory laws and practices should be abolished including those that have caused the destruction of Palestinian houses and property.

6. Everyone has the right to freedom of movement. The past seven years have witnessed profound and flagrant denials of the right to freedom of movement. The closures are a grave human rights violation targeted against Palestinians in the Occupied Territories. The occupied territories have become a land of barriers between town and town and between village and village. Palestinian towns and villages have been cut off from the outside world for days and often weeks; trenches have been dug round Jericho and Ramallah. The great majority of the inhabitants of Gaza have been enclosed for years as though in a prison and Palestinians from the Occupied Territories are unable to enter Jerusalem without a permit. Even those seeking medical treatment have frequently been barred entry. The Israeli Government denies entry to Gaza to its own citizens. These barriers to free movement should now be removed.

7. Everyone has the right to return to his or her country. The right to return is an individual human right, which cannot be given away as a political concession. Palestinians in exile should be given the choice to exercise such a right and return to Israel, the West Bank or Gaza Strip as appropriate. Palestinians should also be allowed to choose other durable solutions, such as integration in their host country or resettlement in a third country. Those who choose not to return are entitled to compensation. Those returning should also receive compensation for lost property. The same rights relating to return and compensation should also be given to Israelis who fled or were forced out of Arab and other countries.

8. Everyone has the right to freedom of thought, opinion and expression. Under the Palestinian Authority critics of the authority or the peace process have been harassed, arrested and imprisoned, often without charge or trial. The Israeli authorities have restricted the movement of human rights activists and journalists have been shot at. Peaceful expression of ideas and opinions which does not constitute advocacy of violence, hatred, slander or libel should be guaranteed and any person detained solely for the expression of conscientiously held beliefs should be released immediately and unconditionally.

9. Women have the right to full equality. The freedom of women is limited by discriminatory codes and practice. Equality of women should be enshrined in law and practice.

10. There should be no impunity for human rights abuses. Allegations of human rights abuses should be promptly, impartially and thoroughly investigated and perpetrators brought to justice in fair proceedings.

Source: Amnesty International, International Secretariat, 1 Easton Street, London WC1X 8DJ. http://www.amnestyusa.org/news/2001/israel03262001.html

Exhibit 3. Universal Declaration of Human Rights adopted by the United Nations (1948)

Preamble

WHEREAS recognition of the inherent dignity and of the equal and inalienable rights of all members of the human family is the foundation of freedom, justice and peace in the world,

WHEREAS disregard and contempt for human rights have resulted in barbarous acts which have outraged the conscience of mankind, and the advent of a world in which human beings shall enjoy freedom of speech and belief and freedom from fear and want has been proclaimed as the highest aspiration of the common people,

WHEREAS it is essential, if man is not to be compelled to have recourse, as a last resort, to rebellion against tyranny and oppression, that human rights should be protected by the rule of law,

WHEREAS it is essential to promote the development of friendly relations between nations,

WHEREAS the peoples of the United Nations have in the Charter reaffirmed their faith in fundamental human rights, in the dignity and worth of the human person and in the equal rights of men and women and have determined to promote social progress and better standards of life in larger freedom,

WHEREAS Member States have pledged themselves to achieve, in co-operation with the United Nations, the promotion of universal respect for and observance of human rights and fundamental freedoms,

WHEREAS a common understanding of these rights and freedoms is of the greatest importance for the full realization of this pledge,

Now, therefore,

The General Assembly proclaims

This Universal Declaration of Human Rights as a common standard of achievement for all peoples and all nations, to the end that every individual and every organ of society, keeping this Declaration constantly in mind, shall strive by teaching and education to promote respect for these rights and freedoms and by progressive measures, national and international, to secure their universal and effective recognition and observance, both among the peoples of Member States themselves and among the peoples of territories under their jurisdiction.

Article I

All human beings are born free and equal in dignity and rights. They are endowed with reason and conscience and should act towards one another in a spirit of brotherhood.

Article 2

Everyone is entitled to all the rights and freedoms set forth in this Declaration, without distinction of any kind, such as race, color, sex, language, religion, political or other opinion, national or social origin, property, birth or other status.

Furthermore, no distinction shall be made on the basis of the political, jurisdictional or international status of the country or territory to which a person belongs, whether it is independent, trust, non-self-governing or under any other limitation of sovereignty.

Article 3

Everyone has the right to life, liberty and security of person.

Article 4

No one shall be held in slavery or servitude; slavery and the slave trade shall be prohibited in all their forms.

Article 5

No one shall be subjected to torture or to cruel, inhuman or degrading treatment or punishment.

Article 6

Everyone has the right to recognition everywhere as a person before the law.

Article 7

All are equal before the law and are entitled without any discrimination to equal protection of the law. All are entitled to equal protection against any discrimination in violation of this Declaration and against any incitement to such discrimination.

Article 8

Everyone has the right to an effective remedy by the competent national tribunals for acts violating the fundamental rights granted him by the constitution or by law.

Article 9

No one shall be subjected to arbitrary arrest, detention or exile.

Article 10

Everyone is entitled in full equality to a fair and public hearing by an independent and impartial tribunal, in the determination of his rights and obligations and of any criminal charge against him.

Article 11

(1) Everyone charged with a penal offence has the right to be presumed innocent until proved guilty according to law in a public trial at which he has had all the guarantees necessary for his defense.

(2) No one shall be held guilty of any penal offense on account of any act or omission which did not constitute a penal offense, under national or international law, at the time when it was committed. Nor shall a heavier penalty be imposed than the one that was applicable at the time the penal offense was committed.

Article 12

No one shall be subjected to arbitrary interference with his privacy, family, home or correspondence, or to attacks upon his honor and reputation. Everyone has the right to the protection of the law against such interference or attacks.

Article 13

(1) Everyone has the right to freedom of movement and residence within the borders of each State.

(2) Everyone has the right to leave any country, including his own, and to return to his country.

Article 14

(1) Everyone has the right to seek and to enjoy in other countries asylum from persecution.

(2) This right may not be invoked in the case of prosecutions genuinely arising from non-political crimes or from acts contrary to the purposes and principles of the United Nations.

Article 15

(1) Everyone has the right to a nationality.

(2) No one shall be arbitrarily deprived of his nationality nor denied the right to change his nationality.

Article 16

(1) Men and women of full age, without any limitation due to race, nationality or religion, have the right to marry and to found a family. They are entitled to equal rights as a marriage, during marriage and at its dissolution.

(2) Marriage shall be entered into only with the free and full consent of the intending spouses.

(3) The family is the natural and fundamental group unit of society and is entitled to protection by society and the State.

Article 17

(1) Everyone has the right to own property alone as well as in association with others.

(2) No one shall be arbitrarily deprived of his property.

Article 18

Everyone has the right to freedom of thought, conscience and religion; this right includes freedom to change his religion or belief, and freedom, either alone or in community with others and in public or private, to manifest his religion or belief in teaching, practice, worship and observance.

Article 19

Everyone has the right to freedom of opinion and expression; this right includes freedom to hold opinions without interference and to seek, receive and impart information and ideas through any media and regardless of frontiers.

Article 20

(1) Everyone has the right to freedom of peaceful assembly and association.

(2) No one may be compelled to belong to an association.

Article 21

(1) Everyone has the right to take part in the government of his country, directly or through freely chosen representatives.

(2) Everyone has the right of equal access to public service in his country.

(3) The will of the people shall be the basis of the authority of the government; this will shall be expressed in periodic and genuine elections which shall be by universal and equal suffrage and shall be held by secret vote or by equivalent free voting procedures.

Article 22

Everyone, as a member of society, has the right to social security and is entitled to realization, through national effort and international co-operation and in accordance with the organization and resources of each State, of the economic, social and cultural rights indispensable for his dignity and the free development of his personality.

Article 23

(1) Everyone has the right to work, to free choice of employment, to just and favorable conditions of work and to protection against unemployment.

(2) Everyone, without any discrimination, has the right to equal pay for equal work.

(3) Everyone who works has the right to just and favorable remuneration ensuring for himself and his family an existence worthy of human dignity, and supplemented, if necessary, by other means of social protection.

(4) Everyone has the right to form and to join trade unions for the protection of his interests.

Article 24

Everyone has the right to rest and leisure, including reasonable limitation of working hours and periodic holidays with pay.

Article 25

(1) Everyone has the right to a standard of living adequate for the health and well-being of himself and of his family, including food, clothing, housing, and medical care and necessary social services, and the right to security in the event of unemployment, sickness, disability, widowhood, old age, or other lack of livelihood in circumstances beyond his control.

(2) Motherhood and childhood are entitled to special care and assistance. All children, whether born in or out of wedlock, shall enjoy the same social protection.

Article 26

(1) Everyone has the right to education. Education shall be free, at least in the elementary and fundamental stages. Elementary education shall be compulsory. Technical and professional education shall be made generally available and higher education shall be equally accessible to all on the basis of merit.

(2) Education shall be directed to the full development of the human personality and to the strengthening of respect for human rights and fundamental freedoms. It shall promote understanding, tolerance and friendship among all nations, racial or religious groups, and shall further the activities of the United Nations for the maintenance of peace.

(3) Parents have a prior right to choose the kind of education that shall be given to their children.

Article 27

(1) Everyone has the right freely to participate in the cultural life of the community, to enjoy the arts and to share in scientific advancement and its benefits.

(2) Everyone has the right to the protection of the moral and material interests resulting from any scientific, literary or artistic production of which he is the author.

Article 28

Everyone is entitled to a social and international order in which the rights and freedoms set forth in this Declaration can be fully realized.

Article 29

(1) Everyone has duties to the community in which alone the free and full development of his personality is possible.

(2) In the exercise of his rights and freedoms, everyone shall be subject only to such limitations as are determined by law solely for the purpose of securing due recognition and respect for the rights and freedoms and others and of meeting the just requirements of morality, public order and the general welfare in a democratic society.

(3) These rights and freedoms may in no case be exercised contrary to the purposes and principles of the United Nations.

Article 30

Nothing in this Declaration may be interpreted as implying for any State, group or person any right to engage in any activity or to perform any act aimed at the destruction of any of the rights and freedoms set forth herein.

RECOMMENDED READING

Norman Finkelstein, *Image and Reality of the Israel-Palestine Conflict*, new, revised edition (New York: Verso, 2003).

10
The Conflict and
Sustainable Development

The Zionist program has always been built around the concept of 'reclaiming' the ancestral Jewish homeland by building extra-state institutions (World Zionist Organization, Jewish Agency, etc.), establishing Jewish land ownership through various mechanisms (largely by ethnic cleansing of non-Jews), and expanding settlements, borders, and control over land and natural resources. The settlements and borders have continuously expanded in territory of hostile natives. The initial large-scale replacement of the population met with obstacles but still succeeded in transforming the country from a predominantly Arab and Muslim one (with some Christian and Jewish Arabs and others) to a predominantly Ashkenazi-led state with Zionist laws. Yet, Palestine/Israel now has some nine million people and nearly half are Palestinian natives. Israeli leaders are frantically seeking to maintain the demographic 'edge'. A three-pronged program is now in vogue in an attempt to accomplish this seemingly impossible task: a) preventing refugees from returning; b) incentives and other tools to lure as many Jewish (or even non-Jewish but not native) immigrants who identify with Zionism; and c) making life so difficult for the remaining Palestinians that they will leave (or even their outright removal). It was thus inevitable that there would be severe environmental effects on this fragile sliver of land, cut off from its hinterland in the Middle East. Any proposed solution must take these issues into consideration.

THE PALESTINIAN AND ISRAELI ECONOMIES
AND SOCIETIES: SEPARATE AND UNEQUAL

The initial Zionist settlements in Palestine between 1880 and 1917 had only marginal negative effect on some of the fellahin (see Chapter 4). There were no major structural changes in the economy under Ottoman rule and no real modernization. The devastation of the First World War was uniform. However, between 1917 and 1948, major socioeconomic structural changes came about. According to

Dr Sara Roy, 'the evolution of two distinct socioeconomic orbits was neither entirely accidental nor entirely planned, but the result of policies that combined to limit the interaction between Jews and Arabs, and in effect promoted the development of one group at considerablke cost to the other'.[1]

When Israel was established in 1948 only a quarter of the Palestinians remained within the self-defined 'Jewish state'. Those who remained continued to experience separate and unequal treatment (see Chapter 7). The majority made refugees between 1947 and 1949 settled in close proximity to the new borders. Many settled in the West Bank and Gaza Strip within the borders of historic Palestine, an area that was conquered by Israel in 1967. The success in 1947–49 of driving out three-quarters of the local inhabitants empowered Israeli leaders to bring massive waves of Jewish immigrants from all over the world to this tiny piece of land. The process of removing natives and colonizing with immigrants has occurred in other countries, but never in such a concentrated manner and on such a small piece of land with limited resources. In 1967, the second phase of Israeli 'reclamation' commenced as Israel invaded and acquired the West Bank (including East Jerusalem), Gaza, Sinai, and the Golan. This only helped to deepen the environmental and social catastrophe.

After the removal of most of the native Palestinians in 1947–49, early Zionist propaganda promulgated the myth that the area was mostly desert and ignored by the population. A myth was also disseminated that 'Arabs' moved into Palestine because of the economic opportunities created by Zionist immigration. In this regard a comparison with Lebanon is revealing. Lebanon has an area of 10,400 square kilometers and a population of nearly four million, excluding the 350,000 Palestinian refugees living there. In addition, there are more than 3–4 million Lebanese migrants in the Americas (most left Lebanon between 1895 and 1920). The Palestinians number about nine million (including all Christian and Muslim refugees, but excluding Zionist settlers and their progeny in the past 80 years). The area they come from is about 2.5 times the size of Lebanon. The numbers suggest that Lebanon historically had a greater density of population than Palestine. Since no Zionist economic enterprises were developed in Lebanon, one questions the mythology of a mass immigration of 'Arabs' because of Zionist development. We must also look carefully at the impact of the Zionist program on the environment and on the possibility of sustainable development. This topic is important because natural resources and the environment are key to a future of prosperity and peace for all.

When Israel was established in 1948, over 800,000 Palestinians were made homeless. Israel acquired over 100,000 abandoned Palestinian homes, nearly two million acres of their land, thousands of businesses, and all public infrastructure in Palestine. This, together with German reparations, US government and private donations were to become the means to build a westernized state with significant economic and military power. The disparity between the ruling Zionist class and the Palestinians intensified, with income disparity jumping significantly, especially in the 1960s. Israel also wanted to ensure a demographic majority of Jews and in slow stages fulfill the Zionist dream of building a vibrant Jewish nation. Thus, all sorts of incentives, tools, and methods were used to bring the maximum number of Jews to the new state while thinning out any remaining non-Jews. The few remaining Palestinians lost much of their land through additional confiscation (150,000 Palestinians remaining while 800,000 made refugees). Israel confiscated nearly 40 percent of the land of the remaining Palestinians (in addition to the two million acres it had taken from their fleeing relatives). The expropriated land was used by the new Jewish collectives (the kibbutzim and moshavim). However, not all confiscated lands could be used and so much of it, including lands of many of the 500 depopulated Palestinian villages, was turned into parks and woodland. These were designated 'protected public areas' to keep the former owners from coming back and to bring in cash from the forestation programs. They were a good source of additional state income as the Jewish National Fund developed programs to 'plant trees in Israel' and promote the idea of 'turning the desert green'. Non-native trees were planted on fertile Palestinian agricultural lands. The proportion of Palestinian workers working in agriculture fell from 70 percent of all Palestinians in 1948 to below 10 percent of the remaining Palestinians in the 1980s. Further, no industrial development was permitted in the remaining Palestinian villages. Many villages were not even recognized so they receive no government services such as sewerage and water. Palestinians were kept under military rule until 1966 and then a few menial jobs were made available to them in the booming Jewish cities and settlements.

New Jewish immigrants were allocated the lands and property of the displaced Palestinians. However, the decision-makers were Ashkenazi Jews, who had concepts of European cultural and developmental ethos that were very different from those of the Orientals (including Arab Jews). An economic class structure developed with Ashkenazim at the top followed by Jews from Arab countries, and non-Jewish Arabs at the bottom.[2]

This hierarchical power structure added an even lower tier when Israel occupied the West Bank and Gaza. The newly conquered Palestinians occupied the lowest rung on this economic ladder. When Israel's economy improved, there was a little 'trickledown' with the opening up of low-paid jobs (in construction, restaurants, etc.) for the lower rungs of society. When Israel's economy slumped, Palestinians both within and outside the Green Line were first to suffer mass unemployment. Thus, while overall unemployment in Israel in 2002 was some 11 percent, among Palestinians within the Green Line it stood at 25–30 percent and in the occupied territories it was 60–70 percent. The West Bank and Gaza further made a captive market for Israeli goods and services as well as providing a source of cheap labor.

Palestinians who worked in the Gulf states did remit money to their relatives in the occupied territories and this income was used to buy Israeli products made in Ashkenazi-owned factories employing the lower economic classes. Some of these factories have been built inside the occupied areas and employ Palestinians from these areas at below the minimum wage and offer no health or social security benefits.

CHANGES SINCE 1991

After the 1991 Gulf War, economic and political changes on a global scale were evident and Israeli and Palestinian policy and economy had to adapt to them. The Arab world was divided, the PLO was weakened, and Palestinians lost their jobs in the oil-rich Arab countries. Israel's strategy in the early 1990s capitalized on these trends and enshrined once and for all its hegemony in the area between the Mediterranean and the River Jordan. Israeli policy required containment of the Palestinian people's aspirations for independence, globalizing Israel's economy, and ensuring acceptance on the part of the world community of Israel. This is why Israel revived the Allon plan to formulate it in the Oslo Accords signed with a weakened and compromised Palestinian leadership in Tunisia. Israel would be able to continue building and expanding settlements, open its markets, have free access to Arab countries, normalize its relations with countries like India and Pakistan, and yet make sure that Palestinians were isolated in ever-shrinking areas of dense population without any real say in the affairs of the country. For this, the Palestinians would be able to fly their flag in a statelet and run their own vassal state (which would resemble a large prison). Many Israelis are now looking back to these plans and seeing that they were clearly unworkable. Unforeseen changes were set in motion. Isolating the Palestinians dried up the supply of cheap labor. It had to be replaced with foreign workers, both legal and illegal. This added to the societal and environmental stresses in Israeli society. Settlements and settlers in the occupied territories doubled between 1993 and 2000 and Jewish industrial production in these areas also doubled. While some Palestinian leaders signed up to this unworkable scheme in Oslo, it was difficult for Israeli leaders to get these same Palestinian leaders to sign the final bill of surrender (see Chapter 11).

But seduced by the possibility of a resolution of the conflict, the high-tech industry boomed to the benefit of a segment of Israeli society. Israel's isolation from other countries began to dissipate, opening up markets and collaborations in joint projects. Palestinians in the occupied areas by contrast saw the disappearance of even the menial jobs they had had. Palestinians in Israel lost their jobs to Russian immigrants. Control over Palestinians' movement and strict controls on imports and exports, supposedly permitted under the Oslo Accords, ensured the paralysis of any endogenous Palestinian economic development. Thus, Palestinians became more and more dependent on charity from Europe and from the Arab states. Indignities and daily humiliations added to this ticking time bomb and eventually contributed to the Palestinian uprising of late September 2000. The gap between Palestinians in the occupied territories and the Israeli occupiers and settlers continued to grow. Per capita GNP in the West Bank and Gaza even before the current large-scale destruction and restrictions stood at about US$1,500 (US$1,000 in Gaza) per year. This compared to US$19,000 for Israeli Jews and US$7,000 for Israeli Muslims.[3] Among those with Israeli citizenship, disparity and economic inequality continue to grow. Between 1987 and 2002, the number of Israeli citizens living in poverty increased by 250 percent and in 2002, the richest 1 percent controlled more assets than 90 percent of the population.[4]

The situation today is unchanged. There is still an economic hierarchy, with wealthy Ashkenazi Jews controlling most of the nation's assets. At the bottom are the Palestinians in the occupied territories. Between them lie the majority of Israeli Jews, especially the Jews originating from Arab countries, and 'Israeli Arabs'. This situation is certainly not conducive to social stability and is the main reason why violence continues. In the case of Israel/Palestine, the issue of land disparity exacerbates the inequality in the economic class structure.

It took 20 years from 1947 to 1967 to convert a largely Arab Christian and Muslim ownership of the 78 percent of Palestine that came under Israeli rule to a largely Jewish-Israeli owned and operated country. After 1967, the Israeli governments under Labor started to repeat the process in the newly acquired Palestinian territories of the West Bank (including East Jerusalem) and Gaza Strip. In the first decade after 1967, and under successive Labor governments, 57,000 settlers were transferred to the occupied areas funded by lucrative governmental subsidies and incentives. In July 1977, President Jimmy Carter tried to convince the newly elected Likud leader, Menachem Begin, to freeze settlement activity as part of the peace agreements with Egypt. Instead, Begin assigned Ariel Sharon to the task of drafting a program for accelerated settlement activity. According to a report on settlements by the Foundation for Middle East Peace:

Settlements under Likud were designed to bring about a 'demographic transformation' of the territories and a Jewish majority there. The co-chairman of the World Zionist Organization's Settlement Department, Mattityahu Drobless, noted that the Likud plan 'will enable us to bring about the dispersion of the [Jewish] population from the densely populated urban strip of the coastal plain eastward to the presently empty [of Jews] areas of Judea and Samaria.[5]

Between 1977 and 1990, the settler population in the West Bank and Gaza stood at over 200,000 (120,000 Israelis in illegally annexed areas of East Jerusalem). The Declaration of Principles and Oslo Agreements did not prohibit settlement expansion or Israeli colonization efforts in the occupied areas. Between 1993 and 2000, the population of settlers in the occupied areas doubled to over 400,000, despite the fact that international law is unambiguous about the illegality of these settlements. Israel occupied the areas in 1967 in a war and these areas were not and cannot be considered as under its sovereignty. Article 49 of the Fourth Geneva Convention (to which Israel is a signatory) states that 'The Occupying Power shall not deport or transfer parts of its own civilian population into the territory it occupies'.[6]

UN Security Council Resolution 465 of 1980 declares:

> all measures taken by Israel to change the physical character, demographic composition, institutional structure or status of the Palestinian and other Arab territories occupied since 1967, including Jerusalem, or any part thereof, have no legal validity and that Israel's policy and practices of settling parts of its population and new immigrants in those territories constitute a flagrant violation of the Fourth Geneva Convention relative to the Protection of Civilian Persons in Time of War and also constitute a serious obstruction to achieving a comprehensive, just and lasting peace in the Middle East.[7]

The number of settlements in the occupied areas in 2001 was as follows: East Jerusalem 11, West Bank 130, Gaza Strip 16, Golan Heights 33.[8] Sharon's government added a further 35 settlements between 2001 and 2002 according to a report by Peace Now. By the year 2000, 150.5 square km in the West Bank had been appropriated for Jewish settlements.[9] Israel has also built an extensive network of so-called 'bypass' roads in the occupied areas. These were 340 km long in 2000 and have increased significantly since then. They bypass native Palestinian towns and are used to serve the Jewish settlements. Large tracts of lands were confiscated to build the roads, which include a 75-meter strip on either side of the roads as a 'safety buffer'. Trees, hills, and any structure within the 75-meter strips are bulldozed and the areas declared closed military zones to Palestinians. The total area acquired in the West Bank for these roads was 51.2 square km in 2000. Added to the 150.5 square km of built-up areas for the settlements/colonies, we find that over 200 square km of land were 'developed' for settlers/colonists. This land was used by Palestinians for agriculture or was development land to allow for the expansion of villages and towns. Accommodating 200,000 settlers in the built-up areas of the settlements has resulted in a population density of about 1,000 settlers/colonists per square km of developed land. Palestinians in the West Bank comprise 2.5 million people living in a built-up area of 367.7 square km; a density of 6,800 Palestinians per square km. The disparity between settlers and natives in terms of land control, the economy, and access is compounded by disparity in the use of other natural resources, especially water.

WATER

Water in the land of Canaan has always been in limited supply, even before large-scale immigration and settlement activity that constituted the Zionist enterprise. The story of water and its allocation in the land of Canaan does not reflect any rationale based on population needs; nor does it reflect international law governing shared resources. Rather, it reflects an imbalance of power heavily tilted towards Israel.[10] A case in point is the resources of the River Jordan basin. The River Jordan collects its waters from Israel, Palestine, Jordan, Syria, and Lebanon. International law requires equitable and fair use of this resource. Yet, Israel diverts and uses most of the water resources (e.g. to irrigate the Negev region). The same has occurred with the large underground aquifers in the West Bank. The UN Commission on Human Rights reported in 2000 that:

- Occupation practices that affect the natural environment of the occupied territories include degradation of the infrastructure, land confiscation, water depletion, uprooting of trees, dumping of toxic waste and other pollution. This inherent right of the Palestinian people is also the subject of Israel's State obligations under, among others, the International Covenant on Economic, Social and Cultural Rights, which it ratified in 1991.
- Palestinian entitlements for water include the underground water of the West Bank and Gaza aquifers, in addition to their rightful shares in the waters of the Jordan River as riparians. The annual renewable freshwater yield in the occupied territories ranges from 600 million cubic metres to 650 million cubic metres. The West Bank's hydrological system includes three major aquifers: the western, north-eastern and eastern basins.
- The Palestinian use of the Jordan River before 1967 was through 140 pumping units. Israel either confiscated or destroyed all of those pumping units. In addition, Israel closed the large, irrigated areas of the Jordan Valley used by Palestin-

ians, calling them military zones that later were transferred to Israeli settlers.

- At present Israel extracts more than 85 per cent of the Palestinian water from the West Bank aquifers, which accounts for about 25 per cent of Israel's water use. As a result of Israeli restrictions, Palestinians currently use 246 million cubic metres of their water resources to supply nearly 3 million people in both the West Bank and Gaza Strip with their domestic, industrial and agricultural needs. This compares to Israel's use of 1,959 million cubic metres for its population of approximately 6 million. That reduces water consumption by Palestinians to 82 m^3 per capita, as compared with 340 m^3 for Israeli citizens and settlers.
- Israel provides settlers with a continuous and plentiful water supply, largely from Palestinian water resources. The supply to Palestinians is intermittent, especially during summer months, as was the case in 1999.[11]

The River Jordan once had an average flow of 1,250 million m^3 per year at the Allenby Bridge,[12] but now only has less than 200 m^3.[13] This reduced flow is essentially due to the diversion of headwaters for Israeli use. The Palestinian use of the River Jordan before 1967 was through 140 pumping units. Immediately after the occupation these pumping units were destroyed or confiscated by the Israeli authorities. Palestinians are currently utilizing less than 0.5 percent of the River Jordan's waters and Israel, which uses most of this water, would be eligible by its pre-1967 borders to only 3 percent of the Jordan basin area. After a thorough review of the hydrological data, Elmusa concluded:

Since 1967, Israel has had a firm grip over virtually all the ground water resources of geographic Palestine and the Jordan River's head waters ... Israel takes 80–90% of the freshwater resources of geographic Palestine. Included in this figure are the shares of Israel and the West Bank under the Johnston Plan [a US plan for distribution of water based on population]. The disparity in extraction between the two sides has translated into a conspicuous water gap in all sectors. The Palestinian per capita municipal use, irrigation use, and aggregate use are less than 30 percent of Israelis'. In all, the water supply in the West Bank and Gaza is substandard and intermittent. The pipe distribution network is dilapidated and its complements, the sewerage system and water treatment plants, are critically lacking ... The gap is even more conspicuous between the Palestinians and the Israeli settlers who consume five to six times as much per capita as do the Palestinians and are profligate irrigation water users.[14]

While Palestinian land was being confiscated and their water allocation slowly diminished, the area of Israeli-controlled irrigated land grew by 340,000 dunums between 1970 and 1990.[15] In addition to this large-scale diversion of water resources, Israel declared most of the Jordan valley and large tracts of the best agricultural lands in the West Bank as closed military zones, resulting in the shutdown of Palestinian agriculture in the area. These vast tracks of Palestinian agricultural land were then turned over to Jewish settlements.

Final status negotiations became bogged down not just over refugee status and Jerusalem, but also due to Israel's insistence on maintaining leverage and control over most of the water resources. Even the agreements signed in Oslo and the creation of the Palestine Water Authority[16] were, like other Oslo agreements, devoid of any equality or even meaning in terms of enforcement and control. The basic elements of a fair distribution of water based on population are provided by A. Tamimi using data from international treaties. However, Israel controlled water allocation and use in the Palestinian occupied areas very inequitably.[17] The problem is exacerbated because 'the West Bank, Gaza, and Israel have a high degree of hydrological interdependence in the sense that most of the fresh, renewable resources in geographic Palestine are common to both sides' and thus it is difficult to ensure separate and equal resources.[18]

ENVIRONMENTAL DEGRADATION

Israeli colonies in the occupied areas were intended for security and control. Thus, most land confiscation and colonial settlement activity was concentrated on high ground (hills and mountains). For this reason, a runoff of waste water, pollution from industrial colonists in declared 'industrial zones', and soil erosion on the hills have directly impacted Palestinian communities located in the lower areas adjacent to the colonies.[19] The UN Commission on Human Rights documented this in 2000. It stated:

- Israeli settlements in the West Bank and Jerusalem are typically placed on high ground. Wastewater from many settlements is collected and discharged to the nearby valleys without treatment. The Special Rapporteur observed that Kfar Darom Israeli settlement in the Gaza Strip releases its sewage and chemical waste left from the industrial plants to the Palestinian Al-Saqa Valley in the central part of the Gaza Strip.
- Israelis dump solid waste without restriction on Palestinian land, fields, and side roads. The solid waste generated in West Jerusalem, for example, is transferred to an unsanitary dumping site east of Abu Dis. That site in the West Bank overlays the infiltration area of the eastern sector of the water aquifer. Also, the settlements of Ariel, Innab, Homesh Alon Morieh, Qarna Shamron, Kadumim and others dispose of their solid waste in the West Bank, as do military camps and settlements inside the 'green line' (1948 border of Israel).
- The Government of Israel has constructed at least seven industrial zones in the West Bank and two in Gaza. The West Bank zones occupy a total area of approximately 302 hectares. They are located mainly on hilltops, from which they dump industrial wastewater onto adjacent Palestinian lands. Information about industries in the Israeli industrial zones is not accessible to the Palestinians. Palestinian sources estimate that at least 200 Israeli factories operate in the West Bank. Some of the products are identifiable, but detailed information on quantities produced, labour, and waste generated is not available. Aluminium, leather-tanning, textile-dyeing, batteries, fibreglass, plastic, and chemicals are among the known industries within these settlements.
- The Special Rapporteur visited the Barqan industrial zone, in the West Bank, which is a clear example of environmental pollution. Aluminium, fibreglass, plastics, electroplating and military industries are known to operate inside Barqan. The industrial wastewater that flows untreated to the nearby valley damages agricultural land belonging to the neighbouring Palestinian villages of Sarta, Kafr al-Dik, and Burqin, polluting the groundwater with heavy metals.[20]

Israeli colonies were planned for security and ideological reasons and thus built on hilltops across the Palestinian landscape. These colonies fit into a pattern of control of natural resources and the native Palestinian population. Thus, there was no forethought on environmental sustainability or clear ideas about how to ensure population harmony with the resources and the environment. We find that there are settlements in every Palestinian district and facilities such as sewage treatment plants are not made available to Palestinians or settlers. Untreated sewage is discharged and, in most cases, this discharge goes directly to the areas inhabited or farmed by Palestinians.

The occupation of the West Bank and Gaza in 1967 also opened up a window of opportunity for Israeli industries. Many of the worst polluting companies, encouraged by tax incentives, moved to the West Bank and Gaza where Israeli government regulations are more lax. There the companies faced the opposition of native Palestinians only, who had no realistic way to stop them. For example, Geshuri Industries, a manufacturer of pesticides and fertilizers, which faced significant court setbacks in its original plant in Kfar Saba, moved to an area adjacent to Tulkarm in the West Bank in 1987. Significant pollution from this and other companies has damaged citrus trees and vineyards there.

PROSPERITY WITH EQUALITY AND SUSTAINABILITY

Environmental degradation in Palestine began in the nineteenth century with industrialization and large-scale deforestation. Under the Ottoman rule, for example, large tracts of forests in the eastern Mediterranean region were felled for fuel and to make tracks for the railroads (e.g. the Damascus–Hijaz track). During the British Mandate (1917–48), some reforestation was undertaken. In the areas of Palestine that came under Israeli and Jordanian rule (1948–67) reforestation programs were common. When the West Bank and Gaza came under Israeli rule in 1967, all the reforestation programs were halted and the trends reversed, and Israel started to shift its population to settle in the occupied areas. Rules were introduced that prevented Palestinians not only from undertaking much of their usual agriculture but also from managing forested lands. In fact, many forested hills were immediately converted to residential settlement/colonial projects, which generated far more pollution than similar settlements inside Israel proper (where there was more planning regulation). Alon Tal, Founder of the Israel Union for Environmental Defense, acknowledged that 'it's a Zionist paradox. We came here to redeem a land and we end up contaminating it.'[21]

The direct impact of Israeli policies on local Palestinians is illustrated best in the agricultural sector. In 1966–67, just before these areas came under Israeli control, 43 percent of Palestinian employment was in the agricultural sector – specifically on 1,945 square km (or 31.5 percent) of the West Bank and Gaza. By 1994, this had shrunk to less than 22 percent of employment and on 15 percent of the land.[22] The other 16.5 percent is now under the control of the Jewish settlements. As the Israeli population in the occupied areas grew at an annual rate of 8–10 percent between 1995 and 2000 compared to a little over 2 percent within the Green Line, the ecological impact intensified.

Since these areas are now fully colonized, a solution to the environmental issues in the context of a two-state scenario has become virtually impossible. The area is too small and people of all religions are mixed if not fully integrated. A unitary economic and environmental policy must be taken into consideration that fits within the basic elements of justice based on human rights. In the context of a two-state solution, Israel would insist on retaining a Jewish majority and thus on the return of Palestinian refugees to areas in the West Bank and Gaza only. These incidentally happen to be the areas that already have a high density of refugees and displaced people and are areas of extreme environmental stress, as discussed above. They also house over 400,000 Jewish settlers. Some refugees will want to be resettled in other countries. However, those wanting to return to their villages inside the Green Line would do far less environmental damage than forcing them into Gaza or the West Bank would achieve. They would also have a far better economic future in a unitary state than they would in the enclaves, which are envisioned for a Palestinian statelet in the West Bank and Gaza. Adding more Palestinian refugees to the already devastated West Bank and Gaza would do severe environmental damage and affect the quality of life for people throughout geographic Palestine/land of Canaan. Reducing the number of foreign migrants from all over the world would also have better economic and environmental consequences for all who are already in the land of Canaan. A unified policy of distributing people to areas of least environmental impact throughout the region would be far more rational than the destructive policies of the past decades.

There are many other advantages to the solution advocated in this book and by many Israelis and Palestinians. This solution envisions integration and the removal of borders and barriers in the context of sustained regional prosperity and stability. The reasons for this are numerous:

1. This solution provides all people with a stake in ensuring environmental sustainability for their shared space.
2. Building a unified economy reduces redundancy of needed infrastructure.
3. The abandonment of the pressure to bring in immigrants from around the world to keep the demographic 'fight' for maintenance of the elusive 'Jewish majority'.
4. The increased prosperity of existing Palestinians in the area will ultimately result in reduced population growth. It is well documented that poverty is positively correlated with high birth rates (Gaza refugee camps, for example, have the highest birth rates).
5. Peace with justice will bring in outside resources (there is already talk of a 'Marshal-type' plan). These resources will reduce the pressure on locals to engage in environmentally harmful practices and industries, such as the military industry and apartheid walls.

RECOMMENDED READING

Sharif S. Elmusa, *Water Conflict: Economics, Politics, Law and Palestinian-Israeli Water Resources* (Washington, DC: Institute for Palestine Studies, 1998).

Stephen C. Lonergan and David B. Brooks, *Watershed: The Role of Fresh Water in the Israeli-Palestinian Conflict* (Oslo: Unipub, 1995).

Sara Roy and Karen Pfeifer (eds.), *The Economics of Middle East Peace: A Reassessment* (New York: JAI Press, 1999).

11
The Political Context

The tragedy in Palestine is not just a local one; it is a tragedy for the world, because it is an injustice that is a menace to the world's peace.

Arnold J. Toynbee 1968,
quoted in the UN Report on Palestine 1990

A passionate attachment of one nation for another produces a variety of evils. Sympathy for the favorite nation, facilitating the illusion of an imaginary common interest in cases where no real common interest exists, and infusing into one the enmities of the other, betrays the former into a participation in the quarrels and wars of the latter without adequate inducement or justification. It leads also to concessions to the favorite nation of privileges denied to others which is apt doubly to injure the nation making the concessions; by unnecessarily parting with what ought to have been retained, and by exciting jealousy, ill-will, and a disposition to retaliate, in the parties from whom equal privileges are withheld.

George Washington's Farewell Address

War is indeed an extension of the politics of hegemony and control. Understanding the political players and their motivations is important, though not sufficient, to ending the conflict. Like the conflict in South Africa and other conflicts, the conflict in the land of Canaan involves local, regional, and international political dimensions. Understanding one of these dimensions without examining the others can lead to false conclusions about how to resolve the conflict.

NATIVES AND ZIONISTS: AN INEVITABLE CLASH?

The image that looms large in the Knesset and on Israeli currency is that of Theodore Herzl. Although Herzl died long before Israel was established, his views still influence a great many people. In his diaries, this Zionist pioneer's plan for native Palestinians was as follows:

> We shall have to spirit the penniless population across the border by procuring employment for it in the transit countries, while denying it any employment in our own country. Both the process of expropriation and the removal of the poor must be carried out discretely and circumspectly.[1]

Herzl's 'spiriting' of the natives did not materialize. Instead, a violent and large-scale removal of the natives transpired first over the short period between October 1947 and early 1949 (as discussed in Chapter 4) and then slowly over the next 55 years with one spurt of 300,000 removed in June 1967. Yet Herzl's quote is instructive since it illustrates how Palestinian natives were viewed in a similar fashion to the way other colonialists viewed the native populations of the countries they invaded. The earliest Zionist pioneers had a vision of redeeming a land considered 'abandoned' by its rightful owners for 2,000 years. The Palestinians were considered at best squatters in Eretz Yisrael (the Land of Israel), who could be removed. It is as if someone had left their house for a while and returned a few years later to find it infested with pests or at best squatters. Cleansing and redeveloping the land were the main themes, with the Palestinians viewed either as obstacles or even as non-existent. General Rafael Eitan, Chief of Staff of the IDF, stated: 'When we have settled the land, all the Arabs will be able to do will be to scurry around like drugged roaches in a bottle.'[2] A colonial movement must view natives as 'synonymous with everything degraded, fearsome, irrational, and brutal ... [and] ... stood outside, beyond Zionism'.[3]

In the early 1900s, Palestinians were mostly farmers and peasants, with a few nomadic tribes and city dwellers. Under Ottoman rule, they were allowed to elect their parliamentary representatives. The Palestinian representatives had no real political power on the ground, which was exercised by Turkish military officers. These officers encouraged native Palestinians to develop feudal and patriarchal dependency while they simultaneously attempted to subvert nationalistic feelings. This was the case not only in Palestine but also in most of the so-called 'Third World' under Ottoman or other colonial rule. Unlike other nations facing colonial rule, Palestinians had the added and incredible weight of the Zionist program which was working towards creating settlements in the area in order to turn it into a Jewish state. Yet, even as early as the first settlements in Palestine by the Zionist movement around the end of the nineteenth century, two classes of Palestinians had developed and shared a distrust and antagonism to this movement. These were the intellectuals (including the representatives elected to the Ottoman parliament) and the fellahin.

Some 418,100 dunums of land were acquired by Jews in Palestine before 1914; 58 percent of this was purchased by Zionists from absentee landlords who were not Palestinians, 36 percent from Palestinian absentee landlords, and the remaining 6 percent from local landlords and Palestinian fellahin.[4]

The fellahin had farmed these lands for many generations and had assumed *de facto* ownership. Thus the fellahin could not accept new Turkish or British laws that deprived them of their land. The dispossessed fellahin greatly resented the new *de facto* Zionist landlords as well as the Arab elites who collaborated with the changing laws. In fact, the famed martyr Shaykh Iz al-Din Al-Qassam had lived among displaced fellahin for years in the slums of Haifa where he acquired an understanding of their plight.[5]

Khalidi cites an editorial of May 1914 published in the popular newspaper *Filastin* (Palestine) in which the editors of this fiercely nationalistic paper defended their position. The editors attacked the central Ottoman government for its attempt to shut down the newspaper because it portrayed Zionism as a threat to the Palestinian nation (*Al-Umma Al-Falastinia*).[6] But these small pro-Palestinian stirrings were no match for the Great Power plays that were to redraw the Middle East map.

BRITAIN AND FRANCE AND THE ZIONIST PROGRAM

The events leading up to the support of Britain and France for Zionist aspirations have received little discussion. In examining historical documents, we find these nations issuing declarations in support of Zionist aspirations. This came in France first with a letter sent from Jules Cambon, Secretary General of the French Foreign Ministry, to Nahum Sokolow, at the time head of the political wing of the World Zionist Organization (based in London) dated June 4, 1917:

You were kind enough to inform me of your project regarding the expansion of the Jewish colonization of Palestine. You expressed to me that, if the circumstances were allowing for that, and if on another hand, the independency of the holy sites was guaranteed, it would then be a work of justice and retribution for the allied forces to help the renaissance of the Jewish nationality on the land from which the Jewish people was exiled so many centuries ago.

The French Government, which entered this present war to defend a people wrongly attacked, and which continues the struggle to assure victory of right over might, cannot but feel sympathy for your cause, the triumph of which is bound up with that of the Allies.

I am happy to give you herewith such assurance.[7]

Some five months later, on November 2, 1917, the British Foreign Secretary Arthur James Balfour conveyed to Lord Rothschild a similar declaration of sympathy for Zionist aspirations:

His Majesty's Government view with favor the establishment in Palestine of a national home for the Jewish people, and will use their best endeavors to facilitate the achievement of this object, it being clearly understood that nothing shall be done which may prejudice the civil and religious rights of existing non-Jewish communities in Palestine, or the rights and political status enjoyed by Jews in any other country.

Palestinians and others in the Arab world were alarmed. The Declaration was issued at a time when Britain had no jurisdiction over the area, and was done without consulting the inhabitants of the land that was to become a 'national home for the Jewish people'. The Declaration also sought to protect the 'rights and political status' of Jews who chose not to migrate to Palestine. However, the native Palestinians were simply referred to as non-Jews and their political rights were not mentioned, only their 'civic and religious rights'. Lord Balfour wrote in a private memorandum to his successor at the Foreign Office, Lord Curzon (who initially opposed Zionism) on August 11, 1919:

For in Palestine we do not propose to go through the form of consulting the wishes of the present inhabitants ... The four great powers are committed to Zionism and Zionism, be it right or wrong, good or bad, is rooted in age-long tradition, in present needs, in future hopes, of far profounder import than the desires and prejudices of the 700,000 Arabs who now inhabit that ancient land.[8]

The Jules and Balfour Declarations demonstrate the support extended to the Zionist supra-national entity which facilitated giving them control over a land that neither of the two governments had jurisdiction over at the time. Some British authors have explained this support as a *quid pro quo* for Weizman's contribution to the British war effort through the development of chemicals for explosives. Some have argued that it was related to Britain's domestic situation with many Zionists in the government and among the electorate. It could also be argued that Britain and France had more reason to benefit from a revival of their early 1840s desire to settle European Jews in Palestine as a way of achieving a structural remodeling of Middle East geopolitics (see Chapter 6). But undermining the Ottoman Empire, which was then allied with Germany, provides only a partial explanation.

The Jewish population in Palestine at the time was minuscule and hardly in a position to resist the Ottoman Empire. By contrast, nationalistic Arabs in the Arabian Peninsula were willing to oppose the Ottoman Empire and eager to liberate their native lands from the Turks. England in fact promised to support their independence as a result of their convergent interests, as attested by the British correspondence with Sharif Hussain and the memoirs of T.E. Lawrence ('Lawrence of Arabia'). There is much disagreement about the factors and their relative importance that led to the decisions made by the governments in question.

The British had also promised independence to the Arabs if they aided them in opposing the Ottoman Empire. This was one of many 'promises', but it was the one that was to override all others, as concrete actions were to reveal in just a short period of time. It is important to note that these governments declared their public support for Zionism, even while simultaneously making private assurances to the Arabs. British and French public support was later joined by the Americans. Much is now written about how the US entered the war and the possible role of influential corporate interests and US Zionists in bringing the US media and government to support the war efforts.

With the acquiescence of the ailing President Wilson and a US administration slowly retreating into isolationism, the British had free rein to implement their plans in Palestine. Palestinians, both Christians and Muslims, rioted against British forces in Jerusalem on February 27, 1920. The British command in Palestine recommended that the Balfour Declaration be revoked. However, the British leadership in London did not share the views of their military. As soon as Britain had secured the League of Nations mandate, it replaced its military governor there with a Zionist Jew, Sir Herbert Samuel, as the first High Commissioner of Palestine (1920–25). It was Samuel who so effectively coached Weizmann during the Balfour negotiations. After Samuel became High Commissioner, Jewish immigration greatly increased, and with it Palestinian resistance. Samuel and the Zionist-leaning colonial offices in Palestine proceeded to set up the political, legal, and economic underpinning to transform the area into a Jewish state. Britain, with the acquiescence of the other Great Powers, acquired the powers needed for its colonial venture. At the World Zionist Organization meeting held in London in July 1920, a new financial arm, the Keren Hayesod, was established. The British-drafted Palestine mandate referred to this colonial economic structure:

> An appropriate Jewish agency shall be recognised as a public body for the purpose of advising and co-operating with the Administration of Palestine in such economic, social and other matters as may affect the establishment of the Jewish national home and the interests of the Jewish population in Palestine, and, subject always to the control of the Administration to assist and take part in the development of the country. The Zionist organization, so long as its organization and constitution are in the opinion of the Mandatory appropriate, shall be recognised as such agency. It shall take steps in consultation with His Britannic Majesty's Government to secure the co-operation of all Jews who are willing to assist in the establishment of the Jewish national home.[9]

The fund was registered on March 23, 1921 as a British limited company. The executive of the Zionist Organization elected the chairman of the board and its members. Funds raised helped finance two large projects to industrialize Palestine in the late 1920s; the Electric Company and the Palestine Potash Company (PPC).[10] Moshe Novemiesky, a leading Zionist, founded the PPC. In 1929, the British Colonial Office gave a concession to the PPC to develop mineral resources in the Dead Sea. The PPC was instrumental in generating large amounts of money, which were funneled to the Zionist program. In 1952, after the state of Israel was established, the company became an Israeli nationalized agency, and renamed the Dead Sea Works.[11]

Arthur Rogers has described the contribution of this British Concession to financing the Zionist movement after 1929 in his book *The Palestine Mystery*,[12] in which he describes a 1925 report by the Colonial Office on the fabulous wealth to be derived from Dead Sea minerals. There is also a report of a Zionist conference in Australia in 1929 in which Zionists were ecstatic about the fact that Britain had given this concession to a committed Zionist by Moshe Novomiesky.

As early as October 25, 1919 Winston Churchill had predicted that Zionism implied the clearing of the indigenous population: 'there are the Jews, whom we are pledged to introduce into Palestine, and who take it for granted the local population will be cleared out to suit their convenience'.[13] In public, Churchill sought to assure the Arabs that Britain was pursuing a humane policy of limited Jewish immigration, that there was space without displacing native Arabs, and no need for Jewish state. But private Cabinet meeting minutes of October 1941 speak differently:

> I may say at once that if Britain and the United States emerged victorious from the war, the creation of a great Jewish state in Palestine inhabited by millions of Jews will be one of the leading features of the peace conference discussions.[14]

This was contrary to the conclusion reached two years earlier by the British commission of inquiry at the end of the Palestinian uprising of 1936–39. This stated:

> The Royal Commission and previous commissions of enquiry have drawn attention to the ambiguity of certain expressions in the Mandate, such as the expression 'a national home for the Jewish people', and they have found in this ambiguity and the resulting uncertainty as to the objectives of policy a fundamental cause of unrest and hostility between Arabs and Jews.
>
> ... That Palestine was not to be converted into a Jewish State might be held to be implied in the passage from the Command Paper of 1922 which reads as follows 'Unauthorized statements have been made to the effect that the purpose in view is to create

a wholly Jewish Palestine. Phrases have been used such as that 'Palestine is to become as Jewish as England is English.' His Majesty's Government regard any such expectation as impracticable and have no such aim in view. Nor have they at any time contemplated ... The disappearance or the subordination of the Arabic population, language or culture in Palestine. They would draw attention to the fact that the terms of the [Balfour] Declaration referred to do not contemplate that Palestine as a whole should be converted into a Jewish National Home, but that such a Home should be founded *in Palestine.*

But this statement has not removed doubts, and His Majesty's Government therefore now declares unequivocally that it is not part of their policy that Palestine should become a Jewish State. They would indeed regard it as contrary to their obligations to the Arabs under the Mandate, as well as to the assurances which have been given to the Arab people in the past, that the Arab population of Palestine should be made the subjects of a Jewish State against their will. (emphasis in original)[15]

It is clear from this that the British had undertaken obligations under vague (I would argue intentionally vague) wordings likely to give them flexibility in their implementation. The events between 1918 and 1938 had caused them to reconsider their position. However, at this point forces were in motion that made change virtually impossible. The Yishuv were already strong and well armed in Palestine, Britain had entered the Second World War, and Hitler's attacks on Jews made it less likely that the British would begin to enforce their curbs on Jewish migration to Palestine as proposed in the White Paper. One of the first acts of the nascent state of Israel, in addition to instituting laws to prevent native Palestinians from returning to their homes and lands, was to repeal the White Paper.

BRITAIN HANDS THE TORCH TO THE US

During the years between 1939 and 1948 the world was transformed. Britain lost its position of pre-eminence and the US became a superpower and adopted the Zionist cause, which had been nearly orphaned by the British as a result of the White Paper. The US was not involved with Palestine or even generally in the Middle East in the early years of Zionism. US engagement in the conflict in Palestine first materialized after its entry in the First World War.

President Wilson articulated his vision on January 8, 1918 in 14 'peace' points. These included, 'adjustment of colonial claims with concern for the wishes and interests of the inhabitants as well as for the titles of rival claimants'.

In the meantime, Britain was facing difficulties. A Palestinian movement against British colonial rule and Zionist schemes gained momentum and erupted in a mass uprising in 1936.[16] By 1939, the British had put down the uprising in a most brutal way, killing most of its leaders and cadres. Hundreds, perhaps as many as 5,000, of the best Palestinian fighters were killed and the political leadership was decimated. This devastating blow had two simultaneous and interesting effects: it weakened Palestinian political and civil institutions and caused the British to rethink their role in the Zionist program. This did not mean that the British would abandon the Zionist program. Instead, they would provide an international base for the program to mitigate problems created by their sole ownership of the program. Zionists also recognized the shift in world political power structures and began to concentrate their work in the US.

During the late 1930s and early 1940s, there were two branches of Zionism, the traditional and revisionist, which roughly correspond to today's division in Israel between the Labor and Likud Parties. Most discussion on the influence on US policy focused on the Zionist labor movement. But, while less recognized, the revisionists actually had a longer-term effect on US policy. The Republican Party was especially susceptible to their influence. Their ranks included Peter Bergson (who established the Bergson Zionist movement) and Benzion Netanyahu (father of the former Israeli prime minister, Binyamin Netanyahu). They sent money and weapons to Palestine to support the underground terrorist movements.[17]

Although President Truman immediately recognized and supported the nascent Jewish state, he was also interested in Israel fulfilling its obligations vis-à-vis the Palestinian refugees. On September 6, 1948, Truman gave his unconditional support to the proposals of the UN mediator, Count Folke Bernadotte, who asked for repatriation of Palestinian refugees. US Secretary of State, George Marshall, reiterated this in an address to the UN. As we have seen, Bernadotte was assassinated by the Irgun. After the assassination, Truman wrote to Ben-Gurion on May 29, expressing the US's dismay with the Israeli violation of international law and warning that his administration might review its relationship with the Jewish state.

When Israel refused to submit to such pressure, Truman backed down.

ISRAELI POLITICAL DISCOURSE

Much has been written about the 1947–49 period. These were the years of *Al-Nakba* (the catastrophe) as 80 percent of the Palestinians were removed from the 78 percent of Palestine that had become the Jewish state. For Zionists, a new state of Israel was created through a 'war of independence'. Myths abound about this period. Contrary to the published myths, even at the height of participation of the Arab forces, Jewish forces held both a quantitative and qualitative advantage, and much of the fighting was on lands not allocated to the Jewish state by the UN General Assembly recommendations.[18] As noted in Chapter 4, the majority of the Palestinians were ethnically cleansed from the nascent Jewish state by Zionist forces well before the Arab countries sent their relatively smaller forces. Even the feeble attempts at resistance, consolidation, and counter-offensive were undermined by Arab leaders more interested in their own hegemony and power than in the welfare of the Palestinians. This was certainly true of King Abdullah of Jordan, who twice undermined efforts by Hajj Amin Al-Husaini to persuade the Arab League to support the establishment of a Palestinian government in exile.[19]

The Palestinians, mostly leaderless since 1939 and now dispersed with their civil society destroyed, took years to regroup. A new Palestinian national leadership emerged in 1959 with the establishment of Fatah (the acronym of 'Harakat Tahrir Falastin, 'HTF, reversed). Other groups emerged around the same time and proliferated in the early 1960s. Many were motivated by the failed misrepresentation of Palestinian aspirations by some Arab countries. Palestinian political leanings covered a spectrum including Baathism (supporting Iraqi and Syrian-style Arab nationalism), classic Arab nationalism (led by the Egyptian president, Jamal Abdul Nasser), secular mixed (e.g. Fatah), communist, and Islamic. In 1964–65, the Palestine Liberation Organization was established as an umbrella group to bring these factions together. The Palestine National Council became essentially a parliament-in-exile. It was a revolutionary movement in every sense of the word. There was never a movement like this in Arab history. The PLO's Charter called for a secular state in Palestine where Jews, Christians, and Muslims would live together in equality.

It was based on the classic revolutionary movements to liberate countries from colonization, occupation, or puppet dictatorships. Israel's stunning war of 1967 and its subsequent defeat of Egypt, Syria, and Jordan propelled the PLO into prominence as an alternative to the failed policies of the Arab regimes. Israel's occupation of the West Bank, Gaza, Sinai, and the Golan Heights started to galvanize not only Palestinians living in exile but also those now under direct Israeli rule.

Initial Israeli government propaganda claimed that the 1967 war was not started by Israel to grab land but was simply a defensive war after Egypt mobilized and other antagonistic factors. The following tell a different story. Israeli General Matityahu Peled stated: 'The thesis that the danger of genocide was hanging over us in June 1967 and that Israel was fighting for its physical existence is only bluff, which was born and developed after the war', adding, 'to pretend that the Egyptian forces massed on our frontiers and were in a position to threaten the existence of Israel constitutes an insult not only to the intelligence of anyone capable of analyzing this sort of situation, but above all an insult to the Zahal [Israeli Army]'.[20] To confirm Israel's intentions, Israeli governments wasted no time in building settlements in the West Bank immediately after acquiring the territory by force in June 1967. This has continued unabated regardless of the status of peace or war in the Middle East.

But the Palestinians also gained political power and international recognition throughout the years of Israeli occupation. In March 1968 the Israeli Army invading Jordan and met fierce resistance from Palestinian guerrillas aided by Jordanian army units in the area of Karameh. The battle at Karameh catapulted the PLO onto the national and international stage, with Arafat riding a wave of popularity. The Palestinians also developed institutions (education, healthcare, and welfare) and a strong government-in-exile represented by the Palestinian National Council. It was the first time that a group had managed to have a positive effect on the lives of Palestinians both in exile and those remaining in the lands under Israeli occupation. But there were also setbacks and blunders. In 1970–71, the PLO was violently ousted from Jordan. The Israeli Air Force was dispatched to threaten Syrian forces not to intervene in King Hussain's war on the PLO. The presence of Palestinians with considerable power in Jordan was threatening Hussain's regime. Similarly, Palestinians were deemed a threat in Lebanon where they had relocated the majority of their forces in 1971. This resulted in fighting in 1975–76 between segments of the Lebanese militias and the PLO and its Lebanese allies. In both cases, the result has been to increase the power of Palestinian nationalism. As Edward Said declared: 'The Palestinians were assaulted for their extraterritorial presence in Jordan and Lebanon – however different the particular circumstances – and confirmed variously in their circumscribed nationalistic aspirations.'[21] It is thus no coincidence that, in 1974, the PLO was recognized by the Arab states as the 'sole, legitimate representative of the Palestinian people'.

AN ERA OF PEACE?

Following the Arab–Israeli war of 1973, a faction in Fatah led by Arafat succumbed to 'moderate' Arab states and agreed to a two-state solution to make rapprochement with the US and its interests in the region. This entailed a significant willingness to compromise. As Alan Hart wrote:

> Arafat and most of his senior colleagues in the leadership knew they needed time to sell it to the rank and file of the liberation movement. If, in 1974, Arafat and his colleagues had openly admitted the true extent of the compromise they were prepared to make, they would have been repudiated and rejected by an easy majority of the Palestinians.[22]

Arafat, perhaps naively, believed he could get the United States to put pressure on Israel to compromise. But essentially every US peace initiative has been rebuffed by Israel since the Rogers plan – even those written by Israel and presented as American plans were later repudiated by incoming Israeli governments.[23]

Egypt and Israel signed a peace accord on September 17, 1978. Returning an illegally occupied Sinai, Israel was able to obtain significant benefit. Israel neutralized the largest Arab country, signed a full peace agreement, and demilitarized the Sinai Peninsula. Israel also gained free movement in the Suez Canal and the Gulf of Aqaba, billions of dollars of US aid, a guaranteed oil supply from the United States despite US oil shortages, and many other benefits. Relevant to the Palestinian 'problem', the agreements included the following brief statements:

1) Israel, Jordan and Egypt supervising elections in Gaza and the West Bank (in exchange of letters, Begin and Carter clarified this means 'Judea and Samaria').

2) These representatives of the local Palestinians (in exchange of letters, Begin and Carter clarified this means 'Palestinian Arabs') will then negotiate final status over a five-year period.

On May 15, 1989, an Israeli 'peace initiative' based on the Camp David Accords between Israel and Egypt was formulated by Prime Minister Shamir (of the Likud Party) and Defense Minister Rabin (of the Labor Party) and 'represents the consensus of Israel policy in the National unity government'. It was initiated following considerable bloodshed in the territories occupied by Israel (during the Palestinian Intifada) in which Palestinian youth were being killed daily. The initiative is based on two stages:

Stage A – A transitional period for an interim agreement.
Stage B – A permanent solution.
The interlock between the stages is a timetable on which the Plan is built: the peace process delineated by the initiative is based on Resolutions 242 and 338 upon which the Camp David accords are founded.[24]

Note that, with the exception of dealing with the PLO, this is what Israel wanted in the 1978 Israel/Egypt accords and what it got in the subsequent 1993 Oslo Accords. In 1993, following secret negotiations between Israel and the PLO leadership in Oslo, agreements were reached to set up five years of interim self-rule for the Palestinians. The plan was predicated on a staged pullback from the West Bank and Gaza and steps to negotiate final settlement issues later. The issues deferred included borders, Israeli settlements, and Palestinian refugees. Immediately after a ceremony on the White House lawn, supervised meticulously by President Bill Clinton, three key things started to happen almost simultaneously with the very slow withdrawal of Israeli forces from Palestinian population centers:

1. Israel embarked on its most ambitious settlement activity, resulting in a doubling of the population of illegal settlers and increasing the areas under control threefold.

2. The nascent Palestinian Authority, with help and prodding by the CIA and the Israeli Mossad, embarked on building a police authority with such things as 'security courts' (insisted on by the Americans), which were not only intended to suppress resistance to the occupation but also to ensure 'tranquility' (obedience) in the local Palestinian people.
3. The US increased its military assistance to Israel with at least two dozen new deals. This included the April 11, 1994 sale of up to 25 F-15I fighter-bombers and spare parts worth US$2.4 billion.[25]

Israel, according to the protocols, continued to be responsible for security, foreign affairs, and all matters concerning Israeli citizens in 'Judea, Samaria, and the Gaza district'. That is precisely what Israel had insisted on in 1978 and was now accepted by Arafat. The 1993 Declaration of Principles thus left the door open for Israel to continue its land confiscation and settlement activity, actually doubling them between 1993 and 2000.

These are the things the Palestinian representatives from the West Bank and Gaza rejected in Madrid in 1991. The representatives presented very unpalatable conditions to Israel, including internationally recognized rights to self-determination, the repatriation of refugees, and the freezing of new Israeli settlement activity. Rabin and Peres concluded that opening a secret channel of communications at Oslo was likely to lead to capitulation. Arafat was discredited internationally yet highly respected locally and, more importantly, Arafat has been ready to deal since 1974. Giving him recognition was something that Israel could use as a carrot to extract concessions on the key issues. That is indeed what happened.

The original Allon plan consisted of the annexation of 35–40 percent of the territories to Israel, and self-rule or Jordanian/Palestinian confederation on the land on which the Palestinians actually live. This plan originated with those who thought that it was impossible to repeat the 1948 'solution' of mass expulsion, for moral as well as world public opinion considerations. The second view, whose principal spokesman was Sharon, assumed that it is possible to find more acceptable and sophisticated ways to achieve a 1948-style 'solution' – it is necessary only to find another country for the Palestinians, such as Jordan, and to make sure that as many Palestinians as possible move there. This was a part of Sharon's global worldview by which Israel can establish 'new orders' in the region (the Lebanon war). In Oslo, the Allon plan route triumphed.[26] The Allon plan was thus a cornerstone of Israeli policy and negotiations in the 1970s with Egypt, in Israel's 'peace' proposal of 1989, and in their approach to Madrid in 1991. The Israelis finally succeeded in getting Arafat to accept it in the 1993 Declaration of Principles (DOP). Edward Said has described the DOP as a 'document of surrender'. Ariel Sharon modified the Allon guidelines to define these key Zionist red lines:

1. Greater Jerusalem, united and undivided, must be the eternal capital of Israel and under full Israeli sovereignty.
2. Israel will retain under its full control sufficiently wide security zones – in both the East and the West. The Jordan Valley, in its broadest sense, as defined by the Allon plan, will be the eastern security zone of Israel. ... The western security zone will include the line of hills commanding the coastal plain and controlling Israel's vital underground water sources. Strategic routes will be retained under Israel's control.
3. Jewish towns, villages and communities in Judea, Samaria, and Gaza, as well as access roads leading to them, including sufficient security margins along them, will remain under full Israeli control.
4. The solution to the problem of Palestinian refugees from 1948–67 will be based on their resettlement and rehabilitation in the places where they live today (Jordan, Syria, Lebanon, etc.). Israel does not accept under any circumstances the Palestinian demand for the right of return. Israel bears no moral or economic responsibility for the refugees' predicament.
5. As a vital existential need, Israel must continue to control the underground fresh water aquifers in western Samaria [the northern part of the West Bank], which provide a major portion of Israel's water. The Palestinians are obligated to prevent contamination of Israel's water resources.
6. Security arrangements: All the territories under control of the Palestinian Authority will be demilitarized. The Palestinians will not have an army; only a police force. Israel will maintain complete control of the whole air space over Judea, Samaria and Gaza.[27]

In addition, 'any government in Israel that will adopt and implement these principles will strengthen Israel's deterrence and could reach a better, more secure peace, one that will ensure Israel's long-term national strategic interests'. These plans were well laid out and understood even by the so-called 'doves' in Israeli politics. As Rabin put it, Oslo was a method to achieve 'traditional [Israeli] objectives'. The Minister of Internal Security, historian, and 'peace advocate' Shlomo Ben-Ami stated that 'in practice, the Oslo Agreements were founded on a neo-colonialist basis, on a life dependence of one on the other forever'.[28] So how did Arafat and company end up in this predicament?

PALESTINIAN POLITICAL DISCOURSE

The reshaping of the Palestinian landscape and of Israel's attitude towards the PLO took place between 1988 and 1993 following a number of events. First, the Palestinian uprising of the 1980s made significant gains in shaping public opinion throughout the world (including in Israel itself) about the limits to which occupied people can be expected to tolerate. Israel's brutal suppression of the uprising generated sympathy for Palestinians suffering under the occupation. Despite massive propaganda efforts, Israel could not continue to sustain the myth of being the underdog fighting for its survival. Instead, it was seen more and more as analogous to South Africa under apartheid. The uprising resulted in the development of a strong local political leadership in the West Bank and Gaza who were not necessarily toeing the Fatah/Arafat line, although they did recognize the PLO (now headquartered in Tunis) as the legitimate Palestinian representative. A second factor was Jordan's relinquishing its claim on the West Bank followed by the PLO's Declaration of Independence in 1988. The Declaration made it clear that the Palestinian leadership was finally ready for statehood alongside the state of Israel (based on UN resolutions) and paved the way for talks between the United States and the PLO in December 1988. Here are relevant sections from the PLO's Declaration of Independence:

Despite the historical injustice inflicted on the Palestinian Arab people resulting in their dispersion and depriving them of their right to self-determination, following upon UN General Assembly Resolution 181 (1947), which partitioned Palestine into two states, one Arab, one Jewish, yet it is this resolution that still provides those conditions of international legitimacy that ensure the right of the Palestinian Arab people to sovereignty. By stages, the occupation of Palestine and parts of other Arab territories by Israeli forces, the willed dispossession and expulsion from their ancestral homes of the majority of Palestine's civilian inhabitants was achieved by organized terror; those Palestinians who remained, as a vestige subjugated in its homeland, were persecuted and forced to endure the destruction of their national life.

Thus were principles of international legitimacy violated. Thus were the Charter of the United Nations and its resolutions disfigured, for they had recognized the Palestinian Arab people's national rights, including the right of Return, the right to independence, the right to sovereignty over territory and homeland ...

Now by virtue of natural, historical and legal rights, and the sacrifices of successive generations who gave of themselves in defense of the freedom and independence of their homeland. In pursuance of Resolutions adopted by Arab Summit Conferences and relying on the authority bestowed by international legitimacy as embodied in the resolutions of the United Nations Organization since 1947; And in exercise by the Palestinian Arab people of its rights to self-determination, political independence, and sovereignty over its territory ...[29]

Accepting the patently unjust UN General Assembly Resolution 181 is a major concession by the PLO.

The third factor leading to further PLO retrenchment from its original goals was the 1990–91 Gulf War. The strategic and political reverberations of this on the Israeli–Palestinian situation should not be underestimated. The consequences included the lowest standing ever for the PLO not only in the West countries but also among its own people.[30] The issue was not simply that Arafat supported Iraq; many other Arab countries did so, including Jordan, as did the average Palestinian and Jordanian. The reasons for the decline in support for Arafat among the Palestinians included the weakening prestige and ability of the PLO to help its own people. The removal of over 350,000 Palestinians from Kuwait was devastating. These are people whose money was used to help other Palestinians through the PLO. Now they themselves needed help and the PLO was in no position to offer it. A depletion of sources of support for Palestinians living in refugee camps and elsewhere (in Jordan, the West Bank, and Gaza) also worsened following the drying up of most sources of funding for the PLO. The movement of these people into already impoverished areas of Jordan, the West Bank, and Gaza led to significant economic hardships.

The support from Gulf states to mainstream Palestinian factions (like Fatah and Arafat) fell significantly due not merely to Arafat's support for Saddam Hussein, but to geopolitical realignments which gave Israel's patron, the United States, more power. The extension of US power and prestige in the Middle East for the first time brought military bases inside countries like Saudi Arabia. The climate during this time was one of weakening links between the PLO in Tunisia and events in Palestine, strengthening Palestinian resistance on the ground, and the disillusionment of many Palestinians and citizens of many Arab countries. In addition, Palestinian anger against the United States increased, not only for its support of Israel but for causing massive civilian deaths and suffering in Iraq. It is evident why Israel thought this was the best time to strike a deal with Arafat and bypass the tougher Palestinian negotiators who were negotiating in meetings at Madrid and Washington (Haidar Abdul-Shafi, Hanan Ashrawi, etc.). Without consulting these negotiators who were living under the occupation, Arafat authorized secret talks in Oslo between his representatives and the Israeli government.

THE OSLO ACCORDS

It is not clear that Arafat foresaw the extent of the damage to both Palestinians and Israelis that was to be inflicted by agreeing to abandon international law and international auspices and enter into capitulation agreements with Israel, with its backer the United States acting as a 'guide'. There are five agreements that Arafat signed which collectively make up the legal framework for what became known as the Oslo peace process: Declaration of Principles (Oslo I, September 1993), Protocols on Economic Relations (Paris Agreement, April 1994), Gaza Strip/Jericho agreement (Cairo Agreement, May 1994), the 'Interim Agreement on the West Bank and Gaza' (Oslo II, 1995), and the Hebron Accords (1997). None of these agreements addressed basic international law, except selectively referring to UN Security Council Resolutions 242 and 338, which the US and Israel had by now interpreted as not requiring the complete withdrawal of Israeli forces from the occupied areas.

Fundamentally, Israel and the US defied international law as the basis for peace negotiations when the Madrid tracts switched to

Oslo. Israel, a belligerent occupier, refused to acknowledge the application of the Fourth Geneva Convention Relative to the Protection of Civilian Persons in Time of War, to the Occupied Palestinian Territories. This despite repeated affirmation by the international community, including the US, beginning with UN Security Council Resolution 237 of June 14, 1967.

The agreements were entered into following the resignation of countless Palestine National Congress members in protest at the unilateral decision by Arafat to enter into capitulation agreements that would not protect human rights or be based on basic principles of international law. Legal experts from the Palestinian side were not consulted and many experts on geography, settlement activity, and international law were excluded from the decision-making process. None of the agreements was to be subjected to a referendum of the occupied Palestinians. Oslo II was not even published in Arabic lest the public saw the capitulation it entailed. The biggest hurdle for acceptance by the Palestinian people was that the Oslo agreements provide Israel with a legal basis to occupy parts of the West Bank. Here is the relevant section:

Article XVII. Section 4
(a) Israel, through its military government, has the authority over areas that are not under the territorial jurisdiction of the Council, powers and responsibilities not transferred to the Council and Israelis.
(b) To this end, the Israeli military government shall retain the necessary legislative, judicial and executive powers and responsibilities, in accordance with international law. This provision shall not derogate from Israel's applicable legislation over Israelis ...

The agreement never explicitly referred to the West Bank and Gaza as occupied territories, and did not mention the Fourth Geneva Convention. Israel is the only country that does not recognize the Convention's applicability to the occupied areas (see Chapter 12). The agreement contains a vague statement about not changing the character of the West Bank and Gaza and keeping their territorial integrity, but this could later be argued to mean not stopping settlement activities, land confiscation, and other blatant violations of international conventions.

The texts of Oslo were thus purposefully vague concerning Palestinian rights while precise on the powers and authorities retained by Israel. As Shahak put it, 'The deeper intention of the [Oslo] Accord is to create an apartheid regime in which the Autonomy Council in the Territories [the Palestinian Authority] will in effect relieve Israel from any duties towards the population.'[31] In the meantime, Rabin and Peres began implementing the plan, first envisaged by Ariel Sharon in 1977, of developing bypass roads to the settlements, and isolating Palestinian towns and villages from one another by a network of settlements, military areas, and bypass roads. This in effect develops 'control from outside' and thus a cantonization or ghettoization of the Palestinian areas. As this plan was put into effect, the 'peace' government of Rabin and Peres increased subsidies to the settlers and implemented programs that enticed settler populations into the occupied territories. Their numbers consequently increased from 200,000 to 400,000 while the area of the settlements controlled tripled. Tanya Reinhardt states:

> The meaning of the plan is that we will solve the problem of two million Palestinians in the territories by imprisoning them in ghettos, starving them, and turning them into beggars. But instead of calling it an occupation, we will present it as a step toward a Palestinian state. We will crush Palestinian throats with our boots while smiling at them nicely.[32]

It also means granting the Palestinians a legislative council, but stating (in Article 18) that 'Legislation, including legislation which amends or abrogates existing laws or military orders, which exceeds the jurisdiction of the Council or which is otherwise inconsistent with the provisions of the DOP, this Agreement, or of any other agreement that may be reached between the two sides during the interim period, shall have no effect and shall be void ab initio.' In other words, no new legislation can challenge the occupation.

Oslo II ominously absolved Israel of any legal liability arising from its occupation. In Article 20, it is stated that

a. Any financial claim made in this regard against Israel will be referred to the [Palestinian] Council

...

e. In the event that an award is made against Israel by any court or tribunal in respect of such a claim, the Council shall immediately reimburse Israel the full amount of the award.

Oslo II even required the Palestinians to 'respect the property and legal rights' of Israeli individuals and corporations in all areas of the West Bank and Gaza (Articles 16 and 22) in contravention of the Fourth Geneva Convention. There was no parallel commitment by the 'Israeli side' to respect the property and legal rights of Palestinians. The agreements demanded specific concessions from the Palestinians on issues ranging from security to economic relations to travel permits, but left it to the will of the Israeli government to do what it wants in the occupied areas.

On April 21, 1996 the Palestine National Council (PNC) held its twenty-first session in Gaza City for the first time since 1964. It decided by a majority vote to 'abrogate the provisions of the PLO Charter that are contrary to the exchanged letters between the PLO and the Government of Israel of 9 and 10 September 1993'. The letter from Arafat to Rabin recognized Israel's right to exist in peace and security. De facto, this ratified Oslo by the Palestinian National Council although the legality of that meeting is challenged.

The Israel/PLO agreements separated the Palestinians into four groups:

1. Residents of Area A and Area B (less than 40 percent of the West Bank/Gaza area). Those people live in the major population centers and Israel wanted Arafat's authority to police and take over civil responsibility.
2. Area C residents: Those in the areas of the West Bank (especially East Jerusalem and anywhere near the hundreds of Israeli settlements) who will be under direct Israeli brutality (including home demolitions, etc.) and the PA was not to have anything to do with those. Israel intended to thin this population outpost also and step up the settlement drive on Palestinian lands.
3. Refugees: Those will be 'final status issues'. It was already decided that their right of return, even though Internationally recognized, is a 'red line' for Israel.
4. 'Israeli Arabs': they were not to be dealt with and the racism and discrimination against them (one fourth internally displaced, over 100 unrecognized villages, etc.) were to be considered internal Israeli issues.

This fractionation had a devastating psychological and material impact on Palestinians both under occupation and in the diaspora. The Hebron accord, for example, made legal and normalized the illegal Jewish settlements in and around Hebron. Four hundred Jews in Hebron were allowed to remain and administer the area of Hebron populated by 40,000 Palestinians and designated by these accords as H-2. 'Israel will retail all powers and responsibilities for internal security and public order in Area H-2 [and] will continue to carry out the responsibility of overall security of Israelis' (Section 2b). During the recent Intifada, the 40,000 residents of the old city of Hebron were subjected to weeks, and sometimes months, of curfews while the 400 settlers were subject to no restrictions. This was all due to the agreement made by Arafat. While the Geneva conventions prohibit collective punishments, the Oslo II agreements made this easy for Israel.

In addition to these restrictions, the Palestinian Authority (PA) was required to keep law and order and provide security to Israel. The more Israel intensified its settlement activity and occupation practices, the more Palestinians withdrew support for Arafat and the PA and switched support to the opposition parties (mistakenly labeled 'rejectionists'). Palestinians who benefited from the Oslo agreements included Arafat and the thousands of his associates and activists allowed to return to the occupied territories. They were given lucrative jobs and positions of authority, thereby causing further tension. Of course, there were gains for other segments of society: increased aid (especially from the European Union), upgrading infrastructure, pride and hope for a better future, and ameliorating a conflict among people weary of continued violence. Cosmetic changes were visible everywhere. On the Allenby Bridge, which links Jordan to the West Bank, there was now Palestinian police. They would take your documents and then hand them to Israeli soldiers behind a one-way mirror. It was later recognized as a charade that was intended to give the illusion of autonomy and even independence, when the reality was continued subjugation, control, and Israeli management of Palestinian affairs. Under the economic agreements signed by Arafat, the Authority cannot sign or engage in any independent economic activity with a third country. Israel retains control of exports and imports into the Palestinian areas. The agreements made it possible and even legal for Israel to split the territories into cantons with limited movement allowed only at Israel's discretion. These units were to have each a separate and highly dependent economy, primarily based on handouts from the West.

The so-called Palestinian Authority had no power or authority over economic policy, foreign policy, natural resources, or even entry and exit in the disjointed territories. It was merely slated to administer a restless and disgruntled native population in these separate enclaves and prevent them from attacking the colonizers. But the shifting political landscape continued and new Palestinian leaderships started to emerge in competition for a post-Oslo leadership. Fatah leader Marwan Barghouti emerged as leader of the uprising. His distant relative Dr Mustapha Barghouti emerged as a leader of non-violent resistance and civil disobedience. The security chiefs Jabroul and Dahlan, in the West Bank and Gaza respectively, were following in the footsteps of Arafat. Hamas and Islamic Jihad as political organizations were driven underground after being targeted as 'terrorist organizations', but continued to gain support among the increasingly disenfranchised and oppressed Palestinians. The leader of the Popular Front for the Liberation of Palestine retired and elections resulted in a smooth transition of leadership by democratic means. However, Israeli forces in Ramallah assassinated this leader and the PFLP elected a new leader, who was later arrested by Arafat's forces. The Democratic Front for the Liberation of Palestine and other groups continue their struggle.

After Oslo, the administration of Bill Clinton proceeded to drop its support for important and relevant UN resolutions and international law. This started with the pivotal Resolution 194 of 1948, which was authored by the US and reaffirmed with US support every year. On December 8, 1993 in withholding its vote, the US administration 'explained' that the September 1993 Israeli–PLO accords have made all previous resolutions 'obsolete and anachronistic'. Secretary of State Madeleine Albright summed up her government's position on the refugees in a letter to members of the General Assembly dated August 8, 1994; 'We believe that resolution language referring the "final status" issues should be dropped ... These include refugees.'

On March 7, 1997, the US vetoed a Security Council draft resolution on Jerusalem, presented by the four European members of the Council. The resolution calls on Israel to abandon its impending construction of a new settlement at Jabal Abu Ghneim, to the south of East Jerusalem. On March 21, 1997, the US again vetoed a Security Council resolution calling on Israel to halt the construction at Jabal Abu Ghneim. On April 24–25, the UN General Assembly, in reaction to the two US vetoes, convened an Emergency Special

Session (ESS) for the first time in 15 years to consider 'Illegal Israeli Actions in Occupied East Jerusalem and the Rest of the Occupied Palestinian Territory'. It overwhelmingly adopted resolution ES (Emergency Session) 10/2 condemning Israel's construction at Jabal Abu Ghneim and demanding cessation of all illegal Israeli actions. Israel ignored the resolution with the support of the US.

Albright frequently called Israeli war crimes simply acts that are 'unhelpful' or that 'Palestinians find objectionable'. In one of her many pronouncements she stated that Israel is encouraged to refrain from doing 'what Palestinians see as the provocative expansion of settlements, land confiscation, house demolitions and confiscation of IDs'.[33] Palestinians do not see these acts as provocative. They are illegal according to international law and basic human rights laws and constitute war crimes. The US under Clinton/Albright thus abandoned international law, the Fourth Geneva Convention and took Israel's side as an occupier and an aggressor. Thus, it was ironic that this most Zionist-tilting administration in US history would present itself to the world as an 'honest broker' for final peace agreements between Israel and the Palestinians at Camp David. The pressure both Clinton and Barak exerted to bring Arafat to Camp David and force him into a deal that sells out self-determination, international law, and human rights (including the rights of refugees) is well documented, despite the media soundbites of 'Barak's generous offer'. The protection and support of the Clinton administration allowed Israel to engage in its most ambitious settlement activity in the occupied areas (1993–2000).

Contrary to media reports and emboldened by US support, Barak did not add anything to what Israel has proposed since the mid-1970s (centered on Israel's perceived self-interest to relieve Israeli forces from policing Palestinians while maintaining rule). Barak never agreed to relinquish settlement blocs, which, combined with the bypass roads between them, would leave only 60 percent of the area of the West Bank and Gaza (or about 13 percent of the total land mass of Palestine) to return to the Palestinians. These would also be in the form of Palestinian cantons cut off from each other, and with movement controlled by Israel. Barak was uncompromising on Jerusalem. West Jerusalem was illegally occupied by Israel in 1948 and Palestinian landowners were expelled, and East Jerusalem was illegally occupied in 1967. UN Security Council Resolution 242 reaffirmed the illegality of holding the occupied territory by force. An even earlier frame of reference is UN General Assembly

Resolution 181, which provided for the partition in Palestine, with Jerusalem to be held under international rule. Israel engaged and continues to engage in blatantly illegal acts, including revoking residency rights, demolishing homes, preventing refugees from returning, barricading the city from surrounding Palestinian areas, and other acts described as 'Judaicizing' the city. Finally, Barak, Beilin, and other architects of the Oslo approach denied any Israeli responsibility for the Palestinian refugee problem and agreed only to token 'family reunification' with no time limits.

President Jimmy Carter wrote that 'an underlying reason that years of U.S. diplomacy have failed and violence in the Middle East persists is that some Israeli leaders continue to "create facts" by building settlements in occupied territory'.[34] What he failed to mention is that they can do this precisely because of US help and complicity cowed by influence of a special interest. Admiral Thomas Moorer of the Joint Chiefs of Staff has written:

> I've never seen a president – I don't care who he is – stand up to them [the Israelis]. It just boggles your mind. They always get what they want. The Israelis know what's going on all the time. I got to the point where I wasn't writing anything down. If the American people understood what grip those people have on our government, they would rise up in arms. Our citizens don't have any idea what goes on. (Washington Report 12/1999, p.124, quoting Andrew Hurley's *One Nation under Israel*)

In similar vein, Senator William Fulbright wrote:

> For many years I have felt that the situation in the Middle East was very nearly hopeless. The fundamental problem for us is that we have lost our freedom of action in the Middle East and are committed to policies that promote neither our own national interest nor the cause of peace. AIPAC [the American–Israeli Public Affairs Committee] and its allied organizations have effective working control of the electoral process. They can elect or defeat nearly any congressman or senator that they wish, with their money and coordinated organization.[35]

With the exception of several members voting according to their conscience, US politicians seem to march to a different drumbeat from the rest of the world. It would be a mistake to attribute all of this to the Israeli lobby. That lobby is influential, but US policy is also dictated by a small group of elites running the oil and arms industries. Their interest is simply to 'manage' the Middle East and maintain the status quo. This policy tolerates low-level conflicts and sometimes encourages them (as in the case of the Iran–Iraq war where these elite interests supported both sides) or even initiates them (as in the recent invasion of Iraq). As usually happens though, management by imperial powers fails over the long term. Often the superpowers overplay their hand, with the result that the conflicts widen more than anticipated and in a direct impact on their own population. In the US, there is now a grassroots movement against multinational corporate hegemony. The movement is rapidly growing and slowly changing the dynamics of the power structure. The fallout from recent events such as the Enron debacle, the September 11 attacks, the illegal attack on Iraq, among others, are still to come.

MIGHT MAKES RIGHT?

Israel, whether under Labor or Likud leadership, continued the traditional Zionist program that thought only in terms of military power and a zero-sum strategy based on the notion that Israel must take land and keep it to remain a 'winner'. Settlements and land confiscation expanded unchecked under both parties and peace was considered undesirable. Ben-Gurion recorded in his war diary that Abba Eban, Israel's Ambassador to the UN, 'sees no need to run after peace. The armistice is sufficient for us; if we run after peace, the Arabs will demand a price of us: borders [that is, in terms of territory] or refugees [that is, repatriation] or both. Let us wait a few years'.[36]

According to Israeli leaders, including Ben-Gurion, peace would mean fixing borders for Israel and the return of Palestinian refugees to their stolen homes and lands. Restoring usurped Palestinian rights would mean the end of the 'Zionist dream'. This was the reason behind the failure of all the peace initiatives. The Zionists employed stalling tactics so that they could expand their territorial boundaries, on the one hand, and avoid any return of the refugees, on the other. Thus, the native Palestinians, whether refugees or 'stragglers', were at best ignored and at worst considered a nuisance. 'Managing' them was analogous to managing other challenges facing the building of a Jewish state (getting weapons, increasing Jewish immigration, etc.).

At times the amount of damage to the Palestinians was more under Labor than under the Likud leadership because of Labor's 'diplomatic' and less confrontational approach. Part of the reasons for this is that Israel's original Zionist agenda was based on force. Some Israelis are actually proud of being larger and stronger in their military power than that of any European NATO state.[37] Israeli forces are now stationed in Turkey and have demonstrated their reach hundreds of miles outside of their bases. Combined with submarines and nuclear power, Israel is now truly a formidable world power. However, that power is still susceptible to one basic threat: the demands of the native Palestinians based on natural and international law. Most Israeli leaders are military people and many prime ministers were former Israeli generals. Their concept of peace is a peace made by 'management' of the Palestinian problem. Occasional flexibility in policy was accepted as long as it did not affect the overall well-articulated Zionist program and with the full understanding that only power and continued settlement and expansion can maintain Israel's elusive 'security'. Palestinian resistance in this context merely elicited stronger management tactics. The few voices within the Israeli government advocating peace were thus essentially ignored. The Israeli public was misled into believing that security could be achieved without justice or equality for the Palestinians.

The Palestinians had their best leadership decimated by the British in 1936–39. Since then, and until the PLO was established, Arab countries (Jordan, Egypt, Syria) took on the task of representing Palestinians. Until Oslo, Arafat and the PLO represented the aspirations for freedom and peace of the Palestinian people as a whole. The PLO attempted with varying success to maintain independence and representation (through the Palestinian National Council). After Oslo, they were relegated to the role of subcontractors for the occupation to maintain Israeli security in the occupied areas. This was done very efficiently especially in the first three years (1993–96). In those years, some saw a significant development of civilian infrastructure in the areas under Palestinian control, some decline in unemployment, and an improvement of the standard of living. But this only affected those not in the majority of the lands occupied in 1967. In those areas (primarily Area C and in East Jerusalem which together make up 60 percent of the West Bank), settlement activity, home demolitions, occupation, dispossession, and other violations of the Fourth Geneva Convention intensified. Further, for the first time since 1967, the territorial integrity of the West Bank was shattered. Israel used to have roadblocks which people could drive around and get from one part of the West Bank to another and even to Jerusalem. This was not to be the case after Oslo. Israel immediately instituted policies of closure, encircle-ments, and bypass roads for Jewish settlers that surrounded Pales-tinian towns. Palestinian extremists fed up with this situation did commit terrorist acts inside Israel in 1996. Both Israel's and Arafat's security forces failed to deal with the violence and its root cause remained: the continued occupation and dispossession of the Pal-estinians. Arafat was reduced to managing one crisis after another. For example, mismanagement of money and resources by people around him resulted in a significant rebellion. Arafat continued to deal with this by various methods he was well known for, ranging from minor shifts in strategy to co-opting people by offering them positions within his organization.

Since 1974, Arafat and the close circle around him believed that the only leverage against the overwhelming Israeli military power is international diplomatic support for the Palestinian cause. The international community outside of Israel since the 1970s has voiced remarkable support for the Palestinian cause with one notable exception: the United States. Arafat's biggest failure was failing to effect change in US foreign policy, the main obstacle to peace in the Middle East. This failure was most profound at the Camp David negotiations of July 2000.

US President Clinton under Israeli influence called for the Camp David meetings of July 2000 in order to end the conflict once and for all. These were defining moments for Arafat. Here, he was slated to sign yet another agreement similar to others he had signed over seven years that consolidated and strengthened apartheid and occupation. In this instance adding the coveted 'end of conflict' agreement which would end all future claims for Palestinian rights. This includes once and for all nullifying international law, the fourth Geneva convention, relevant clauses of the Universal Decla-ration of Human Rights, and even Israel's own signed agreements. Akram Hanieh, an advisor to Arafat at the Camp David talks, wrote a report that revealed what really happened. Arafat was reluctant to go because he felt the parties concerned, especially the Israelis, were not ready for final agreements. He was concerned about what failure might bring. Clinton insisted and promised that there would be no blame attributed if the talks failed. Arafat attended and, according to Hanieh, it became quickly obvious that Clinton was interested only in advancing the Israeli position on all issues.[38] The result was the failure of the summit and the increased belief in Israel that a military solution to the Palestinian problem is the only viable solution. Ariel Sharon, a war criminal by all definitions, successfully ignited the Intifada and acquired the position of prime minister. His election promise of security and peace went unfulfilled. Arafat continued to negotiate at Taba and beyond. The 'Palestinian Authority' was carefully being first cornered and then entirely disbanded before his eyes. Here we saw a dramatic transformation of Arafat from a freedom fighter and revolutionary leader to a weak and subservient leader relying on the US and Israel. Peace under these conditions became more elusive than ever.

According to the Congressional Research Service's annual report on conventional arms sales, the US delivered $26.4 billion in arms to the Middle East in 1997–2000, or just over 62 percent of all US deliveries to developing countries. Saudi Arabia ($16.2 billion), Israel ($3.9 billion), Egypt ($3.6 billion), and Kuwait ($1.5 billion) were the largest buyers. All these are repressive regimes with well-documented records of human rights violations. The US continues to adhere to its strategy of maintaining Israel's qualitative edge over any possible combined forces in the region. While countries like Saudi Arabia spend billions on American weapons, Israel is largely funded and subsidized by the US. The signals Washington sends with its support are also relevant. Three days after Mohammad Al-Durra was killed by Israeli forces near the illegal settlement of Netzarim, the US made arrangements to supply Israel with 50 advanced Apache helicopters. At the height of the Israeli assault on Palestinian areas on June 20, 2001 Israeli Minister of Defense Binyamin Ben-Eliezer struck a deal with Lockheed Martin to purchase more than 50 F-16I fighter jets, a deal valued at over $2 billion. This follows Israel's initial order of 50 jets in 1999, which cost approximately $2.5 billion. All such deals are financed through US military aid of almost $2 billion annually to Israel. Deliveries of the new fighter jets will commence in 2006 and conclude in 2009.

More US aid goes to Israel than to any other country. In total, the US gives Israel more than 30 percent of its total foreign aid budget, even though Israel has just 0.1 percent of the world population. Each year the US gives $2 billion in direct military aid, $840 million in direct economic aid, over $1 billion in indirect aid (contracts and free weapons shipments), and $1–2 billion in other tax-free support.

The US does not provide this aid in installments as is the case with other countries but in a lump sum at the beginning of each year. The US thus has to borrow the money it gives to Israel and pay interest on it. Interest losses are estimated at over $50 billion. In total this aid has cost taxpayers over $140 billion in the past three decades, which is equivalent to over $30,000 for every Israeli. This aid would be enough to provide clean drinking water to the 1.2 billion people who have no access to a safe water supply.[39]

US aid literally pays for the occupation of the West Bank, Gaza Strip, and East Jerusalem and is the key to Israel's continued belligerence and defiance of human rights and international law. US law ostensibly prohibits the president from furnishing military aid to any country 'which engages in a consistent pattern of gross violations of internationally recognized human rights'.[40] As the US State Department determines annually, Israel has committed and continues to commit such acts. But violations of this law and other problems with this aid are rarely questioned in Washington. Aid was initiated immediately after Israel attacked the USS *Liberty* in international waters in 1967 killing 34 US servicemen. It is believed this attack was to prevent the US from finding out what Israel was doing in the Sinai (including executing prisoners of war as later admitted). All remaining servicemen have and continue to reject the subsequent cover-up by the Navy. It is unprecedented that such an attack on a US ship did not generate a congressional investigation.[41] A report was aired on the History Channel on August 9, 2001, 35 years after the attack and after significant and unexplained 'delays'.

More recently, the US government has pushed hard for a 'road map' to peace, which calls for the establishment of a Palestinian state. In the 2,221 words of this road map, a few key words are missing. Of these the most egregious omissions are 'human rights' and 'international law'. Even then, the Israeli government got private assurances from Washington that 14 'reservations' it had about the road map would be taken into consideration in implementation. A document sent by American Zionists to Prime Minister Netanyahu in 1996 was titled 'A Clean Break: A New Strategy for Securing the Realm'.[42] The realm is the Israeli one in the Middle East. They called for regime change in Iraq led by the US followed by acts directed at Iran and Syria, and they spoke of 'alliances' with Turkey and India. Chaired by Richard Perle, chief architect of the most recent US war on Iraq, the group included James Colbert (from the Jewish Institute for National Security Affairs), Paul Wolfowitz (now Assistant Defense

Secretary), David Wurmser, and William Kristol. Another project of these 'neo-conservatives' who are so powerful in Washington is the so-called 'Project for a New American Century'.[43] Common denominators characterize these and similar plans: all written by neo-conservative ideologues who either worked for or still work on behalf of Israeli and/or corporate interests, all pre-date September 11, 2001, and all call for reshaping the Middle East to enhance Israel's security by claiming aligned US and Israeli interests.

At every turn, the US, under heavy influence of those with Israeli ties, tried to ignore public sentiments and cultivate and encourage dictatorial regimes. Yet, this has been an utter failure as is evident in the Gulf War, the attempt to protect Israel at every turn, and the massive resistance generated in the Muslim and Arab world. The Arab countries that are run by dictators supported by the US similarly cannot last indefinitely. The unresolved Palestine–Israel conflict is the Achilles' heel of US policy in the Middle East. The model of the toppling of the US-supported Shah regime in Iran is a good lesson to local peoples and to the United States. Finally, it is important to remember that after the grassroots economic pressures on apartheid South Africa the US government was one of the last to realize the bankruptcy of its support for the apartheid regime. It is time for a similar revolution in thinking.

RECOMMENDED READING

Nasser Aruri, *Dishonest Broker: The Role of the United States in Palestine and Israel* (Cambridge, Mass.: South End Press, 2003).

Gary M. Burge, *Whose Land? Whose Promise?: What Christians Are Not Being Told about Israel and the Palestinians* (Cleveland, Ohio: Pilgrim Press, 2003).

Noam Chomsky, *Middle East Illusions* (Lanham, Md: Rowman & Littlefield, 2003).

12
The International Context and International Law

> We the people of the United Nations determine to save succeeding generations from the scourge of war, which twice in our lifetime has brought untold sorrow to mankind, and to reaffirm faith in fundamental human rights, in the dignity and worth of the human person, in the equal rights of men and women, and of nations large and small, and to establish conditions under which justice and respect for the obligations arising from treaties and other sources of international law can be maintained, and to promote social progress and better standards of life in larger freedom.
>
> United Nations Charter, Article 1

A solution to the competing claims and aspirations of different people in the land of Canaan can take two possible scenarios. One can discuss solutions based on power and politics, in which case the stronger party will prevail over the weaker. This is not a recipe for long-term stability, especially since political and military powers can and do shift. Alternatively, one can apply a just and uniform set of laws to all nations and peoples. Skeptics may argue that the application of such a set of laws is flawed because the superpowers can still dominate international bodies. An example of this would be pressure exerted by Britain and now the United States to advance a Zionist agenda (see Chapter 11). Yet, international law at some point must begin to serve its lofty ideals as enshrined in the Universal Declaration of Human Rights and the United Nations Charter. Lessons from its failures should be learnt to improve the system not to abandon it.

EARLY INTERNATIONAL FAILURES

The British–French memorandum of understanding, known as the Sykes–Picot agreement of 1916, divided the Arabian Peninsula and the eastern Mediterranean region between France and Britain, while Britain made promises to the Arab people and to the Zionist movement. The agreements and promises were incompatible. These issues later had to be settled through an international body capable of reconciling or at least covering up British blunders. Such a resolution through the League of Nations was attempted for Palestine. The League was dominated by the victorious powers of the First World War. The Covenant of the League of Nations thus stated in Article 22:

> To those colonies and territories which as a consequence of the late war have ceased to be under the sovereignty of the States which formerly governed them and which are inhabited by peoples not yet able to stand by themselves under the strenuous conditions of the modern world, there should be applied the principle that the well-being and development of such peoples form a sacred trust of civilization and that securities for the performance of this trust should be embodied in this Covenant.
>
> The best method of giving practical effect to this principle is that the tutelage of such peoples should be entrusted to advanced nations who by reason of their resources, their experience or their geographical position can best undertake this responsibility, and who are willing to accept it, and that this tutelage should be exercised by them as Mandatories on behalf of the League.

The colonial language is obvious today, but at least in this document there is a recognition of the right of native inhabitants to remain in their lands. What was unique about the Palestine mandate was that it was made clear that 'tutelage' entailed a commitment to run the country for the purpose of creating a Jewish national homeland in Palestine. This was in accordance with the British desire expressed in the Balfour Declaration. While insisting this would not affect the 'rights' of natives, none of the arrangements proposed for the 'Palestine issue' were to be undertaken in consultation with Palestinians. Here are relevant clauses from the League's Palestine Mandate (July 24, 1922):

> Whereas the Principal Allied Powers have agreed, for the purpose of giving effect to the provisions of Article 22 of the Covenant of the League of Nations, to entrust to a Mandatory selected by the said Powers the administration of the territory of Palestine, which formerly belonged to the Turkish Empire, within such boundaries as may be fixed by them; and

Whereas the Principal Allied powers have also agreed that the Mandatory should be responsible for putting into effect the declaration originally made on November 2nd, 1917, by the Government of His Britannic Majesty, and adopted by the said Powers, in favor of the establishment in Palestine of a national home for the Jewish people, it being clearly understood that nothing should be done which might prejudice the civil and religious rights of existing non-Jewish communities in Palestine, or the rights and political status enjoyed by Jews in any other country; and

Whereas recognition has thereby been given to the historical connection of the Jewish people with Palestine and to the grounds for reconstituting their national home in that country; and

Whereas the Principal Allied Powers have selected His Britannic Majesty as the Mandatory for Palestine; and confirming the said Mandate, defines its terms as follows:

ARTICLE 1

The Mandatory shall have full powers of legislation and of administration, save as they may be limited by the terms of this mandate.

ARTICLE 2

The Mandatory shall be responsible for placing the country under such political, administrative and economic conditions as will secure the establishment of the Jewish national home, as laid down in the preamble, and the development of self-governing institutions, and also for safeguarding the civil and religious rights of all the inhabitants of Palestine, irrespective of race and religion.

ARTICLE 3

The Mandatory shall, so far as circumstances permit, encourage local autonomy.

ARTICLE 4

An appropriate Jewish agency shall be recognized as a public body for the purpose of advising and co-operating with the Adminis-tration of Palestine in such economic, social and other matters as may affect the establishment of the Jewish national home and the interests of the Jewish population in Palestine, and, subject always to the control of the Administration to assist and take part in the development of the country.

The Zionist organization, so long as its organization and constitution are in the opinion of the Mandatory appropriate, shall be recognized as such agency. It shall take steps in consultation with His Britannic Majesty's Government to secure the co-operation of all Jews who are willing to assist in the establishment of the Jewish national home.

ARTICLE 6

The Administration of Palestine, while *ensuring that the rights and position of other sections of the population are not prejudiced,* shall facilitate Jewish immigration under suitable conditions and shall encourage, in co-operation with the Jewish agency referred to in Article 4, close settlement by Jews on the land, including State lands and waste lands not required for public purposes. [emphasis added]

ARTICLE 7

The Administration of Palestine shall be responsible for enacting a nationality law. There shall be included in this law provisions framed so as to facilitate the acquisition of Palestinian citizenship by Jews who take up their permanent residence in Palestine.

ARTICLE 11

The Administration of Palestine shall take all necessary measures to safeguard the interests of the community in connection with the development of the country, and, subject to any international obligations accepted by the Mandatory, shall have full power to provide for public ownership or control of any of the natural resources of the country or of the public works, services and utilities established or to be established therein. It shall introduce a land system appropriate to the needs of the country, having regarded, among other things, to the desirability of promoting the close settlement and intensive cultivation of the land.

The Administration may arrange with the Jewish agency mentioned in Article 4 to construct or operate, upon fair and equitable terms, any public works, services and utilities, and to develop any of the natural resources of the country, in so far as these matters are not directly undertaken by the Administration. Any such arrangements shall provide that no profits distributed by such agency, directly or indirectly, shall exceed a reasonable rate of interest on the capital, and any further profits shall be utilized by it for the benefit of the country in a manner approved by the Administration.

Note the colonial thinking, that the native population are merely passive recipients of wisdom and control from outside. Yet ostensibly, the administration is responsible for 'ensuring that the rights and position of other sections of the population are not prejudiced'. Unfortunately, this did not happen, as we saw in the discussion of the appointment in 1922 of Sir Herbert Samuel, a Zionist, to oversee the Mandate.

The concept of respecting the rights of inhabitants existed long before the twentieth century. Agreements between the US and Russia on acquiring Alaska, between the US and Spain on acquiring Florida and many other agreements made clear that land ownership and other rights of the native inhabitants should be protected.[1]

AN ILLEGAL PARTITION

After the Second World War, peoples and nations sought to develop a better system to govern international relations based on the lessons learnt from the mistakes and horrors of war. The creation of the United Nations was a moment of collective hope. The UN's Charter was strengthened with a number of agreements, including the Universal Declaration of Human Rights (see Exhibit 3) and the Fourth Geneva Convention of 1949. While the UN was not immune from committing some of the mistakes the League of Nations had made in regards to Palestine, its Charter and treaties were attempts at resolution despite pressures from the same self-seeking powers of the day, notably the five permanent members of the UN Security Council. As an example of the flawed process, the UN Special Committee on Palestine (UNSCOP) included eleven members and traveled to the area in 1946, but included no Palestinian members. Palestinians (natives) could not present their case to the committee unlike the well-organized representation of Zionist groups and individuals, including Ben-Gurion. The committee visited representatives of so-called Arab states in Beirut and were unimpressed by their commitment to Palestine, according to accounts from the committee members' book.[2] The committee spent considerable time interviewing European Jews in displaced people's camps in meetings that were coached by the Jewish Agency, which persuaded them that the overwhelming majority of the Jews wanted to live in Palestine.[3]

The UN resolution on the Partition of Palestine (UN General Assembly Resolution 181) of November 29, 1947 came after significant lobbying by Zionist, US, and other world leaders.[4] The UN Charter which came into force on October 24, 1945 was clearly violated by this resolution. Among the purposes of the UN Charter, as outlined in Chapter 1, Article 1 is 'to develop friendly relations among nations based on respect for the principle of equal rights and self-determination of peoples, and to take other appropriate measures to strengthen universal peace'. However, the partition resolution was the first instance in UN history of the people of the land being partitioned not being afforded self-determination.

While it was illegitimate and contrary to the UN Charter, it is not correct to claim that this resolution is irrelevant today; nor is it correct to claim that Zionists accepted the partition while the 'Arabs' rejected it. Zionist leaders accepted only the part of the UN partition resolution calling for a Jewish state in the already heavily populated area of Palestine. They rejected the rest, including the proposed borders, the internationalization of Jerusalem, economic union, and, most importantly, the prohibition on removing native people. Israel was established not by implementation of this resolution, which called for specific ways to implement it, but by force of arms and with the massive support of other colonial powers. In the process of establishing the state of Israel, the largest post-Second World War refugee population was created by a process that today is called ethnic cleansing. Israel was admitted to the UN only after giving assurances on the implementation of Resolutions 181 and 194. UN General Assembly resolutions violated by Israel started with these two resolutions and extend to over 100 others and over 70 passed in the UN Security Council. UN General Assembly Resolution 194, for example, calls for the return of Palestinian refugees and compensation to those 'choosing not to return'. Israel has yet to abide by that resolution, which has been reaffirmed practically every year since it was made over a span of 55 years. In paragraph 11, Resolution 194 reads:

> Resolves that the refugees wishing to return to their homes and live at peace with their neighbors should be permitted to do so

at the earliest practicable date, and that compensation should be paid or the property of those choosing not to return and for loss of or damage to property which, under principles of international law or in equity, should be made good by the Governments or authorities responsible;

Instructs the Conciliation Commission [France, Turkey, and the United States] to facilitate the repatriation, resettlement and economic and social rehabilitation of the refugees and the payment of compensation, and to maintain close relations with the Director of the United Nations Relief for Palestine Refugees and, through him, with the appropriate organs and agencies of the United Nations ...

Ben-Gurion considered a Jewish state in part of Palestine as the first step towards the fulfillment of larger ambitions. His vision was spelled out in a letter to his son, Amos:

A partial Jewish State is not the end, but only the beginning ... We shall bring into the state all the Jews it is possible to bring ... We shall establish a multi-faceted Jewish economy – agricultural, industrial, and maritime. We shall organize a modern defense force, a select army ... and then I am certain that we will not be prevented from settling in the other parts of the country, either by mutual agreement with our Arab neighbors or by some other means. Our ability to penetrate the country will increase if there is a state.[5]

A letter was sent from the 'Agent of the Provisional Government of Israel' to the President of the United States, dated May 15, 1948, requesting recognition. It stated:

MY DEAR MR. PRESIDENT: I have the honor to notify you that the state of Israel has been proclaimed as an independent republic within frontiers approved by the General Assembly of the United Nations in its Resolution of November 29, 1947, and that a provisional government has been charged to assume the rights and duties of government for preserving law and order within the boundaries of Israel, for defending the state against external aggression, and for discharging the obligations of Israel to the other nations of the world in accordance with international law.[6]

However, Israel did not exist within these frontiers (55 percent of Palestine, as spelled out in UN General Assembly Resolution 181) but had 78 percent of Palestine. Also, Israel failed to fulfill its obligations to international law – even those minimal obligations set by the colonial-minded superpowers Britain and the US. For example, the resolution to allow refugees to return to their homes and lands was violated by Israel introducing laws to ensure they never came back. On the ground, the first task of the conquering Israeli Army was to erase any remnant of the 530 'vacated' Palestinian towns and villages. Regardless of how they were removed (discussed in detail in Chapter 4), international law is very clear on their right of return. The late W.T. Mallison, Professor of Law and Director of the International and Comparative Law programs at the George Washington University wrote (in collaboration with Sally Mallison, a research associate) in 1986:

> For most individuals the practice of returning to one's home or country is so commonplace ... that the right of return as a legal concept is given little attention. ... This usual state practice is so uncontroversial that it is not the subject of diplomatic and juridical contention. The Palestinians however, are in an unusual situation because their right of return has been systematically denied to them ever since the events of 1947 and 1948. ... Historically, the right of return was so universally accepted and practiced that it was not deemed necessary to prescribe or codify it in a formal manner. In 1215, at a time when rights were being questioned in England, the MAGNA CARTA was agreed to by King John. It provided that: 'It shall be lawful in the future for anyone ... to leave our kingdom and to return, safe and secure by land and water.'[7]

THE FOURTH GENEVA CONVENTION

The Fourth Geneva Convention of August 12, 1949, and entered into force on October 21, 1950, is particularly relevant since Israel and the US are signatories to it.[8] Israel is in violation of several of its articles. These violations have been documented by the International Committee of the Red Cross, which is charged with reporting to the high contracting parties. Particularly egregious violations are noted for these articles:

Section III. Occupied Territories

- Article 47: Establishes that persons in the Occupied Territories must not be deprived of the protections laid down in the Geneva Convention; i.e. the protections granted to victims of war.
- Article 49: Prohibits under all circumstances deportations, individual or mass forcible transfers to other countries. Additionally, and significantly, article 49 states that the Occupying power [Israel] shall not transfer parts of its own civilian population [Israelis] into the territory it occupies. This renders all Jewish settlements illegal.
- Article 50: Forbids closing educational institutions in occupied area. Israel routinely does that.
- Article 53: Forbids the destruction of homes, land, property, crops, and other individual or community property of protected members (individuals under occupation). Israel again routinely violates this.
- Article 76 (Detained individuals): Makes it illegal to take people accused of offences outside of the areas of occupation (i.e. they must remain in their own land). They must be given food and resources necessary to ensure proper health and must receive medical attention if necessary. They also have the right to receive religious or spiritual assistance; Minors must be treated with proper regard; Women shall be confined in separate quarters and supervised by other women; and delegates of a protecting power or of the International Committee of the Red Cross have the right to visit all detainees. Individual or mass forcible transfers as well as deportations of protected persons from occupied territory to the territory of the Occupying Power or to that of any other country, occupied or not, are prohibited, regardless of motive.[9]

The Israeli authorities initially applied the convention to the areas they occupied in 1967 and instructed their army to observe it, but the order was revoked five months later.[10] The Israeli government then in 1971 entrusted Attorney General Meir Shamgar to find a way to circumvent the convention. Shamgar's principal argument centered on the assertion that there was no previous sovereign rule in those areas and thus the population is not occupied but simply being administrated.[11] Following Israeli briefings the US media parroted the concept that the area was 'disputed' or being 'administered'. However, other countries, including Israel's staunchest ally and patron the United States, did not accept this political maneuver in full. It is thus disturbing that the Oslo process does not refer anywhere to occupied areas or the Israeli occupation of the West Bank and Gaza. (The capitulations made at Oslo are discussed in more detail in Chapter 11.)

Other international covenants and laws are pertinent here. The Universal Declaration of Human Rights states, in Article 13:

> Everyone has the right to freedom of movement and residence within the borders of each State. (2) Everyone has the right to leave any country, including his own, and to return to his country.[12]

Israel has violated this article repeatedly, and continues to do so.

UN General Assembly Resolution 273 (III) admitted Israel to the 'family of nations' on May 11, 1949. This resolution was approved after Israel consented to implement other UN resolutions (including Resolution 181 on partition and Resolution 194 on refugees' return). Specifically, it stated:

> Having received the report of the Security Council on the application of Israel for membership in the United Nations.
>
> Noting that, in the judgment of the Security Council, Israel is a peace-loving State and is able and willing to carry out the obligations contained in the Charter,
>
> Noting that the Security Council has recommended to the General Assembly that it admit Israel to membership in the United Nations,
>
> Noting furthermore the declaration by the State of Israel that it 'unreservedly accepts the obligations of the United Nations Charter and undertakes to honor them from the day when it becomes a Member of the United Nations,
>
> Recalling its resolutions of 29 November 1947 [UN Resolution 181] and 11 December 1948 [UN Resolution 194] and taking note of the declarations and explanations made by the representative of the Government of Israel before the ad hoc Political Committee in respect of the implementation of the said resolutions,
>
> The General Assembly,
> Acting in discharge of its functions under Article 4 of the Charter and rule 125 of its rules of procedure,

1. Decides that Israel is a peace-loving state which accepts the obligations contained in the Charter and is able and willing to carry out those obligations;
2. Decides to admit Israel to membership in the United Nations.

Israel not only refused to comply with its obligations, but relied heavily on its two patrons, Britain and the US, to ensure protection at the UN, through the frequent resort to the veto and by intimidation of smaller countries. This worked well in the Security Council, which started to gain more and more powers at the expense of the UN General Assembly. This was precisely because the great powers could veto resolutions in the Security Council and thus prevent action by the majority. Yet, although more and more countries have voted in the General Assembly against Israel's continued intransigence over the years, from 1948 to 1967, the US succeeded in blocking any UN Security Council resolution that reiterated a General Assembly resolution or tried to press Israel to comply with the terms of its admittance to the UN.

UN SECURITY COUNCIL RESOLUTIONS 242, 338, AND MORE

UN Security Council Resolution 242 was issued following the 1967 Arab–Israeli war. It was passed unanimously at the 1,382nd meeting after language modification to suit the US. Here is what it said:

The Security Council,
Expressing its continuing concern with the grave situation in the Middle East,
    Emphasizing the inadmissibility of the acquisition of territory by war and the need to work for a just and lasting peace in which every State in the area can live in security,
    Emphasizing further that all Member States in their acceptance of the Charter of the United Nations have undertaken a commitment to act in accordance with Article 2 of the Charter,

1. Affirms that the fulfillment of Charter principles requires the establishment of a just and lasting peace in the Middle East which should include the application of both the following principles:

(i)   Withdrawal of Israel armed forces from territories occupied in the recent conflict;

(ii) Termination of all claims or states of belligerency and respect for and acknowledgment of the sovereignty, territorial integrity and political independence of every State in the area and their right to live in peace within secure and recognized boundaries free from threats or acts of force;

2.   Affirms further the necessity

(a)   For guaranteeing freedom of navigation through international waterways in the area;

(b)   For achieving a just settlement of the refugee problem;

(c)   For guaranteeing the territorial inviolability and political independence of every State in the area, through measures including the establishment of demilitarized zones;

3.   Requests the Secretary-General to designate a Special Representative to proceed to the Middle East to establish and maintain contacts with the States concerned in order to promote agreement and assist efforts to achieve a peaceful and accepted settlement in accordance with the provisions and principles in this resolution;

4.   Requests the Secretary-General to report to the Security Council on the progress of the efforts of the Special Representative as soon as possible.

Note that the preamble speaks of the 'inadmissibility of the acquisition of territory by war', yet nowhere in the resolution was there a statement as to its enforceability. Contrast this with the UN Security Council resolution on Iraq's occupation of Kuwait, which basically authorized the US to take any measures to ensure compliance. The resolution also speaks about a 'just settlement of the refugee problem'. No other UN resolution contains a vaguer statement on refugees. UN resolutions on Kosovo, for example, were very specific about insisting that refugees be allowed to return to their homes and lands. It is also notable that this resolution refers to Article 2 of the UN Charter, which deals mostly with peaceful settlement of disputes between nations, and not to Article 1, where we find such statements as 'To develop friendly relations among nations based on respect for the principle of equal rights and self-determination of peoples'. Self-determination for Palestinians was thus made an exception.

UN Security Council Resolution 338 was passed following the October 1973 Arab–Israeli war. It stated:

> The Security Council,
> Calls upon all parties to present fighting to cease all firing and terminate all military activity immediately, no later than 12 hours after the moment of the adoption of this decision, in the positions after the moment of the adoption of this decision, in the positions they now occupy; Calls upon all parties concerned to start immediately after the cease-fire the implementation of Security Council Resolution 242 (1967) in all of its parts;
> Decides that, immediately and concurrently with the cease-fire, negotiations start between the parties concerned under appropriate auspices aimed at establishing a just and durable peace in the Middle East.

The 'just and durable peace' was again to be left to the parties themselves, with no enforcement mechanism or a discussion of self-determination or human rights. With clear US support for Israel's military superiority, this effectively left it to Israel to decide how peace would be formulated.

UN Security Council Resolution 446 of March 22, 1979 reaffirmed that the Jewish settlements in the Occupied Territories (including the Golan Heights) 'have no legal validity and constitute a serious obstruction to achieving a comprehensive, just and lasting peace in the Middle East'. It calls on Israel as an occupying power to abide by the Fourth Geneva Convention and to desist from taking any action that changes the legal status or the demographic profile of the Occupied Territories, including Jerusalem. The UN Security Council adopted a similar resolution on July 20, 1979. Again no enforcement mechanisms were included due to US pressure and threats of a veto.

The language in these UN Security Council resolutions is mild in comparison to other General Assembly resolutions. Contrast, for example, UN Security Council Resolution 446, which states that these settlements 'constitute a serious obstruction to achieving a comprehensive, just and lasting peace in the Middle East', with UN General Assembly Resolution 2727 of December 5, 1970. Item (2):

> Calls upon the Government of Israel immediately ... to comply with its obligations under the Geneva Convention relative to the

Protection of Civilian Persons in Time of War, of 12 August 1949, the Universal Declaration of Human Rights and the relevant resolutions adopted by the various international organizations.

The Fourth Geneva Convention expressly prohibits an occupying power from transferring its own population into occupied areas.

More recent UN Security Council resolutions, when not vetoed by the United States, can be problematic to some Israeli officials. UN Security Council Resolution 1322(2000) was voted in by 14 to 0, with the US abstaining. The US could have exercised its veto but did not; thus the US allowed it to become binding in international law. In paragraph 1 of UN Security Council Resolution 1322 the Security Council: 'Deplores the provocation carried out at Al-Harem al-Sharif [site of the Al-Aqsa mosque and the Dome of the Rock] in Jerusalem on 28 September 2000 and the subsequent violence there ...' This provocation was inflicted by General Ariel Sharon, now Israel's prime minister, with the full support of the then prime minister, General Barak. These men must have known that such a desecration, which includes the killing of several unarmed Palestinians by Israeli soldiers, would set off another uprising, which became known as the Al-Aqsa Intifada, or the uprising in support of the Al-Aqsa mosque. But, more importantly, UN Security Council Resolution 1322 'Calls upon Israel, the Occupying Power to abide scrupulously by its legal obligations and responsibilities under the Fourth Geneva Convention relative to the Protection of Civilian Persons in a Time of War, 12 August 1949 ...'

The US has blocked 35 resolutions critical of Israel in the Security Council. However, the remaining Security Council resolutions and basic international law are sufficient to make the following unacceptable:

1. The refusal of Israel to withdraw from the areas occupied in 1967 or even comply with the Geneva Convention in these areas (e.g. settlements are completely illegal).
2. The refusal of Israel to implement UN Resolution 181, on which the creation of a State of Israel in Palestine was based.
3. The refusal of Israel to allow refugees to return to their homes and lands and compensate them for lost property and for their suffering.[13]

Working against compliance with these international laws center on the US's protection of Israel for internal political considerations. However, the failure to accept the rights of the Palestinians, some of whose rights are enshrined in international laws and treaties, has been key to the continued bloodshed and mayhem in the land of Canaan and beyond. In the final chapter, I will address a durable solution that takes into account international law and human rights and addresses the legitimate needs and aspirations of people of the land of Canaan.

Exhibit 4. Other Relevant UN General Assembly Resolutions Passed by Overwhelming Majorities

UN General Assembly Resolution 3236 of November 22, 1974, on the Question of Palestine:

> 1) Reaffirms the inalienable rights of the Palestinian people in Palestine, including, (a) the right to self-determination without external interference; (b) the right to national independence and sovereignty; 2) Reaffirms also the inalienable right of the Palestinians to return to their homes and property from which they have been displaced and uprooted, and calls for their return; 3) Emphasizes that full respect for and the realization of these inalienable rights of the Palestinian people are indispensable for the solution of the question of Palestine.

UN General Assembly Resolution 42/159 of December 7, 1987:

> Supports the right of peoples living under occupation to resist that occupation and to seek and receive support of outside parties. Thus, groups that have resisted Israeli occupation in the past (such as Hizbullah in Lebanon), and those groups that continue to resist Israeli occupation in the present (such as Islamic Jihad, Hamas, the PFLP, the DFLP, Fatah, and others) are legitimate resistance movements rather than 'terrorist' organizations. Offensive actions such as suicide bombings against civilians, however, are considered illegitimate means of resistance, i.e. criminal acts of aggression.

UN General Assembly Resolution 51/124 of December 13, 1996:

> Notes with regret that repatriation or compensation of the refugees, as provided for in paragraph 11 of its resolution 194 ... has not yet been effected and that, therefore, the situation of the refugees continues to be a matter of concern.

UN General Assembly Resolution 51/126 of December 13, 1996:

> (1) Reaffirms the right of all persons displaced as a result of the June 1967 and subsequent hostilities to return to their homes or former places of residence in the territories occupied by Israel since 1967. (2) Expresses the hope for an

accelerated return of displaced persons through the mechanism agreed upon by the parties in article XII of the Declaration of Principles on interim self-government Arrangements; and (3) Endorses ... the efforts of the ... United Nations Relief and Works Agency (UNRWA) for Palestine Refugees in the Near East to continue to provide humanitarian assistance ...

UN General Assembly Resolution 51/129 of December 13, 1996:

(1) Reaffirms that the Palestine Arab refugees are entitled to their property and to the income derived there from, in conformity with the principles of justice and equity; (2) Requests the Secretary-General to take all appropriate steps, in consultation with the United Nations Conciliation Commission for Palestine, for the protection of Arab property, assets and property rights in Israel and to preserve and modernize these existing records.

UN General Assembly Resolution 52/114 of 52nd Session, 1997:

Affirms, yet again, the right of the Palestinian people to self-determination.

RECOMMENDED READING

Francis Boyle, *Palestine, Palestinians & International Law* (Atlanta: Clarity Press, 2003).

John Quigley, 'The Role of Law in a Palestinian-Israeli Accommodation', *Case Western Reserve Journal of International Law*, Vol. 31, Nos. 2–3 (Spring/Summer 1999).

13
Peace Can be Based on Human Rights and International Law

We will have to face the reality that Israel is neither innocent, nor redemptive. And that in its creation, and expansion; we as Jews, have caused what we historically have suffered; a refugee population in diaspora.

Martin Buber, March 1949

> Give birth to me again
> Give birth to me again that I may know
> In which land I will die, in which land
> I will come to live again.
>
> Mahmud Darwish

In 1947, the United States, the Soviet Union, and France pushed for a plan in the United Nations for the partitioning of Palestine.[1] This plan was put forward without consulting the Palestinians who inhabited the area. At the same time, the Arab countries presented a plan to the UN based on federalism. The *New York Times* published an article detailing this proposal:

A few minutes before the Assembly convened Arab spokesmen announced that they had drawn up a new six-point program in twenty-four hours of conferences. The program involved this formula:

(1) A federal independent state of Palestine shall be created not later than Aug. 1, 1949.
(2) The Government of Palestine shall be constituted on a federal basis and shall include a federal government and governments for Arab and Jewish countries.
(3) Boundaries of the cantons will be fixed so as to include a federal basis and shall include a federal government and governments for Arab and Jewish countries.

(4) The population of Palestine shall elect by universal, direct suffrage a Constituent Assembly, which shall draft the Constitution of the future federated state of Palestine. The Constituent Assembly shall be composed of all elements of the population in proportion to the number of their respective citizens.

(5) The Constituent Assembly, in defining the attributes of the federated government of Palestine as well as of its legislative and judiciary organs and the attributes of the governments of the cantons and of the relation of the governments of these cantons with the federal government, shall draw its inspiration chiefly from the principles of the Constitution of the United States as well as from the organization of laws in the states of the United States.

(6) The Constitution will provide, among other things, for protection of the holy places, liberty of access to visit the holy places and freedom of religion as well as safeguarding of the rights of religious establishments of all nationalities in Palestine.[2]

This plan was not successful as the competing proposal embodied in what was to become Resolution 181 was vigorously promoted by the two great powers of the time, the United States and the Soviet Union. Zionist leaders went forward and even violated this resolution by a unilateral declaration of statehood, ethnically cleansing the areas recommended for them and more, and preventing the return of the refugees. Zionism then controlled 78 percent of the territory as opposed to the 55 percent set out in Resolution 181. In 1967, Israel forcibly took the rest of Palestine. Resolution 181 is used to give legal cover for the creation and maintenance of the state of Israel. As noted earlier, it was passed with pressure and contrary to the UN Charter. It was never implemented in the sense that it sets a program for implementation and had clear parameters for its implementation. When Israel was admitted to the UN, it was with the assurances that it would implement this and other resolutions (including Resolution 194). Thus, Israel's borders would be those shown on the maps of Resolution 181 (55 percent of Palestine), there would be an economic union, and an internationalized Jerusalem. More importantly, there would be safe return for refugees to their native lands and respect for other elements of international law, including the Universal Declaration of Human Rights. In fact, strict adherence to international law would require that Israel be expelled from the UN and sanctioned until it agrees to comply with its obligations. This pertains especially to allowing refugees to return to their homes and lands and compensating them for their losses and suffering. Since this is the only legal and moral solution, Zionism would have to be rethought.

ZIONIST DISCOURSE

The militant Zionism of the nineteenth and twentieth centuries succeeded in creating a strong nation and in bringing in millions of Jewish immigrants. Zionism failed to conquer and completely cleanse the whole area, to crush Palestinian national aspirations, and to create a safe and secure state with normal relations with other states in the Middle East. Its primary victims were the native Palestinians who were ethnically cleansed. Yet, the return of Palestinian refugees is not only legal and moral but also feasible (see Chapter 4). The obstacles are a set of philosophical beliefs that are not rooted in logic or equality (see Chapters 6 and 7). Zionism has also failed to deliver what it promised the Jews of the world: security and a sense of being in control of their destiny. The few Zionist successes came from cultural Zionism and go largely undiscussed. For example, the forging of a Hebrew-speaking Israelite nation from an Ashkenazi and Yiddish-speaking people has been accomplished. There are now two generations of Israelis whose mother tongue is Hebrew. They even have a unique accent when speaking a second language. Yet Israeli leaders and militant Zionist leaders still refuse to recognize this and insist on the concept of a 'Jewish nation', ignoring the new and remarkable development of an Israeli nation with its flaws and strengths. Some Palestinians in turn still dream of restoring an 'Arab Palestine'. Both are living in the past and both ignore the possibilities of a post-Zionist evolutionary world that can create true stability and peace with justice.

This brings us to what initially seemed to a majority on both sides a pragmatic solution: the two-state solution. The Palestinian leadership agreed on a historic compromise by accepting this notion. Here is what the PLO Negotiations Affairs Department articulated as a summary of those compromising Palestinian positions:

Borders:
The Palestine Liberation Organization's position regarding the issue of borders is straightforward: the international borders

between the States of Palestine and Israel shall be the armistice cease-fire lines in effect on June 4, 1967. Both states shall be entitled to live in peace and security within these recognized borders. The primary bases for this Palestinian position are: United Nations Security Council Resolution 242, which emphasizes the inadmissibility of the acquisition of territory by war and calls for the withdrawal of Israel armed forces from territories occupied in the 1967 war; and the internationally recognized Palestinian right to self-determination. The West Bank and the Gaza Strip together constitute only 22% of historic Palestine. The PLO's acceptance of the June 4, 1967 borders represents an extraordinary compromise. Any further Israeli incursions into Palestinian territory will not only result in widespread disillusionment and disaffection, but will also diminish the viability of Palestinian statehood.

Statehood:
By virtue of their right to self-determination, the Palestinian people possess sovereignty over the West Bank (including East Jerusalem) and the Gaza Strip and, accordingly, have the right to establish an independent State on that territory. The decision of when to declare that state and what the institutions of that state will be is a decision that rests solely with the Palestinian people. The PLO, as the sole legitimate representative of the Palestinian people, is the vehicle through which they express their political decisions. While Israel has exercised control over the West Bank and the Gaza Strip since the 1967 war, the international community regards Israel as a belligerent occupant with no rights to the territory.

Jerusalem:
As stated in the 1993 Declaration of Principles on Interim Self-Government Arrangements, Jerusalem (and not merely East Jerusalem) is the subject of permanent status negotiations. As part of the territory occupied in 1967, East Jerusalem is subject to United Nations Security Council 242. It is part of the territory over which the Palestinian state shall exercise sovereignty upon its establishment. The State of Palestine shall declare Jerusalem as its capital. Jerusalem should be an open city. Within Jerusalem, irrespective of the resolution of the question of sovereignty, there should be no physical partition that would prevent the free circulation of persons within it. As to sites of religious significance, most of which are located within the Old City in East Jerusalem,

Palestine shall be committed to guaranteeing freedom of worship and access there. Palestine will take all possible measures to protect such sites and preserve their dignity.

Settlements:
Settlements are illegal and must be dismantled. The corollary of the prohibition against the acquisition of territory by force is the Fourth Geneva Convention's stipulation against settling civilians of an occupying power in occupied territories. Israel sought to consolidate its acquisition of the occupied territories by settling large numbers of its civilians in the West Bank (including East Jerusalem) and the Gaza Strip, thereby creating 'facts on the ground.' In United Nations Security Council Resolution 465 (1980), the Security Council demanded that Israel 'dismantle the existing settlements and in particular to cease, on an urgent basis, the establishment, construction of planning of settlements in the Arab territories occupied since 1967, including Jerusalem.' Israeli settlements geographically fragment the West Bank and the Gaza Strip and thus undermine the viability of Palestinian statehood. Israeli settlements also place intolerable burdens on Palestinian movement and development, in significant part by depriving the Palestinian people of important land and water resources. Israel has created two sets of law in the occupied territories – one for settlers and one for Palestinians – thereby institutionalizing discrimination.

Refugees:
Every Palestinian refugee has the right to return to his or her home. Every Palestinian refugee also has the right to compensation for their losses arising from their dispossession and displacement. The Palestinian position on refugees is based on UN General Assembly Resolution 194 (1948), calling for the return of the refugees and their compensation. Resolution 194 was affirmed practically every year since with almost universal acceptance – the one consistent exception being Israel. The Palestinian side proposes to develop, in coordination with the relevant parties, a detailed repatriation plan that includes the modalities, timetables and numbers for a phased return of the refugees. This plan must ensure the safety and dignity of return in accordance with international human rights norms.

Water:

Palestinian sovereignty over the territory of the West Bank and the Gaza Strip has direct implications for Palestinian sovereign rights to natural resources. In the case of water, the State of Palestine is entitled to an equitable and reasonable share of international aquifers in the West Bank and the Jordan River, and to sole control over water systems located wholly within Palestinian borders. During its occupation, Israel tightly controlled Palestinian access to water, while allocating the lion's share of high-quality water to Israelis, including settlers. Currently, Israelis consume three to four times as much water as Palestinians do per capita. Palestine needs its rightful share of water to provide for the drinking and sanitation needs of a growing Palestinian population and to allow our agricultural sector to achieve its full potential.

Security:

The PLO seeks to structure security relations between the States of Palestine and Israel in ways that will: promote good neighborly relations between the States, provide effective responses to specific threats, create mechanisms for ongoing cooperation, and show due regard for international human rights standards. Security relations between the states of Palestine and Israel must be structured to reflect not only the security concerns of the Israeli people, but also the rights and interests of the Palestinian people. In particular, no security relations should prejudice or undermine Palestinian sovereignty and control over our territory.

Relations with Neighbors:

The State of Palestine as a sovereign state has the right independently to define and conduct its foreign relations. The PLO will nevertheless seek to promote cooperation among Israel, Palestine, and neighboring States in fields of common interest. In order to promote cooperation among Israel, Palestine, and neighboring States, Palestine will seek cooperation in numerous fields, including: agriculture, aquaculture and marine matters, arms control, communications, crime prevention, culture, economic relations, energy, environment, exploitation of natural resources, health, security, social security and welfare, sports, tourism and transportation.[3]

The Palestinians then compromised further in the maps proposed at Camp David in July 2000 and at Taba in January 2001. In short, the Palestinian leadership was willing to:

1. Give up 78 percent of their country to new immigrants against the wishes of the natives.
2. Give up the demand for a secular state for all its people and in essence accepting a racist Zionist state that considers itself a nation 'for the Jewish people' and not for its citizens and has promulgated a set of racist laws that ensure continued discrimination and dispossession of non-Jews (see Chapter 7 for details).
3. Accept to work out a phased repatriation of refugees to take into consideration Israeli government fears of upsetting demographic structure (i.e. to insist on keeping a Jewish majority, a racist view).
4. Accept to exchange land of equal value so that the majority of the settlement (illegal by international law) can be annexed to Israel.
5. Agree to share water that belongs to the indigenous people.
6. Abandon UN Resolution 181 which gave 55 percent of Palestine to a 'Jewish state' and 45 percent to an 'Arab state' against the wishes of the natives (and pushed by imperial US interests). Yet it specifically prohibited population transfer (which is precisely what happened). The borders defined therein are however, the only ones that provide any legal framework (however unfair) for a two-state solution. Yet Palestinians were willing to accept the cease-fire borders which would give the 'Jewish state' not 55 percent of the land but 78 percent of the land of Palestine.
7. Agree to share Jerusalem (including the old city) and even a priori agree to leave West Jerusalem under full Israeli sovereignty (Resolution 181 on partition calls for an internationalized Jerusalem).

REALITY IS NOT CONDUCIVE TO A TWO-STATE SOLUTION

The reality on the ground is not conducive to this historic Palestinian compromise because, first and foremost, any regression of Zionist expansion is perceived to weaken its original purpose and goals. In coming to terms with abandoning the two-state solution in favor of a bi-national state, Haim Hanegbi stated:

Everyone with eyes to see and ears to hear has to understand that only a binational partnership can save us. That is the only way to transform ourselves from being strangers in our land into native sons ... I realized that the reason it is so tremendously difficult for Israel to dismantle settlements is that any recognition that the settlements in the West Bank exist on plundered Palestinian land will also cast a threatening shadow over the Jezreel Valley, and over the moral status of Beit Alfa and Ein Harod. I understood that a very deep pattern was at work here. That there is one historical continuum that runs from Kibbutz Beit Hashita to the illegal settler outposts; from Moshav Nahalal to the Gush Katif settlements in the Gaza Strip. And that continuity apparently cannot be broken. It's a continuity that takes us back to the very beginning, to the incipient moment ... [see Figure 2]

I'm not crazy. I don't think that it will be possible to enlist thousands of people in the cause of a binational state tomorrow morning. But when I consider that Meron Benvenisti was right in saying that the occupation has become irreversible, and when I see where the madness of sovereignty is leading good Israelis, I raise my own little banner again. I do so without illusions. I am not part of any army. I am not the leader of any army. In the meantime our act is that of a few people. But I think it's important to place this idea on the table now.[4]

One of the key issues to prevent a two-state compromise is the current demographics. The Jewish population of Israel and the occupied territories now exceeds five million. The Palestinian population in Israel (within the Green Line) is 1.3 million. In the proposed Palestinian 'state' of the West Bank and Gaza there are more than four million Palestinians and 400,000 Jewish settlers. Thus, there is already, even without any returning refugees, a rough parity between the number of non-Jews and Jews west of the River Jordan in an area of 84,000 square km. The Palestinian population in the Hashemite Kingdom of Jordan (Trans Jordan) is over two-thirds of the population. These are densely populated areas, with about 3,000 individuals per square km. A partition into two viable states – the key word here is viable – is rendered impossible by the already mixed population in every part of the country and the inequality of areas allotted to the two states (78 percent to 22 percent). Canaan is indeed a single country composed of Israelis and Palestinians for all practical purposes. A single pluralistic and democratic state of Palestine/Israel or a joint confederation with Jordan/Israel/Palestine is feasible and reasonable. The demographic and social and environmental issues discussed in Chapter 10 are also factors, as are others:

1. The old PLO structure, the PNA, the Oslo Accords (predicated on an assumption of a two-state solution), and certainly the Israeli state have failed to achieve:
    (a) Palestinian rights including their inalienable right to return to their homes and lands;
    (b) Basic equality and dignity to all people;
    (c) An historic reconciliation that brings peace, justice, tranquility, and prosperity to people of the Middle East;
    (d) Security and safety for all inhabitants;
2. Even a truly sovereign Palestinian state on the whole of the West Bank and Gaza with East Jerusalem as its capital is not possible (400,000 settlers), and will not be viable.
3. Such a mini-state will exacerbate the problems of the Palestinians living in Israel. After giving up these areas, Israeli society would become more acutely aware and vindicated in its need of being a 'Jewish state'.
4. Recent events on the ground and internationally have forced a rethinking regarding the futility of a forced solution, the futility of apartheid systems, and the need for justice and equality. With intertwined economies, the rapid growth of the Palestinian population within and outside the Green Line, limited resources, and massive expenditure on defense instead of economic development.
5. Recent polls of Israelis and Palestinians reveal a growing disillusionment of the two-state solution as a viable means of stabilizing the area let alone having this solution achieve a long lasting peace. In a recent survey, over a third of Palestinians polled called for a democratic secular state even without this being formalized by any Palestinian organizational structure. The Israeli public is also disillusioned with the two-state solution.

THE POLITICS OF JUSTICE

A movement against Israeli apartheid must offer rational alternative structure in a post-Zionist era that would replace the current narrow, nationalistic, and racist structure. This alternative, based on human rights, equality, and justice, could attract wide support, from Jews and Israelis.

Many intellectuals correctly point out all the faults of the current proposed solutions and the reasons for the failures of earlier peace initiatives and organizational activities. However, the Palestinian movement needs to organize to offer viable and credible alternatives to those criticized plans. All interested parties need to get together to bring about a transition to a working solution that respects human rights. This includes people of different religions and currently different national identification/designations, whether Palestinian refugees, Israelis, displaced people, 'present absentees', Palestinians in the occupied areas, Jordanians of Palestinian descent, or Jordanians. Indeed, there are some signs that this rethinking is taking place.

A group of prominent Israeli artists issued the following statement:

> If the state of Israel aspires to perceive itself as a democracy, it should abandon once and for all, any legal and ideological foundation of religious, ethnic, and demographic discrimination. The state of Israel should strive to become the state of all its citizens. We call for the annulment of all laws that make Israel an apartheid state, including the Jewish law of return in its present form.[5]

Similarly, new associations for one pluralistic state have been set up by groups of Palestinians and Israelis.[6]

My primary intention in writing this book was to explore a durable solution to a difficult problem by using the key concepts of human rights and international law. Yet, these concepts are difficult to understand when so much fear and mythology abound. Some political ideologies that deal with these issues from many standpoints lead inevitably to the conclusion of accommodation and coexistence. An example of such trend is the ease with which socialist viewpoints translate into one-state solutions.[7] Coexistence and equality are also compatible with some pan-Arabic or pan-Islamic strands of thought. But even a conservative right political philosophy can lead to peaceful coexistence (in order to free markets, exchange goods and services, etc.). However, coexistence and equality are more difficult to accommodate within certain neo-conservative trends and certain branches of Zionism. A new conservative cadre of thinkers and leaders, now in power in Washington, mostly derive their philosophy from the work of such political scholars as Leo Strauss (1899–1973). Strauss has had significant impact on very influential followers, ranging from neo-conservatives in Washington like Irving Kristol and his son William Kristol, to Likud leaders like Binyamin Netanyahu. Strauss believed that the concepts of right and wrong should be transmitted by strong statesmen who guide large segments of society.[8] This in essence is a deterministic agenda of 'survival of the fittest', as opposed to an evolving caring one, based on human needs.

Strauss's influence has left an indelible mark on US foreign policy, ranging from the Reagan era contract with America to hawkish views on a 'clash of civilizations'.[9] The differences in philosophies should not be distilled to a difference of determinism versus relativism. The difference is more fundamental than that. It is a difference between people whose experiences are shaped by violence and might and those who believe that humanity can evolve through a paradigm of tolerance and coexistence. Those who have attempted to straddle the two philosophies have found it difficult to maintain a balance. A good example is to look at the declining fortunes of the so-called 'Liberal Zionists'. These Zionists find it easy to defend Palestinians in the West Bank and Gaza from ethnic cleansing and home demolition, while they cannot endorse the right of Palestinian refugees to return to their homes and lands inside Israel. They want some semblance of equality for Palestinians with Israeli citizenship but will defend the discriminatory 'Law of [Jewish] Return' which states that any Jew, including converts, can become an Israeli citizen, a 'right' denied to thousands of non-Jewish people born there. This duality leaves many attempting to understand this view perplexed. Finding this position untenable over the long term, many move towards liberalism or towards the conservative agenda. Under the mostly capitalist systems of Israel and the US, conservatives unencumbered by altruism or a spirit of sharing, climb to the highest level of the corporate, financial, and political structures. This power is self-perpetuating as it is relatively simple to turn such financial, political, and media capital into votes. Looking at it from this perspective, one may become despondent. But other factors need to be considered.

ALTRUISM IS PRAGMATIC

Altruism and species survival are intimately linked. In an era where technology allows a few individuals to kill millions and where the world is connected in a way previously inconceivable, a Straussian model is no longer credible. Biology shows that altruism can evolve naturally in populations and can aid the survival of these populations. In the twenty-first century, borders are dissolving; communication, intermarriage, and relocation are creating a new world. The Internet and globalization are making irreversible changes in what used to be thought of as important and unchangeable, including need for nationalities, borders, and even separate languages and currencies. Even those 'Liberal Zionists' who agree with this vision but claim that Zionism must be supported now until humanity evolves more miss the point. Humans with a vision of plurality and democracy must strive to shorten the time to achieve this vision rather than fight it or waiting for it to materialize spontaneously.

In the context of the Arabic and Islamic world, a transformation is also happening. Some Arabs think regressively to narrow nationalism or political and religious exclusivity; this is essentially a Straussian model. Yet many draw on concepts of inclusion and openness which guided much of the progress of Al-Andalus/Spain under the more liberal Islamic leaders of the time.

Of course, there are many concerns regarding such visions of inclusive, pluralistic, and caring societies. Palestinians may fear losing their rights to the already more dominant segments of the society. But I would argue that implementing these rights could only occur while working hand in hand with an enlightened Israeli public towards a common goal. The absence of democracy in many states in the area is a matter of concern to the Israeli and Palestinian population, and encompasses fears that joining forces may lead to majority rule, which could turn into the dictatorship of one group over another. These fears should be dispelled not by words or utopian dreams but by a program based on partnership, concrete laws, international guarantees, and the separation of powers. For a program like the one proposed here to succeed, efforts must be intensified (by Christians, Muslims, Jews, and others, who have reached the conclusion that peace is not only possible but essential).

It is clear that the conflict is not primarily religious. Founding Zionists were never religious and many even despised religious Jews. We also need to dispel the myth that a solution based on military might is possible. The numerous wars fought demonstrate that there will not be a final day of victory and an end to war with the triumph of one side over the other. An individual like Ariel Sharon who tries to impose a military solution or to 'defeat the enemy' has already been shown to be ignorant of history.

Another way to look at the situation in the Middle East is to identify who the beneficiaries are from a lack of a peaceful and just resolution. Such a resolution could result in economic development, respect for human rights, and the removal of barriers to exchange of people and of information. Such a resolution could be a threat to the following groups:

1. The arms industry: The US is the largest exporter of weapons in the world and over 60 percent of US weapons exports go to the Middle East.
2. The oil industry: Less US involvement in the Middle East could spell an end to US dependency on oil, development of alternative energy sources, and energy conservation.
3. 'Think tanks' and their employees primarily located in Washington DC. No fewer than two dozen such groups operate and receive a lot of funding from specialized interests, ranging from oil and military industries to lobbies for Israel and other countries. Without some conflict to write and push position papers for, their jobs would be jeopardized.
4. Many Zionist leaders. Individually, they get significant attention and support, hefty lecture fees, good positions, and many write books and receive adulation. Collectively, they can maintain the 'Jewish character' of the state of Israel under their 'guidance' and avoid possible democratic reforms, the separation of state and religion, and economic development that they will not control.
5. Religious zealots, whether Christians, Jews, or Muslims, who believe in doomsday scenarios or an apocalyptic ending. For them, humans should just accept certain 'truths' such as God 'testing' his faithful by providing them with an enemy so that if they are to triumph, they have to be ever more religious and 'strong'. Of course, they simultaneously must also ignore the admonitions in these religions calling for mercy, love, and respect for others and embrace only the worst elements of their religion. The fanatical Jewish colonizers/settlers in Hebron are a good example of this, as are people like Osama Bin Laden.

6. Many Arab leaders (Saudi Arabia, Jordan, Syria, Egypt, etc.). A resolution could take away the only crutch left for their dictatorial powers which benefit immensely from lucrative oil and arms deals. With their people not distracted by the conflict outside their borders, they would demand freedom, responsible economic development, the elimination of corruption, a better societal infrastructure, and jobs.

7. US elected representatives who receive millions of dollars in election donations from pro-Zionist and other groups listed above who benefit from the status quo. Absence of the conflict in the Middle East could deprive them of ways to solicit funding from rich and politically active segments of their voter pool.

Three facts remain and provide the kernel for a re-evaluation of the current direction of political policy. First, these 'beneficiaries' are a tiny minority of the mass of humanity adversely affected by the continuation of this conflict. Second, five of the eight million Palestinians remain refugees or displaced people prevented from going back to their homes and lands. Third, Israel, established to provide a safe haven for Jews, is ironically the only place where Jews are under threat and subjected to violence.

It is time for the remainder of us, who do not benefit from the continuation of this tragic conflict, to support a solution based on human rights and not the current balance of power. This, by definition, implies basic rights such as the right of refugees to return to their homes and lands, abandoning nationalistic and supremacist philosophies, and building pluralistic societies. If this is achieved in Israel/Palestine it will result in a domino effect that will cause a dramatic shift in the repressive Arab regimes which will no longer have that most crucial 'crutch'. But even if they resist change, the tremendous savings and economic development released by the two most highly educated people in the Middle East (the Israelis and Palestinians) will undoubtedly result in dramatic and positive ripples across the globe. There need not be any losers but only winners. Understanding the obstacles is a first step towards a solution.

WE HAVE BEEN THERE, DONE THAT

A historian records events in the past and makes comparisons. Politicians try to do their bit to address conflicts based on their nationalistic, religious, or other narrow interests. Intellectuals try to dissect motivations, shed some light on events, and understand things based on their readings. The media present things in ways that sometimes are clearly biased, sometimes fair, and most of the time superficial. Activists of different persuasions try to influence perceptions and the course of future events. It is to this last group I believe all of us should belong.

The history of the Holy Land over the past 100 years and histories of similar struggles in South Africa and elsewhere prove the futility of:

- Acquisition of territory by force;
- Suppression, removal, and isolation of natives;
- Attempts to claim divine or other religious 'rights' to land;
- Ignorance of human rights and basic legal standards (including international law);
- Violence as a method of terrorizing, control, and/or suppression of resistance;
- Ignoring the potential of multiethnic, multi-religious, and multicultural societies with basic human rights protected.

Yet, this history also proves the power of ideas, compassion, and collective work in advancing agendas (good or bad). It is time for the people of the land of Canaan (Israel/Palestine), with the support of all peace- and justice-loving people across the globe, to work to ensure peace, justice, and equality among all the people. An example manifesto of ten principles/sections that provides a framework for peace is shown in Exhibit 5. This draft is just one of many possible scenarios for coexistence and equality. Solutions based on human rights require very hard work and will run against opposition. Grass-root activism by non-violent means (boycotts, education, etc.) can make human rights a centerpiece for future arrangements for a peaceful resolution.

Earlier chapters have detailed, as Amnesty International has stated, that peace is elusive because the program imposed in Oslo ignores basic human rights and international law (see Chapters 11 and 12). To obtain peace, we have to address basic human rights as enunciated in the Universal Declaration of Human Rights. These rights may occasionally conflict with some interpretations or applications of narrow nationalism. In the opening chapters of this book, we described the background to the Israel/Palestine question, and in Chapters 6 and 7 we discussed the issues surrounding Zionism as a failed solution to the problem of anti-Jewish sentiment and how Zionism in practice has produced a set of laws that are discriminatory to non-Jews and are the mirror image of South African apartheid laws. Chapter 10 showed the environmental and societal impact of the conflict, especially in terms of putting political causes ahead of sustainable development in the tiny area of Israel/Palestine. We also explained how the Israeli, US, British, and Arab governments have largely played a negative role in bringing about peace in the Middle East, simply because they put narrow political interests and narrow nationalistic agendas ahead of human rights, sustainable development, and international collaboration. The world is moving towards dissolving borders, more international collaboration, and more communications. Some, like many in the US government, want to maintain narrow nationalism while implementing capital globalization to benefit multinational corporations. Others want this trend to move towards curbing multinational corporations, redistributing wealth, and ensuring sustainable global development (e.g. the Kyoto Accords). This is not the place to discuss these but I would only say that regardless of power plays, borders are dissolving, nationalism is becoming less important, and populations are mixing as never before. This is a trend that I think all agree will continue.

In light of this, let us examine what it means to be a Zionist or a Palestinian Arab nationalist. Zionists include Christian Zionists who support the ingathering of the Jews for their own reasons. To Zionists, whether secular or religious Jews, Israel means having a nation, a center of passion and attachment, a revived language (Hebrew), and all the benefits of a modern state that is 'ours' (as Zionists like to explain). It also means investing assets, whether donated by Jews or received from the West, in a 'Jewish homeland'. These funds and energies have been channeled into building institutions, infrastructure, an army, and all the trappings of a nation-state. This has already succeeded regardless of whether the non-Jewish natives of Palestine have had to pay the price and regardless of what the future holds. Israel is now well established as a nation with a language and a culture, regardless of what one thinks about the legitimacy of this establishment and its colonizing activities. Yes, Israel was established by the aggressive and the violent brand of Zionism initiated in the 1840s by Britain and later encouraged and supported by the western countries. And yes, after the Nazi era, the western countries were more amenable to support the Zionist program and the Zionist program took on a life of its own. On occasion this program even came into conflict with its western parents (e.g. Britain in 1939 and the US in 1956). Yet, western countries have avoided any serious challenge to Israeli policy and refrained from talking about human rights when that means Palestinian human rights.

This has created a sense of invincibility and power among Israeli leaders that has allowed them to ignore international law and human rights even in agreements they have signed (e.g. the Fourth Geneva Convention, the Oslo Accords). On occasion Israeli leaders have even challenged the great powers that make their existence possible. This is seen in the challenge to the British White Paper of 1939 and settlement expansion against the wishes of the US government. Yet, Israel exists as a Jewish state because Levi Eshkol's and Martin Buber's brand of Zionism failed. Zionism without massive ethnic cleansing of the Palestinian natives, a Zionism that is of a humane, multicultural, and multi-religious nature would not have allowed for the establishment of a Jewish state in a land already occupied. The mainstream Zionists (whether Labor or Likud, Ben-Gurion or Sharon) with help from Christian Zionists and non-Zionists wanted not only a Zionist culture and language and economy but also military power. Power they achieved. But mainstream Zionists also wanted a state that would be a safe haven for Jews and eventually become 'normalized'. Early Zionist visions were based on a strong, safe state as an antidote to anti-Semitism. In this goal, one could argue that the presence of Israel does not contribute to dispelling anti-Jewish feelings and that hatred will continue to grow unless justice is enacted for the victims of Zionism, the Palestinians. Israel in a sea of dispossessed and disenfranchised Palestinians simply cannot survive, while a state with equality and justice for the Palestinians can expand and grow economically and spiritually and in every other way.

Palestinians for their part were mostly a peasant society but with enough intellectuals and leaders to realize at an early stage what the Zionist plans were. Palestinians were simply in the way of realizing the Zionist visions of a country that is entirely Jewish 'like England is English'. This would be a nation in which Jews are in the majority, run the affairs of government, and have unique laws such as considering land ownership for the Jewish nation (Am Yisrael), and are granted automatic citizenship and automatic rights to land and subsidies denied to non-Jews. As explained earlier, Eretz Yisrael (the Land of Israel, really the land of Canaan) was densely populated by the descendants of the Canaanites and other groups. These are natives who mostly spoke Arabic and who identified with Judaism, Christianity, or Islam. As a result of the Zionist program, the population of Christians and Muslims in Palestine/the land of Canaan became refugees or dispossessed people. Palestinians stubbornly demanded their rights enshrined in international law and UN resolutions (including the right of return and self-determination). While it would be a mischaracterization to state that Israel has always been the belligerent party or that Palestinians and Arab countries are always innocent, it would be equally wrong to state that somehow there is parity between Israelis and Palestinians or between the colonizers and the colonized. Having said that, what do Palestinians want and what will they be content with? The simple answer is given by looking at where they are now: nine million people without a country of their own, most of them dispossessed of their lands and properties, and most of them impoverished. A basic element of justice would be to restore what was taken from them. Understanding history is important to understanding how to resolve the key issues of refugees, borders, settlements, self-determination, and equality.

THE POWER OF COEXISTENCE AND NON-VIOLENT DIRECT ACTION

The Palestinians, as victims of dispossession, have negligible military power and are dispersed and impoverished. But even if they acquire some might, they would be wise to recognize the power of non-violent actions, the power of coexistence, and grassroots empowerment among all people fighting for their basic rights. Israelis, having accumulated tremendous political, military, and economic might, must realize the limits of this power and the futility of continued oppression and domination. They too must learn to use the power of non-violence, the power of logic and coexistence, rather than the power of tanks and missiles. As Edward Said wrote:

> The third way avoids both the bankruptcy of Oslo and the retrograde policies of total boycotts. It must begin in terms of the idea of citizenship, not nationalism, since the notion of separation (Oslo) and of triumphalist unilateral theocratic nationalism whether Jewish or Muslim simply does not deal with the realities before us. Therefore, a concept of citizenship whereby

every individual has the same citizen's rights, based not on race or religion, but on equal justice for each person guaranteed by a constitution, must replace all our outmoded notions of how Palestine will be cleansed of the others' enemies.[10]

Since its inception, Zionism has relied on the western powers to grant it legitimacy and keep it alive. This started with Great Britain in the 1840s through the Balfour Declaration of 1917 and continued with US support in the UN Security Council. Having actively participated in 'cleansing' the land of its native inhabitants to set the stage for increased Zionist colonization, Israeli leaders dealt with all issues efficiently except the persistent problem of a Palestinian presence. Interestingly, while ignoring the remaining Palestinians and discriminating against them, the same leadership may have left open the option of coexistence and of returning Palestinians expelled. After all, how does one explain that the majority of Palestinian village lands are still vacant, including Deir Yassin? Many have been turned into national parks and 'green areas'. One would hope that deep down the Israeli leadership realize that Israel will remain ephemeral no matter how strong it becomes unless justice is restored. They perhaps know that one day, a post-Zionist era will come and which will liberate them from dependence on the West. While initially believing Palestinians were an 'inconvenience' or that the refugees would eventually settle elsewhere, Israeli leaders were unpleasantly surprised at the turn of events and the strength of the Palestinian will not only to survive as individuals, but also as a people.

Many in Israeli society remain isolated, protected, and ignorant of what it takes to bring peace. Many thus simply have given up and see solutions based on continued domination or separation, expulsions, building walls, and other harsh means. These moves are justified by arguing that the demands of the other side are too extreme. Reconciling the two groups requires rethinking assumptions and mythologies as we attempted to do in earlier chapters. To Israeli Jews, 1948 was the birth of a new nation, a heroic war of independence. To Palestinians, May 14, 1948 marks *Al-Nakba* (the catastrophe) when they commemorate their expulsion, lost lands, homes, relatives and a country. To those who believe in Zionism, Zionist aspirations created a Jewish homeland that connected it to Israelite history. Old Zionist hearts still beat stronger every time they set foot in Ben-Gurion International airport after a trip abroad.

To Palestinians, their exclusion, alienation, and subjugation are so strong that their heart beats faster when they see a Palestinian flag or symbolism of Zionist success, whether the flag of the Star of David or a border crossing with Israeli soldiers or a settlement on Palestinian land.

In his excellent analysis *The Question of Palestine*, Edward Said concluded:

> The irreducible and functional meaning of being a Palestinian has meant living through Zionism first as a method of acquiring Palestine, second as a method for dispossessing and exiling Palestinians, and third as a method for maintaining Israel as a state in which Palestinians are treated as non-Jews, and from which politically they remain exiles despite (in the case of the 650,000 Israeli-Palestinian citizens) [now 1.3 million] their continued presence on the land.[11]

A large segment of the population on both sides still lives in the past. Many Israeli Jews believe they can maintain racist laws in a western-implemented, self-proclaimed 'democratic Jewish state', while ignoring, or at best managing, the Palestinians. Many Palestinians still believe that it is possible to reconstitute an Arab or even a wholly Muslim Palestine and reverse the wheels of history.

PSYCHOLOGICAL AND PHYSICAL APARTHEID

Adding to the physical apartheid implemented by Israel and documented in detail elsewhere in this book, there is a great deal of psychological apartheid. Unlike the physical apartheid constructed unilaterally, psychological apartheid has walls constructed from both sides. These shield people from the reality of the other side and also prevent introspection on their own shortcomings. Both the psychological and physical apartheid walls must be removed if there is ever to be a viable future for all.

Palestinians have been subjected to cruel and unreasonable treatment for so many years that many have begun to doubt that justice is achievable and many certainly believe coexistence impossible. Similarly, in so far as many Israelis have felt embattled and attacked many also feel that coexistence is impossible. A defeatist attitude has developed and envelops some Palestinians and Israelis and many of their supporters. But if the societies do not coexist peacefully, they will perish as rival primitive societies.

There appears to have been little thought given to what is best for the community as a whole, which would then also benefit the individual. The resources are foolishly perceived as finite and many ideologues perceive the conflict as a zero-sum game. A few politically oriented people are viciously fighting over control and power instead of devoting their efforts to providing for economic growth, employment, and other features of a viable society.

A sense of hopelessness and desperation leaves many looking for 'crumbs' of both material and psychological 'food'. This is especially stressful when combined with the deep commitment by many to historical myths of grandeur or glory. I am not going to spend much time on the history of the Jewish, Arabic, and Islamic civilizations (volumes have been written on these). Suffice it to say that our psychological profile is one that contrasts our existing condition with the perceived greatness of our ancestors and prophets. We thus assume that we are a privileged group but this immediately contrasts with what we observe to be the difficult current situation described throughout this book. This is especially true for the Palestinian people who are dispossessed. We can address the bigger issues of why 1.3 billion Muslims or 300 million Arabs (Muslims and Christians) have so little to say in the direction of world economies and social and cultural developments so dominated now by the US as the sole remaining superpower. But perhaps this too can be resolved once the friction in Israel/Palestine is resolved. Imagine the example set if this one place, previously an example of violence, endemic hatred, and tribalism, could transcend all this to build a truly shining example of coexistence and non-violence. Imagine the billions of dollars spent on armaments going to desalinate seawater, build high-tech industries, and truly harness the great minds of the inhabitants (Jews, Christians, and Muslims) for positive developments.

Of course, people do cling to the past, their emotions, and their tribalism. They cannot simply discard all connection to the past and suddenly adopt logical and pragmatic approaches to solve conflicts. But fortunately it is possible to evolve gradually as we appear to be doing in this new information age. We need not ignore history, but we do need to decide what to emphasize in this history. Should we emphasize the prosperity, peace, and unity that Islam and the Arabic civilization brought to the Middle East? Or should we mourn the loss of the diversity of languages and cultures that existed before that? Should we emphasize the tolerance and coexistence of Jews, Christians, and Muslims (e.g. in Spain or Al-Andalus)? Or should we emphasize the oppression of Assyrian Christians and the genocide of Romanian Christians by the Ottoman Turks? Should we discuss the ethnic cleansing of some Canaanites by invading Hebrews? Or should we talk about the coexistence, trade, and neighborly relations in the Kingdom of Israel at the time of Solomon and David? Should we talk about the golden era of Arab sciences, mathematics, medicine, astronomy, and law? Or should we speak of the occasional problematical behavior of some Muslim rulers (e.g. in India with the suppression of Buddhism and Hinduism)? Should we celebrate the incredible ability of the monotheistic religions to make people work together for good deeds and as a team of devout people looking to better human life on this earth? Or should we mourn the loss of individualism that ensues from the dogmatic practices of these religions? Or should we talk about how all religions have been used to abuse basic human rights and to engage in war crimes. Examples include the Crusades, the colonization of the so-called New World under the banner of Christianity, ethnic cleansing by Israel of non-Jews in 1947–49 under the banner of Judaism, Taliban atrocities in Afghanistan, and Osama Bin Laden under the banner of Islam.

Perhaps we need to teach children to value themselves, value teamwork, respect others, and defend the rights of minorities. This is not as simple as it seems. Adults need to learn to accept, in a very positive fashion, views that are foreign to them. In other words, someone who expresses his views should be listened to and respected regardless of how sacred the 'holy cows' are. Would you be willing to listen rationally to a view radically different from your own on your religion or your way of doing things? Would you be willing to defend wholeheartedly the right of that person to present his view?

Truth is usually the first casualty of war. Few ask why Palestinians are resisting, why Israelis are so fearful, what really separates them, and what really unites them. While fixated on 'violence', history and context are lost, as is rational discourse. Investigations by Amnesty International, Human Rights Watch, Physicians for Human Rights, the UN, and Israeli human rights groups go unreported and their recommendations unheeded. Even details of what has taken place in the negotiations and the core issues remain hidden from public view and replaced by rhetoric and political babble.

The people in the land of Canaan and even in the US have been shielded from reality, from the importance of human rights and developing enforced international legal norms. Thus it is not surprising that when asked, 'do you support or oppose the continuing assassination policy in the territories by Israeli security forces?' 77 percent of Israeli Jews said yes. Assassinations are prohibited under international law. The majority of Israeli Jews supported the incursions into Lebanese and Palestinian territory even when these resulted in massive civilian deaths. It is instructive that 56 percent believed that the main purpose of the incursions of April 2001 was to warn the Palestinians (i.e. collective punishment), while 26 percent believed the main purpose was the elimination of the terrorist infrastructure, and 13 percent believed the operation had both purposes. The rest had no view on the matter. Sixty-one percent of Israeli Jews believe that all means are legitimate in the 'war against terror', even those forbidden by law, while 34 percent believe that the means must be legal.[12] Similarly, the majority of Palestinians under Israeli occupation supported suicide bombings inside Israel in polls conducted in 2001 (the reverse of 1996). These statistics afford some understanding of how mass psychology can be so easily manipulated to ignore human rights.

AN INEVITABLE SOLUTION

A just peace based on self-determination and the right of return was proposed in a UN General Assembly resolution on July 21, 1976. During the first phase of the plan, Palestinians displaced in 1967 would be allowed to return immediately to the occupied West Bank, including eastern Jerusalem, and the Gaza Strip. At the same time, preparations would be made for the return of Palestinians displaced in 1948 to their places of origin inside Israel. These would include designation or creation of a competent agency to be entrusted with the organizational and logistical aspects of the mass return of displaced Palestinians; creation and financing of a fund for that purpose; and registration of displaced Palestinians other than those already registered with UNRWA. Following the completion of these preparations the second phase of the plan would facilitate the return of refugees to their places of origin now inside Israel. Palestinians not choosing to return would be paid just and equitable compensation, as provided for in UN Resolution 194.

There are three possible resolutions to a colonialist situation. The first is to expel the colonizers and return sovereignty to the natives, as happened in Algeria. The second is the complete or near-complete annihilation of the native population, as happened in Australia and North America. The third is the abolition of the privileges of the colonizers and the creation of a democratic, egalitarian system anchored in a constitution guaranteeing equality, with the complete abolition of all forms of discrimination against the natives, along with the establishment of a framework capable of creating a pluralistic society. It is this process that is currently evolving in South Africa.

As the economies of Palestine and Israel continue to suffer and the illusions of peace based on apartheid dissipate, more people will come to see the futility of the previously offered scenarios. Some still cling to the notion that colonizers can be removed as the Algerians did with the French settlers and Palestine will be redeemed as an Arab Islamic state. In the meantime, the Zionist state of Israel is unable to comply with democratic standards or extricate itself from an ever-deepening quagmire. It chooses neither to evolve into a pluralistic society nor to repeat its methods of ethnic cleansing practiced in 1947–49. Many still delude themselves that Israel is a 'Jewish democracy'. In South Africa, the cooperation of some whites and blacks with economic pressure from outside was needed to move South Africa to a post-apartheid state. In the land of Canaan, Jews, Christians, and Muslims working together to make the change with pressure from outside is needed and is beginning to show some progress. A durable peace can and should be based on an elemental understanding of history, reality, morality, and justice. More and more people are beginning to see the outline of how this peace can be achieved. I have drafted such an outline based on discussion with hundreds of activists over the years (see Exhibit 5). This is merely to open the discussion and provide points for visualizing a new land of Canaan.

Those who think the Israeli/Palestinian conflict is a never-ending war because 'these people have been killing each other for ages' or that such visions are too idealistic are ignorant of history. Britain and France have fought each other in many wars, including the 100 Years War, but now it is unthinkable to imagine a resurgence of conflict between those two great powers. The Berlin Wall came down and apartheid in South Africa was dismantled. The 100-year conflict in the Middle East remains one of the few conflicts of the twenty-first century left to be resolved but is not unresolvable. I argue that a grass-roots movement can effect change that will result in a win-win situation for people of the land of Canaan. The guiding goals of such a grass-roots movement for peace should be based on justice and equality. Here are the goals:

Ultimate Goals:
1. The right of return for refugees to their homes, farms, businesses, and lands (include restitution, and compensation for suffering).
2. A pluralistic democracy in Israel/Palestine with equality and human rights for all.
3. An end to all acts of violence.

Intermediate Goals:
1. To develop more governmental and public support for the ultimate goals. Currently, significant support exists in most places except the governments and media of Israel and the US.
2. To use economic and public relations tools of divestment and economic boycotts (as happened in South Africa)
3. To press governments providing military and economic aid to stop military aid and condition economic aid on implementation of international law and human rights.

Short-term Goals:
1. To develop community members and structures to identify with this vision.
2. To engage in efforts of education and alliance building.
3. To ensure fair media coverage and exposure with a concerted media strategy and action.
4. To provide direct relief and humanitarian aid to those suffering from human rights abuses.

Breaking through the conundrums humans have created is not easy. It requires transcending a part of our selves that may seem familiar and reassuring. Learning to live together, while initially uncomfortable, can lead to a new way of thinking. Joseph Campbell wrote in 1968:

Today, the walls and towers of the culture-world that then were in the building are dissolving ... But of course, on the other hand, for those who can still contrive to live within the fold of a traditional mythology of some kind, protection is still afforded against the dangers of an individual life; and for many the possibility of adhering in this way to established formulas is a birthright they rightly cherish, since it will contribute meaning and nobility to their unadventured lives, ... and to those for whom such protection seems a prospect worthy of all sacrifice, and orthodox mythology will afford both the patterns and the sentiments of a lifetime of good repute.

However, for those to whom such living would be not life, but anticipated death, the circumvallating mountains that to others appear to be of stone are recognized as of the mist of dream, and precisely between their God and Devil, heaven and hell, white and black, the man of heart walks through. Out beyond those walls, in the uncharted forest night, where the terrible wind of God blows directly on the questing undefended soul, tangled ways may lead to madness. They may also lead, however, as one of the greatest poets of the Middle Ages tells, to 'all those things that go to make heaven and earth.'[13]

It is indeed a journey of awakening at the individual level that is not only spiritual, but requires concrete action to bring true peace and justice to fruition. We Canaanites, who invented the alphabet, domesticated animals and developed agriculture, and made this arid land into a land of milk and honey, surely can do this. An Arab poet wrote '*Itha Asha'bu yawman Arad al-hayata fala budda an Yastijeeb al-qadar. Wala budda lillayal an Yanjali wala budda li-thulm an yankasir.*' Roughly translated, it means: If the people one day strive for life, then ultimately destiny will respond and the night will give way and the injustice will be broken. The path to peace is not served by the creation of more states or unjust 'fixes' to perceived demographic 'problems'. It has to do with justice and the implementation of human rights and international law. It requires grass-roots action to accelerate its arrival but it is the only solution possible in the long tern. We can either remain locked in our old mythological and tribal ways, or we can envision a better future and work for it. The choice is obvious.

Exhibit 5. Draft Framework

Section 1. The Land and the People: The land of Canaan includes as a minimum the land west of the River Jordan bordered in the east by Jordan, in the south by Egypt, on the north by Lebanon and Syria. Including Jordan in this arrangement is highly desirable. The people of this land are those who resided in this area naturally, including Palestinian refugees and their descendants. International law recognizes the right of refugees to return to their homes and lands. While native rights supersede any privilege or land given to immigrants who came under the banner of Zionism by the unjust Israeli 'law of [Jewish] return', the new immigrants who arrived as such and willing to coexist as equal will be recognized and treated equally under the laws. While correcting past injustices, appropriate measures will be taken to ensure minimal internal dislocation and no external dislocation for anyone wishing to continue to reside in peace and equality in the state.

Section 2. Equality before the law: All instituted laws that discriminate among citizens based on religion, ethnicity, gender, or age are considered null and void. Based on constitutional principles, all individuals must and will be treated equally.

Section 3. Self-determination and self-governance: Self-determination is a key concept in international law and the UN Charter. Since the two-state resolution adopted by the UN in 1947 violated this principle by not consulting the local inhabitants and later events made it impossible to implement, it is not considered a basis for a solution. The people of the land (Palestinians and Israelis) will be reconstituted with the rights of the dispossessed Palestinians to return to their homes and lands. At that point, all the people will have the right of collective self-determination with guarantees by the international community for plurality and democracy.

Section 4. Freedom of religion: The state throughout its institutions shall uphold freedom of religion and worship. Holy sites for all religions will be protected by law. Custody of holy sites shall be with the respective religious authorities with any disputes addressed through an independent judiciary system (see section 6).

Section 5. Relationship of state and religious institutions: There shall be separation between religious matter and governmental state matters. No person shall have privilege (in employment, housing, access to government, services, or any other privilege) based on religious beliefs or lack thereof. Religious institutions and the state authorities shall be free to operate within the boundaries of the adopted constitution without infringing individual or religious rights. Parliament shall prohibit parties from running unless their membership is open to people of all religions.

Section 6. State powers: There shall be legislative, executive, and judiciary powers each separate and independent.

6.1. A democratically elected legislative council (parliament) shall decide laws pertaining to all aspects of state without infringement on the rights of minorities or instituting any laws that violate basic human rights as declared by the Universal Declaration of Human Rights (which shall be considered part of this framework). The parliament shall also select any state insignia, national regalia, or other symbolic structures as deemed appropriate, but without infringing on the rights of one or other ethnic or religious groups.

6.2. Executive power shall be vested in the office of the elected president and the cabinet. The cabinet and the president shall run the affairs of the state in accordance with state laws and in compliance with relevant international laws.

6.3. Judiciary: The judicial power shall be vested in one Supreme Court and all state courts as ordained and established by the parliament. Judges for the Supreme Court shall be elected by the parliament. Term of office will be decided by the constitution. The judicial power shall cover all cases arising as a result of the constitution adopted by parliament, other adopted laws by parliament (including judging if such laws violate constitutional principles), and issues under obligation of international treaties.

Section 7. People first: The purpose of state government is government by the people and for the people. Human rights shall be the foundation of state laws. Many of these inalienable human rights are codified in the Universal Declaration of Human Rights (UDHR). Adherence to all provisions of the UDHR shall be a primary objective in building a constitution with a bill of rights.

Section 8. Truth Commission: Upon return of displaced persons and refugees, abolition of discriminatory laws, and elections to a national parliament, a truth commission will be established (elected by members of the new parliament) which will address all issues of injustices committed. This includes acts of violence committed against civilians, forced removal, property rights, and any other issues that may be brought before it for adjuration. It will be charged with minimizing any repercussions and forgiving individuals who committed crimes for which they now freely admit.

Section 9. Violence: We recognize acts of terrors as reprehensible whether exploding bombs in civilian areas, shelling neighborhoods, demolishing homes or any other act of terror. The Israeli occupation and colonization practices are by definition violence. Assassination (extra-judicial execution) is violence prohibited by international law. Having nuclear weapons, biological and chemical warfare capabilities is also abhorrent. We are not naive to believe that it is possible to obtain and implement a mutual renunciation of all violence especially while occupation and oppression remains. But efforts must be made to reduce the violence by implementing justice and equality and building trust. We believe the alternative vision and program presented above is the best course of action to move in that direction.

Section 10. International guarantees and place in the world: Our land and people are integral part of the area of the Middle East broadly defined with significant cultural, religious, and ethnic ties to other parts of the Middle East. This is also an area of great significance to Christianity, Islam, and Judaism. Thus, there must be effective guarantees of security, liberties and freedoms not only for the local people but also by them with international guarantees, support, and guidance for other interests and access to this center of human heritage. Further, this conflict was used as pretext for lack of progress to democracy in the region. By showing the example of living together in harmony, equality, and democracy, we can provide an example to a world ravaged by lack of democracy, and ethnic, religious, and national strife. Truly, we then can become what many religious traditions instruct: an example to the world.

RECOMMENDED READING

Naim Stifan Ateek and Rosemary Radford Ruether, *Justice and Only Justice: A Palestinian Theology of Liberation* (New York: Orbis Books, 1990).

Alice and Staughton Lynd (eds.), *Nonviolence in America: A Documentary History* (New York: Orbis Books, 1995).

Tanya Reinhart, *Israel/Palestine: How to End the War of 1948* (New York: Seven Stories Press, 2002).

Gene Sharp, *The Politics of Nonviolent Action* (Boston: Porter-Sargent, 1973).

Nancy Stohlman and Laurieann Aladin, *Live from Palestine: International and Palestinian Direct Action against the Occupation* (Cambridge, Mass.: South End Press, 2003).

Notes

CHAPTER 2

1. Good summaries can be found in Nelson Glueck, *Deities and Dolphins: The Story of the Nabataeans* (New York: Farrar, Straus & Giroux, Inc., 1965); Philip C. Hammond, *The Nabataeans: Their History, Culture and Archaeology* (Philadelphia: Coronet Books, 1973).
2. Jean Starcky, 'The Nabateans: A Historical Sketch', *The Biblical Archaeologist*, Vol. XVIII (December 1955).
3. Beatrice Gruendler, *Development of the Arabic Scripts: From the Nabatean Era to the First Islamic Century According to Dated Texts* (Otterup: Scholars Press, 1993).
4. Donald Harden, *The Phoenicians* (New York: Frederick A. Praeger, 1962).
5. Walter E. Rast, *Through the Ages in Palestinian Archaeology* (Philadelphia: Trinity Press International, 1992).
6. Donald B. Redford, *Egypt, Canaan and Israel in Ancient Times* (Princeton, NJ: Princeton University Press, 1992).
7. See, for instance, Israel Finkelstein and Neil Asher Silberman, *The Bible Unearthed: Archaeology's New Vision of Ancient Israel and the Origin of Its Sacred Texts* (New York: The Free Press, 2001); A.D. Marcus, *The View from Nebo, How Archeology is Rewriting the Bible and Reshaping the Middle East* (Boston: Little, Brown, 2000); Thomas L. Thompson, *The Mythic Past: Biblical Archaeology and the Myth of Israel* (New York: Basic Books, 2000); Keith W. Whitelam, *The Invention of Ancient Israel: The Silencing of Palestinian History* (London and New York: Routledge, 1996).
8. Karen Armstrong, *A History of God: the 4000-year Quest of Judaism, Christianity, and Islam* (New York: Alfred A. Knopf, 1993).
9. Ibid., p. 23.
10. John W. Mulhall, CSP, *America and the Founding of Israel: An Investigation of the Morality of America's Role*; available at http://www.al-bushra.org/America/0america.html.
11. F. Donner McGraw, *The Early Islamic Conquests* (Princeton, NJ: Princeton University Press, 1981).
12. M. Gill, *A History of Palestine* (Cambridge: Cambridge University Press, 1992), pp. 643–1099. Also S. Hadawi, *Bitter Harvest, A Modern History of Palestine*, fourth edition (New York: Olive Branch Press, 1991).
13. Edward W. Said, *The Question of Palestine* (New York: Vintage Books, 1992), pp. 10–11.
14. http://www.palestinecostumearchive.org/; see also Leila El Khalidi, *The Art of Palestinian Embroidery* (London: Saqi Books, 2000); Shelagh Weir and Serene Shahid, *Palestinian Embroidery* (London: British Museum, 1988); and Jehan Rajab, *Palestinian Costume* (London: Kegan Paul,

1989).   http://palestinianembroider.tripod.com/.   http://www.fortune city.com/boozers/durham/224/dresses.html.

15. Ahad Ha-Am, 1891, quoted in Rashid Khalidi, *Palestinian Identity: The Construction of Modern National Consciousness* (New York: Columbia University Press, 1997), p. 101.

CHAPTER 3

1. Promotional material from The Centre for Genetic Anthropology, Departments of Anthropology and of Biology, University College London. Posted at http://www.ucl.ac.uk/tcga/.

2. Robin McKie, 'Journal Axes Gene Research on Jews and Palestinians', *Observer*, November 25, 2001. Also available at http://www.observer. co.uk/international/story/0,6903,605798,00.html.

3. Antonion Arnaiz-Villena et al., 'The Origin of Palestinians and their Genetic Relatedness with other Mediterranean Populations', *Human Immunology*, Vol. 62, No. 9 (2001), pp. 889–900.

4. Avraham Amar et al., 'Molecular Analysis of HLA Class II Polymorphisms among Different Ethnic Groups in Israel', *Human Immunology*, Vol. 60 (1999), pp. 723–30.

5. Marc Perelman, 'Palestinian Gene Study Breeds Scandal', *Forward*, November 30, 2001, pp. 7–18, available also at http://www.forward. com/issues/2001/01.11.30/news7.html.

6. *Jewish Genetic Diseases: A Mazornet Guide*. Available in publication form and also at http://www.mazornet.com/genetics/.

7. Batsheva Bonne-Tamir and Avinoam Adam, *Genetic Diversity among Jews: Diseases and Markers at the DNA Level* (Oxford: Oxford University Press, 1992).

8. Center for Jewish Genetic Diseases, Mount Sinai School of Medicine. Promotional material and web at http://www.nfjgd.org/.

9. J. Travis, *Science News 151* (February 15, 1997), p. 106.

10. *New York Times*, May 9, 2000.

11. M.F. Hammer et al., 'Jewish and Middle Eastern non-Jewish Populations Share a Common Pool of Y-chromosome Biallelic Haplotypes', *Proceedings of the National Academy of Science*, Vol. 97, No. 12 (2000), pp. 6769–74. http://www.pnas.org/cgi/content/full/97/12/6769.

12. Almut Nebel et al., 'The Y Chromosome Pool of Jews as Part of the Genetic Landscape of the Middle East', *American Journal of Human Genetics*, Vol. 69, No. 5 (2001), pp. 1095–112.

13. K. Skorecki et al., 'Y Chromosomes of Jewish Priests', *Nature*, Vol. 385 (1997), p. 32.

14. M.G. Thomas et al., 'Origins of Old Testament Priests', *Nature*, Vol. 394 (1998), p. 138.

15. *Jerusalem Post*, February 28, 2001.

16. A. Zoossmann-Diskin, 'Are Today's Jewish Priests Descended from the Old Ones?' [Stammen die heutigen jüdischen Priester von den alten ab?], *HOMO: Journal of Comparative Human Biology* [*Zeitschrift fuer Vergleichende Biologie des Menschen*], Vol. 51, Nos. 2–3 (2000), pp. 156–62.

17. Hammer et al., 'Jewish and Middle Eastern non-Jewish Populations ...'.
18. Martin Richards, 'Beware the Gene Genies', *Guardian*, February 21, 2003. See also The American Center of Khazar Studies for compilation of genetic data. http://www.khazaria.com.
19. E.S. Poloni, O. Semino, G. Passarino, A.S. Santachiara Benercetti, I. DuPanloup, A. Langaney, and L. Excoffier, 'Human Genetic Affinities for Y Chromosome p49a,f/TaqI Haplotypes Show Strong Correspondence with Linguistics', *American Journal of Human Genetics*, Vol. 61, No. 5 (1997), pp. 1015–935.
20. Arthur Koestler, *The Thirteenth Tribe: The Khazar Empire and its Heritage* (London: Random House, 1976).
21. Kevin Brook, *The Khazars: A European Experiment in Jewish Statecraft*. Published on the web by the Hagshama Department of the World Zionist Organization. See http://www.wzo.org.il/en/resources/view.asp?id=140, and also Kevin Brook, *Are Russian Jews Descended from the Khazars? A Reassessment Based upon the Latest Historical, Archaeological, Linguistic, and Genetic Evidence*, posted at http://www.khazaria.com/khazar-diaspora.html.

CHAPTER 4

1. Nur Masalha, *Expulsion of the Palestinians: The Concept of 'Transfer' in Zionist Political Thought, 1882–1948* (Washington, DC: Institute for Palestine Studies, 1992).
2. Justin McCarthy, *The Population of Palestine* (New York: Columbia University Press, 1980), p.10, quoting adjusted Ottoman figures; Clifford A. Wright, *Facts and Fables: The Arab–Israeli Conflict* (London and New York: Kegan Paul International, 1989); Rashid Khalidi, in Edward Said and Christopher Hitchens (eds.), *Blaming the Victims* (London and New York: Verso Books, 2001).
3. Michael J. Cohen, *The Origin and Evolution of the Arab–Zionist Conflict* (Berkeley: The University of California Press, 1989), p. 90.
4. Salman Abu Sitta, *The Palestinian Nakba 1948, The Register of Depopulated Localities in Palestine* (London: The Palestinian Return Centre, 2000).
5. Benny Morris, *The Birth of the Palestinian Refugee Problem, 1947–1949* (New York: Cambridge University Press, 1987).
6. Benny Morris, *Israel's Border Wars, 1949–1956: Arab Infiltration, Israeli Retaliation and the Countdown to the Suez War* (Oxford: Clarendon Press, 1993); Benny Morris, *The Birth of the Palestinian Refugee Problem, 1947–1948* (Cambridge: Middle East Library, 1987, 1989); Bennis Morris, *Correcting a Mistake – Jews and Arabs in Palestine/Israel, 1936–1956* (Tel Aviv: Am Oved Publishers, 2000).
7. Menachem Begin, *The Revolt: Story of the Irgun* (New York: Henry Shuman Inc., 1951); also cited in Fawaz Turki, *The Disinherited: Journal of a Palestinian Exile*, second edition (New York: Monthly Review Press, 1974), p. 20.
8. Morris, *The Birth of the Palestinian Refugee Problem*, p. 27, and Masalha, *Expulsion of the Palestinians*, pp. 131–2.

9. Joseph Weitz, *Ha-Ma'avak 'al ha-adamah* (*The Struggle for the Land*), in Hebrew (Tel Aviv: N. Tverski, 1950), p. 6.

10. Masalha, *Expulsion of the Palestinians*, p. 117 quoting from Protocol of the Jewish Agency Executive meeting of June 12, 1938, Vol. 28, No. 53, Central Zionist Archives.

11. *Davar*, June 9, 1979.

12. Morris, *The Birth of the Palestinian Refugee Problem*, p. 222.

13. Salman Abu Sitta, 'Traces of Poison', *Al-Ahram*, February 27–March 5, 2003, http://weekly.ahram.org.eg/2003/627/focus.htm. Also in *Al-Haya*, February 1, 2003 [in Arabic]. Israel was the first to develop and use biological warfare in the Middle East.

14. Benny Morris, 'Response to Finkelstein and Masalha', *Journal of Palestine Studies*, Vol. 21, No. 1 (1991), pp. 98–114.

15. Benny Morris, 'Revisiting the Palestinian Exodus of 1948', in E.L. Rogan and A. Schlaim (eds.), *The War for Palestine: Rewriting the History of 1948* (New York: Cambridge University Press, 2001), pp. 37–59.

16. Joseph Weitz, *My Diary and Letters to the Children* (Ramat Gan, 1965), Vol. 2, p. 293.

17. *Haaretz*, November 3, 2000.

18. Dan Kurzman, *Soldier of Peace: The Life of Yitzhak Rabin, 1922–1995* (New York: HarperCollins, 1998), pp. 140–1.

19. Armitzur Ilan, *The Origin of the Arab–Israeli Arms Race: Arms, Embargo, Military Power and Decision in the 1948 Palestine War* (New York: New York University Press, 1996), p. 62.

20. David Ben-Gurion, IDF Archives, 121/50/172, translated and cited in Marwan Bishara, *Palestine/Israel: Peace or Apartheid* (London: Zed Books, 2001).

21. Don Peretz, 'The Arab Refugee Dilemma', *Foreign Affairs*, October 1954, pp. 137–8; cited in Turki, *The Disinherited*, pp. 22–3.

22. Tom Segev, *1949: The First Israelis*, trans. Arlen Neal Weinstein (New York: The Free Press, 1986).

23. Sami Hadawi, *Palestinian Rights and Losses in 1948* (London: Saqi Books, 1988).

24. Meron Benvenisti, *Sacred Landscape: The Buried History of the Holy Land since 1948* (Berkeley: University of California Press, 2000), p. 156.

25. Yoseph Elgazi in *Zo Hadareh*, July 30, 1975.

26. Israel Land Authority Report, Jerusalem 1962, quoted in Barukh Kimmerling, 'Land Conflict and Nation Building: A Sociological Study of the Territorial Factors in the Jewish–Arab Conflict' (Hebrew University thesis, mimeo, 1976), p. 233.

27. *Kol Ha'ir* Weekly Magazine, July 26, 2001, in Hebrew, translation at http://oznik.com/kolhair02.html.

28. UN Doc. Al 648, 1948.

29. *Jewish Newsletter*, New York, February 9, 1959, cited in Erskine Childers, 'The Other Exodus', *Spectator*, London, May 12, 1961.

30. Turki, *The Disinherited*, p. 77.

31. Surveys cited in Dr Adel Samareh, '*Al-Lajioun Al-Falastinyoun: Haq al-awda wa istidkhal al-hazima* [The Palestinian Refugees and the Inter-

nalization of Defeat] (California: Palestine Publishing Foundation, 2000).

32. The Israel/Palestine Center for Research and Information, August 2001, http://www.ipcri.org.

33. United Nations Economic and Social Council 'Report of the Human Rights Inquiry Commission established pursuant to commission resolution S-5/1 of 19 October 2000' E/CN.4/2001/12 published March 2001. Available at http://www.badil.org/Press/2001/press167-01.htm. But note that Palestinian rights are actually much more than what could be accommodated by paragraph 1D, as Palestinians have political rights, including that of self-determination, which are covered under other statutes of international law.

34. Questions of the violation of human rights in the occupied Arab territories including Palestine: Report on the situation of human rights in the Palestinian territories occupied since 1967, submitted by Mr Giorgio Giacomelli, Special Rapporteur, pursuant to Commission on Human Rights resolution 1993/2 A. See full report at http://www.hri.ca/fortherecord2000/documentation/commission/e-cn4-2000-25.htm.

35. Salman Abu Sitta, *From Refugees to Citizens at Home* (London: Palestine Land Society and the Palestinian Return Centre, 2001).

36. Rosemary Sayigh, *Palestinians: From Peasants to Revolutionaries, a Peoples History* (New York: Zed Books, 1979), p. 75.

37. Erskine B. Childers, 'The Other Exodus', *Spectator*, May 12, 1961, p. 672.

38. Sayigh, *Palestinians*, p. 64.

39. *The Journal of Palestine Studies*, Vol. 1, No. 4 (summer 1972), p. 144, citing *Yediot Aharanot*, April 4, 1972.

40. David Hirst, *The Gun and the Olive Branch: The Roots of Violence in the Middle East* (Berkeley: Thunder's Mouth Press, 2003).

41. Segev, *1949: the First Israelis*.

42. See *Chicago Daily News*, September 10–11, 1977; also see the *Oregonian*, Portland, July 18, 1977.

CHAPTER 5

1. Joseph Campbell, *The Masks of God: Creative Mythology* (New York: Viking Penguin Inc., 1968).

2. Keith W. Whitelam, *The Invention of Ancient Israel: The Silencing of Palestinian History* (London: Routledge, 1997).

3. Karen Armstrong, *Jerusalem: One City Three Faiths* (New York: Knopf, 1996), p. 228.

4. Ibid., p. 330.

5. Michael Bar-Zohar, *Ben-Gurion: A Biography* (New York: Delacorte Press, 1977).

6. Avi Shlaim, *The Politics of Partition: King Abdullah, the Zionist Movement, and Palestine* (Oxford: Oxford University Press, 1990).

7. Avi Shlaim, *Collusion across the Jordan: King Abdullah, the Zionist Movement, and the Partition of Palestine* (New York: Columbia University Press, 1988), p. 139.

8. Armstrong, *Jerusalem*, p. 403.

9. Amir S. Cheshin, Avi Melamed and Bill Hutman, *Separate and Unequal: The Inside Story of Israeli Rule in East Jerusalem* (Cambridge, Mass.: Harvard University Press, 2001).

CHAPTER 6

1. Mohameden Ould-Mey, 'The non-Jewish Origin of Zionism', *The Arab World Geographer*, Vol. 5 (2002), pp. 34–52.

2. Barbara W. Tuchman, *Bible and Sword: England and Palestine from the Bronze Age to Balfour* (New York: Ballantine Books, 1984).

3. 'Restoration of the Jews', *The Times*, August 17, 1840, p. 5, col. 6(f).

4. Lord Lindsay, *Letters on Egypt, Edom, and the Holy Land* (London: Henry Colburn, 1838), pp. 188–90.

5. L.J. Epstein, *Zion's Call: Christian Contributions to the Origins and Development of Israel* (New York: University Press of America, 1984).

6. George Gawler, *Tranquilization of Syria and the East: Observations and Practical Suggestions, in Furtherance of the Establishment of Jewish Colonies in Palestine, the Most Sober and Sensible Remedy for the Miseries of Asiatic Turkey* (1845), quoted in Ould-Mey, 'The non-Jewish Origin of Zionism'.

7. Epstein, *Zion's Call*.

8. 'Zionism versus Bolshevism: A Struggle for the Soul of the Jewish People', *Illustrated Sunday Herald*, February 8, 1920, reproduced in Lenni Brenner, *51 Documents: Zionist Collaboration with the Nazis* (New Jersey: Barricade, 2002), p. 27.

9. Translated from the German by Dr D.S. Blondheim, Federation of American Zionists, 1916, *Essential Texts of Zionism*; Jewish Virtual Library http://www.us-israel.org/jsource/Zionism/pinsker.html.

10. Benny Morris, *Righteous Victims: A History of the Zionist–Arab Conflict, 1881–2001* (New York: Knopf, 2001), p. 21.

11. Israel Ministry of Foreign Affairs web-site: http://www.israel.org/mfa/go.asp?MFAH00ng0.

12. Amnon Rubinstein, *Haaretz*, March 13, 2002.

13. Vladimir Jabotinsky, 'The Iron Wall: We and the Arabs'. First published in Russian under the title 'O Zheleznoi Stene' in Rasswyet', November 4, 1923. Translated by Lenni Brenner. It can be downloaded at http://www.marxists.de/middleast/ironwall/ironwall.htm.

14. Vladimir Jabotinsky, 'A Letter on Autonomy, 1904', reprinted in Brenner, *51 Documents*, p. 10.

15. Adolf Hitler, *Mein Kampf*, reissued edition (Boston: Houghton Mifflin, 1998), p. 56.

16. Memorandum from the Zionist Federation of Germany, June 21, 1933, reprinted in Brenner, *51 Documents*, p. 43.

17. Edwin Black, *The Transfer Agreement: The Untold Story of the Secret Pact Between the Third Reich and Jewish Palestine* (New York: Macmillan; London: Collier Macmillan, 1984).
18. Lenni Brenner, *The Iron Wall: Zionist Revisionism from Jabotinsky to Shamir* (London: Zed Books, 1984), cites as reference no. 23: Yoav Gelber, 'Zionist Policy and the Fate of European Jewry (1939–42)', *Yad Vashem Studies*, Vol. XII (1979), p. 199.
19. Rabbi Moshe Shonfeld, *The Holocaust Victims Accuse* (New York: Neturei Karta, 1977).
20. Sigmund Freud's letter to Dr Chaim Koffler, Keren HaYassod, Vienna: February 26, 1930; posted at the Freud Institute in UK web-site: http://www.freud.org.uk./arab-israeli.html.
21. Hillel Halkin, 'Objectivity is Morally Overrated', *Jerusalem Post*, November 14, 2002. Also on the web at http://www.jpost.com/servlet/Satellite?pagename=JPost/A/JPArticle/ShowFull&cid=1037248935749.
22. Naeim Giladi, *Ben-Gurion's Scandals* (Flushing: Glilit, 1995).

CHAPTER 7

1. 'Racism and the Administration of Justice' (Amnesty International, 2001), also found at http://www.amnestyusa.org/stoptorture/racism report.pdf.
2. For example, see Arye Rattner and Gideon Fishman, *Justice for All? Jews and Arabs in the Israeli Criminal Justice System* (Westport, Conn.: Greenwood Publishing Group, 1998). See also http://www.jr.co.il/hotsites/i-law.htm http://www.kesher.org.il/legal/main.html and http://www.adalah.org.
3. The Knesset's web-site http://www.knesset.gov.il/knesset/.
4. http://www.israel.org/mfa/go.asp?MFAH00mz.
5. *New York Times*, January 21, 1972, p. 14; cited in Oscar Kraines, *The Impossible Dilemma: Who is a Jew in the State of Israel?* (New York: Bloch Publishing, 1976).
6. Tom Segev, *1949: The First Israelis*, trans. Arlen N. Weinstein (New York: Henry Holt, 1998), pp. 80 and 82.
7. Arab Association for Human Rights background report, posted at http://www.arabhra.org.
8. 'Bedouin Probe Seen As "Farce"', *Jewish Week*, August 17, 2001.
9. Noam Arnon, *Haaretz*, August 28, 2002.
10. Visit the web-site of the Jewish Agency for Israel. Their description of the Law of Return is at http://www.jafi.org.il/aliyah/aliyah/law.html.

CHAPTER 8

1. *Webster's Third New International Dictionary*, unabridged on CD-ROM.
2. William Sargant, *Battle of the Mind: A Physiology of Conversion and Brain-washing* (Cambridge: Malor Books, 1957).
3. Simha Flapan, *Zionism and the Palestinians* (New York: St. Martin's Press, 1977), Chapter 2.

4. *The Sunday Times*, September 24, 1972, p. 8.
5. Nahum Barnea and Danny Rubenstein, *Davar*, March 19, 1982.
6. David McDowall, *Palestine and Israel: The Uprising and Beyond* (Berkeley: University of California Press, 1991), p. 262, citing *Haaretz*, May 11, 1984.
7. Fawaz Turki, *The Disinherited*, second edition (New York: Monthly Review Press, 1972), pp. 160–1.
8. Howard Zinn, *You Can't Be Neutral on a Moving Train: A Personal History of Our Times* (Boston: Beacon Press, 2002), p. 208.

CHAPTER 9

1. http://www.amnestyusa.org/news/2001/israel03262001.html.
2. A.R. Chapman, 'Reinterpreting Rights and Responsibilities', in K.W. Hunter and T.C. Mack (eds.), *International Rights and Responsibilities for the Future* (Westport, CT: Praeger, 1996).
3. UN Commission of Human Rights. Fifty-sixth session, *Question of the Violation of Human Rights in the Occupied Arab Territories, Including Palestine*. Report on the situation of human rights in the Palestinian territories occupied since 1967, submitted by Mr Giorgio Giacomelli, Special Rapporteur, pursuant to Commission on Human Rights resolution 1993/2 A. http://www.hri.ca/fortherecord2000/documentation/commission/e-cn4-2000-25.htm.
4. 'Human Rights Monitors Needed in Israeli-Palestinian Conflict'. Open letter from Amnesty International and Human Rights Watch to leaders of the US, EU, Israel, the Palestinian Authority, and UN Secretary-General Kofi Annan (New York and London, July 6, 2001) http://www.hrw.org/press/2001/07/isr-0706-ltr.htm.
5. Elizabeth Olson, 'U.N. Panel on Torture Urges Further Steps by Israel', *New York Times*, November 26, 2001.
6. Associated Press, July 11, 2001.
7. Amnesty International, 'Israel/Occupied Territories: Israel fails to address increasing use of torture'. Press release November 23, 2001, http://www.ppsmo.org/press%20folder/e2001/press11.htm.
8. B'Tselem, 'A Deadly Pattern'. Press release, March 12, 2002, http://www.btselem.org/.
9. http://www.phrusa.org/research/forensics/israel/update_commentary.html.
10. Physicians for Human Rights, 'Medical Group Examines Use of Force in Israel, Gaza and West Bank; Issues Conclusions on Death of "Issam Judeh"'. Press release, November 13, 2000. http://www.phrusa.org/research/forensics/israel/Israel_force.html.
11. Amnesty International, 'Amnesty International Urges Israel to Stop Attacks on Palestinian Areas'. Press release, October 23, 2001, http://www.amnestyusa.org/news/2001/israel10232001.html.
12. Human Rights Watch, 'Israel/Occupied Territories: Jenin War Crimes Investigation Needed. Human Rights Watch Report Finds Laws of War

Violations', May 3, 2002, http://hrw.org/press/2002/05/jenin0503.htm.

13. Amira Hass, 'Don't Shoot Till You Can See They're Over the Age of 12', *Haaretz*, November 20, 2000.

14. *Yediot Aharonot*, Hebrew edition, November 17, 2000.

15. Keith Richburg, *Washington Post*, November 30, 2000, p. A01.

16. Amnesty International, 'Israel and the Occupied Territories: Demolition and Dispossession: The Destruction of Palestinian Homes'. December 8, 1999. Available at http://web.amnesty.org/library/Index/engMDE150591999.

17. Gush Shalom report and maps on the wall, http://gush-shalom.org/thewall.

18. UN Commission of Human Rights. Fifty-sixth session, *Question of the Violation of Human Rights in the Occupied Arab Territories, Including Palestine*.

19. Amnesty International Press Release MDE 15/099/2003, 7 November 2003 Israel/OT: Israel must immediately stop the construction of wall.

CHAPTER 10

1. Sara M. Roy, *The Gaza Strip: The Political Economy of De-Development* (Washington: Institute for Palestine Studies, 1995), p. 51.

2. M. Sachar, *A History of Israel: From the Rise of Zionism to Our Time* (New York: Alfred A. Knopf, 1996).

3. Itzhak Ravid, 'The Demographic Revolution', presented at the Herzliya Conference, December 2001, http://www.herzliyaconference.org.

4. *Haaretz*, December 2, 2002, Report: 'Education Has Contributed to Growing Economic Gaps'. http://www.haaretzdaily.com/hasen/pages/ShArt.jhtml?itemNo=236901&contrassID=1&subContrassID=0&sbSubContrassID=0.

5. *Israeli Settlements in the Occupied Territories: A Guide*. Report of the Foundation for Middle East Peace, March 2002, http://www.fmep.org/reports/2002/sr0203.html.

6. *Fourth Geneva Convention Relative to the Protection of Civilian Persons in Time of War*. Adopted 12 August 1949 by the Diplomatic Conference for the Establishment of International Conventions for the Protection of Victims of War, held in Geneva from April 21 to August 12, 1949 entry into force October 21, 1950. Also available at http://193.194.138.190/html/menu3/b/92.htm.

7. UN Security Council Resolution 465 and other UNSC resolutions are available via UN publications and on the UN web pages.

8. *Israeli Settlements in the Occupied Territories: A Guide*.

9. Built-up area calculations according to Applied Research Institute of Jerusalem, http://www.arij.org.

10. T. Stauffer, *Water and War in the Middle East: The Hydraulic Parameters of Conflict* (Washington, DC: The Center for Policy Analysis on Palestine); J. Isaac, 'The Essentials of Sustainable Water Resource Management

in Israel and Palestine', *Arab Studies Quarterly*, Vol. 22, No. 2 (2000), pp. 13–31.

11. UN Commission of Human Rights. Fifty-sixth session, *Question of the Violation of Human Rights in the Occupied Arab Territories, Including Palestine*. Report on the situation of human rights in the Palestinian territories occupied since 1967, submitted by Mr Giorgio Giacomelli, Special Rapporteur, pursuant to Commission on Human Rights resolution 1993/2 A. http://www.hri.ca/fortherecord2000/document ation/commission/e-cn4-2000-25.htm.

12. C. Main, *The Unified Development of the Water Resources of the Jordan Valley Region* (Tennessee: Tennessee Valley Authority, 1953).

13. A. Soffer, 'The Relevance of Johnston Plan to the Reality of 1993 and Beyond', in J. Isaac and H. Shuval, *Water and Peace in the Middle East* (Amsterdam: Elsevier, 1994).

14. Sharif S. Elmusa, *Water Conflict: Economics, Politics, Law and Palestinian-Israeli Water Resources* (Washington, DC: Institute for Palestine Studies, 1998), p. 351.

15. S. El Musa, *Al Miya fi al Mufawadat al Filistiniyah – al Israiliyah* (Beirut: n.p., 1997), p. 42.

16. See documents posted at the Euro-Mediterranean Information System on the know-how in the water sector. http://www.semide-ps.org/doc umentation.htm.

17. A. Tamimi, 'A Technical Framework for Final-Status Negotiations over Water', *Palestine-Israel Journal*, Vol. III, No. 3/4 (1996), p. 68.

18. Elmusa, *Water Conflict*, p. 348.

19. V. Qumsieh, 'The Environmental Impact of Jewish Settlements in the West Bank, Palestine-Israel', *Journal of Politics, Economics and Culture*, Vol. V, No. 1 (1998), p. 32.

20. UN Commission of Human Rights (see note 11).

21. L. Beyer, 'Trashing the Holy Land', *Time*, September 7, 1998, p. 62.

22. *The Socio-economic Impact of Settlements on Land, Water, and the Palestinian Economy* (Washington, DC: Foundation for Middle East Peace, 1998).

CHAPTER 11

1. Theodore Herzl, *Complete Diaries*, ed. Raphael Patai, trans. Harry Zohn (New York: Herzl Press and T. Yoseloff, 1960), pp. 88–9.

2. Gad Becker, *Yediot Aharonot*, April 13, 1983; *New York Times*, April 14, 1983.

3. Edward Said, *The Question of Palestine* (New York: Vintage Books, 1979), p. 88.

4. Rashid Khalidi, *Palestinian Identity: The Construction of Modern National Consciousness* (New York: Columbia University Press, 1997), pp. 112–13 and references therein.

5. S. Abdullah Schleifer, 'The Life and Thought of 'Izz-id-Din al-Qassam: Preacher and Mujahid', *Islamic Quarterly*, Vol. 22, No. 2 (1979), p. 70.

6. Khalidi, *Palestinian Identity*, p. 155.

7. Jules Cambon, June 4, 1917, letter is posted at the 'Zionist Exposition' of the World Zionist Organization. http://www.wzo.org.il/home/politic/balfour.htm. Translation kindly checked by Jean-Christian Rostagni.
8. Quoted in Christopher Sykes, *Crossroads to Israel 1917–1948* (reprinted Bloomington: Indiana University Press, 1973).
9. Palestine Mandate documents, Article 4, available at the Avalon Project at Yale University.
10. See http://www.kh-uia.org.il/us/history.html.
11. For details, see 'The Building of the Israeli State Sector: Case Study: The Palestine Potash Ltd.', *The Economic Quarterly*, Vol. 41, No. 2 (1994), pp. 263–89; and D. Gavish, 'Salt of the Earth: From the Palestine Potash to the Dead Sea Works', *Yad Izhak Ben-Zvi*, Jerusalem (1995) (in Hebrew).
12. Arthur Rogers, *The Palestine Mystery: Sidelights on a Secret Policy* (London: The Sterling Press, 1948).
13. Nur Masalha, *Expulsion of the Palestinians: The Concept of 'Transfer' in Zionist Political Thought, 1882–1948* (Washington: Institute for Palestine Studies, 1992), p. 15.
14. Benny Morris, *Righteous Victims, A History of the Zionist-Arab Conflict, 1881–2001* (New York: Knopf, 2001), pp. 167–8.
15. Available at Avalon Project, Yale University.
16. Ted Swedenburg, 'The Role of the Palestinian Peasantry in the Great Revolt (1936–9)', in Ilan Pappe (ed.), *Israel/Palestine Question: Rewriting Histories* (London: Routledge, 1999).
17. See Rafael Medoff, *Militant Zionism in America: The Rise and Impact of the Jabotinsky Movement in the United States, 1926–1948* (Birmingham: University of Alabama Press, 2002).
18. Ilan Pappe, *The Making of the Arab-Israeli Conflict 1947–1951* (New York: I.B. Tauris, 1992), p. 65 and references cited therein.
19. Ibid., pp. 74–6.
20. General Matityahu Peled, *Haaretz*, March 19, 1972.
21. Edward Said, *The Question of Palestine* (New York: Vintage Books, 1979), p. 167.
22. Alan Hart, *Arafat: Terrorist or Peacemaker*, revised edition (London: Sidgwick and Jackson, 1988), p. 379.
23. Naseer Aruri, *Dishonest Broker: The Role of the United States in Palestine and Israel* (Cambridge, Mass.: South End Press, 2003).
24. The full proposal is posted at http://www.usembassy-israel.org.il/publish/peace/may89.htm.
25. Federation of American Scientists, http://www.fas.org/asmp/profiles/israel_armstable.htm.
26. Tanya Reinhart, Hebrew edition of *Yediot Aharonot*, June 10, 2001.
27. 'Six Red-lines for Peace', *Jerusalem Post*, July 21, 2000.
28. Cited in Noam Chomsky, *The New Intifada: Resisting Israel's Apartheid*, edited by R. Carey (London: Verso, 2001), p. 20.
29. Palestinian Declaration of Independence, Algiers, November 15, 1988.
30. Lamis Andoni, 'The PLO at the Crossroads', *Journal of Palestine Studies*, Vol. 21, No. 1 (1991), pp. 54–65.

31. Israel Shahak, *Open Secrets: Israeli Nuclear and Foreign Policies* (London: Pluto Press, 1997), p. 164.
32. Tanya Reinhardt, *Yediot Aharonot*, May 1, 1995, quoted by Shahak, *Open Secrets*, pp. 167–8.
33. *New York Times*, October 15, 1997.
34. Jimmy Carter, 'For Israel, Land or Peace', *Washington Post*, November 26, 2000, p. B6.
35. J. William Fulbright, *The Price of Empire* (London: Pantheon Books, 1989), p. 183.
36. Benny Morris, *The Birth of the Palestinian Refugee Problem, 1947–1949* (Cambridge: Cambridge University Press, 1989), p. 22, citing quotations in Avi Shlaim, *Collusion across the Jordan: King Abdullah, the Zionist Movement, and the Partition of Palestine* (New York: Columbia University Press, 1988), p. 465 and citing David Ben-Gurion, *Yoman Hamilhama-Tashah* [The War Diary 1948–9], ed. Gershon Rivlin and Elhannan Orren (Tel Aviv: n.p., 1982), iii, p. 993.
37. Yitzhak ben Israel, *Haaretz*, April 16, 2002, in Hebrew.
38. Akram Hanieh, *Journal of Palestine Studies*, Vol. 30, No. 2 (2001); Robert Malley and Hussein Agha, 'Camp David: A Tragedy of Errors', *New York Review of Books*, June 13, 2002, http://www.nybooks.com/articles/14380.
39. WEHAB Working Group, *A Framework for Action on Water and Sanitation*, World Summit on Sustainable Development – Johannesburg 2002 (New York: United Nations, August 2002).
40. US Congressional Record 22 U.S.C. § 2304(a).
41. James M. Ennes, Jr., *Assault on the Liberty: The True Story of the Israeli Attack on an American Intelligence Ship*, reprint edition (New York: Ivy Books, 1987). Also see http://www.ussliberty.com.
42. The document can be found at http://www.israeleconomy.org/strat1.htm.
43. See http://www.newamericancentury.org.

CHAPTER 12

1. John Quigley, 'The Role of Law in a Palestinian–Israeli Accommodation', *Case Western Reserve Journal of International Law*, Vol. 31, Nos. 2–3 (Spring/Summer 1999).
2. Ilan Pappe, *The Making of the Arab-Israeli Conflict 1947–1951* (New York: I.B. Tauris, 1992).
3. Ibid., p. 27.
4. Ibid., pp. 41–3.
5. Michael Bar-Zohar, *Ben-Gurion: A Biography* (New York: Delacorte Press, 1977), pp. 91–2.
6. Avalon Project archives at Yale University.
7. W.T. Mallison Jr. and Sally V. Mallison, *The Palestine Problem in International Law and World Order* (London: Longman, 1986), Chapter 4.
8. Fourth Geneva Convention Relative to the Protection of Civilian Persons in Time of War, 75 UNTS 287.

9. Richard Falk, 'International Law and the Al-Aqsa Intifada', *Middle East Report*, No. 217 (Winter 2000), pp. 16–18.
10. Allegra Pacheco, in R. Carey (ed.), *The New Intifada: Resisting Israel's Apartheid* (London: Verso Books, 2001), p. 183.
11. M. Shamgar, 'Legal Concepts and Problems of the Israeli Military Government – the Initial Stage', in M. Shamgar (ed.), *Military Government in the Territories Administered by Israel 1967–1980* (Jerusalem: n.p., 1982), pp. 13–14, cited in Pacheco, in Carey, *The New Intifadah*, p. 183.
12. The Universal Declaration of Human Rights. Adopted and Proclaimed by the United Nations on December 10, 1948. Israel signed the declaration.
13. Francis Boyle, *Palestine, Palestinians & International Law* (Atlanta: Clarity Press, 2003).

CHAPTER 13

1. 'Proposal Driven through by U.S. and Soviet Will Set up Two States', *New York Times*, November 30, 1947.
2. *New York Times*, November 29, 1947.
3. http://www.nad-plo.org.
4. 'Cry, the Beloved Two-state Solution', *Haaretz*, August 7, 2003. http://www.haaretz.com/hasen/pages/ShArt.jhtml?itemNo=326324.
5. Israeli Artists Manifesto, *Beit Ha'Am*, cited in Marwan Barghouti, *The New Intifadah: Resisting Israel's Apartheid* (London: Verso, 2001), p. 171.
6. See the Association for One Democratic State in Palestine/Israel http://www.lpj.org/Nonviolence/Sami/OneState/bylawseng.htm and the Action Committee for One Democratic Secular Republic http://www.onerepublic.org, www.palestinenet.org. http://one-democratic-state.org/.
7. Fouzi el-Asmar, Uri Davis and Naim Khader (eds.), *Debate on Palestine* (New York: Ithaca Press, 1981); Fouzi el-Asmar, Uri Davis and Naim Khadr, *Towards a Socialist Republic of Palestine* (New York: Ithaca Press, 1978).
8. Leo Strauss, *Natural Right and History*, reissued edition (Chicago: University of Chicago Press, 1999).
9. Shadia B. Drury, *Leo Strauss and the American Right* (New York: Griffin Trade Paperback, 1999).
10. Edward Said, 'A Reply to Arab Intellectuals', *Le Monde Diplomatique*, August/September 1998.
11. Edward Said, *The Question of Palestine* (New York: Vintage Books, 1979), pp. 180–1.
12. *Haaretz*, November 4, 2001.
13. Joseph Campbell, *The Masks of God: Creative Mythology* (New York: Viking Penguin, 1968), p. 37.

Index

Printed and bound by CPI Group (UK) Ltd, Croydon, CR0 4YY

04/11/2024

14585933-0001